University of
Chester

This book is to be returned on or before the last date stamped below. Overdue charges will be incurred by the late return of books.

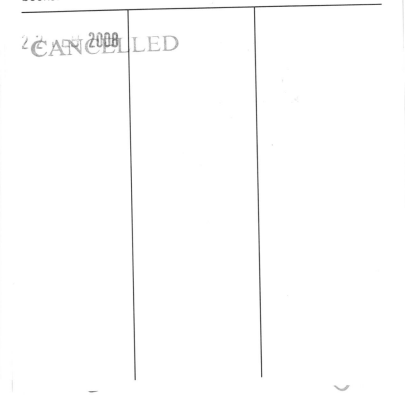

Forensic Focus

Series editor: Gwen Adshead

Originally under the editorship of Murray Cox, this series takes the currently cystallizing field of Forensic Psychotherapy as its focal point, offering a forum for the presentation of theoretical and clinical issues. It also embraces such influential neighbouring disciplines as language, law, literature, criminolgy, ethics and philosophy, as well as psychiatry and psychology, its established progenitors.

Forensic Focus 4

Prison Theatre:
Perspectives and Practices

Edited by James Thompson

Jessica Kingsley Publishers
London and Philadelphia

First published in the United Kingdom in 1998 by
Jessica Kingsley Publishers Ltd
116 Pentonville Road, London N1 9JB, England
and 1900 Frost Road, Suite 101, Bristol PA 19007, USA.

Copyright © 1998 the contributors and the publisher.

Library of Congress Cataloging in Publication Data
A CIP catalogue record for this book is available from the Library of Congress

British Library Cataloguing in Publication Data
Practices and perspectives in prison theatre. – (Forensic focus; 5)
1. Prison theater 2. Drama - Therapeutic use
I. Thompson, James
365.6'6

ISBN 1 85302 417 1

Printed and Bound in Great Britain by
Athenaeum Press, Gateshead, Tyne and Wear

Contents

Part III: Working in the Institution

Part IV: Evaluation and History

To my father

Acknowledgements

I would like to thank all the authors for their time in contributing to this book and their patience in the editing process that often involved cross-Atlantic communication. I would like to thank the staff of the LBJ School of Public Affairs in Austin, Texas where I completed this work and particularly Yayoi Narita who helped translate computer discs, re-type chapters and ease transatlantic confusions. A thank you to Grady Hillman who offered support throughout my year in Texas, and without whom my early forays in to the US field would not have been possible. A big thank you goes out to all at the TIPP Centre – Michael Balfour, Jacqui Burford, Bridget Eadie, Paul Heritage, Kate Lodge and Nic Nuttgens – who allowed me to disappear to Texas for one year. A thank you also to Viv Gardner in the Drama Department at Manchester University whose support has been vital in maintaining positive links between the TIPP Centre and Manchester University. A final and the biggest thank you goes to Debbie, Hannah and Leah. I couldn't have done Texas without you!

James Thompson

Introduction

James Thompson

Two litmus tests collide

The mood and temper of the public in regard to the treatment of crime and criminals is one of the most unfailing tests of the civilisation of any country...the treatment of crime and criminals make and measure the stored-up strength of a nation and are sign and proof of the living virtue in it. (Winston Churchill)[1]

Any community without the arts is a community that will no longer have a soul. (Arne H. Carlson, Governor of Minnesota)[2]

Both the arts and the 'treatment of criminals' are, according to the British and American politicians above, indicators of a community or society's virtue and degree of civilisation. Whilst accepting that the concepts used – virtue, civilisation and soul – are ambiguous, relative and highly contested, these statements do construct two theoretically useful and interesting propositions for a book called *Perspectives and Practices in Prison Theatre*. The arts and criminal justice are given significance beyond the fields themselves; they become indicators or barometers of the 'stored-up strength of a nation'. This book on 'theatre' and 'prison' brings a demonstrator of 'soul' into the place which reflects the degree of our 'civilisation'.[3] It tells the tales of where these the two 'indicators' overlap – where the two litmus tests collide.

Criminal justice therefore is not only an area of public policy in its own right but as presented here by Churchill, it also offers a window through which observers can judge and criticise their society[4]. He makes it clear that the willingness to blame and banish a person illustrates as much about the society doing the blaming and banishing, as it does about the person him/herself. A study of law breakers is simultaneously a study of law makers. A study of the

1   Winston Churchill 1911, whilst Home Secretary, quoted in Miller 1996, p.280.
2   Quoted in *High Performance Magazine* 1997.
3   For a critique of the use of the word 'civilisation' see Garland (1990 p.215).
4   Dostoyevski is famed for a similar view – 'the degree of civilization in a society can be judged by entering its prisons.' (*The House of the Dead* (1985). Cited in Rideau and Wikberg 1992, p.106).

prison is a study of the society in which it stands. The 1.6 million people in American prisons and jails and the rapid retreat from any notion of rehabilitation (*Austin American Statesman* 1996) provides a commentary on the state of the US as a whole.[5] The rising prison numbers in the UK, up approximately 200 per week with the current 60,000 projected to reach 74,500 by 2005, is a similar 'measure' of the nation's 'strength' (*The Times* 1997).

The arts too, as partially stated here by the Republican Minnesota Governor, illustrate the 'stored-up strength' of a country, both by their presence indicating a sense of health but also in their use as another window to view and understand society. I would not choose to use an ambiguous term such as 'soul' but it suggests, even to a spokesperson of the American right, that the arts are a human need or at the core of our humanity. By implication a community without the arts therefore lacks that humanity. To me the arts are both something that we are and need, and also the basis of how we act. The arts are part of the fabric of our daily lives and also how we transform and re-create our daily lives. They demonstrate the ability of humans both to be and reflect on their existence. Paulo Freire comments that humankind is distinguished from the animal kingdom by his/her ability 'to treat not only his (sic) actions but his very self as the object of his reflection' (Freire 1970, p.78). The 'source of knowledge and creation' is men and women's skill in combining 'reflection and action' (Freire 1970, p.78). Theatre, part of Arne's 'soul', from workshop and rehearsal to performance is reflection *in* action – it is the practice of reflecting on and recreating our lives.

So what happens when these two litmus tests are brought together – when 'soul' is brought to the place that measures society's 'virtue'? What happens when they collide? Does theatre bring health to the prison or does it provide a basic human need? Does it bring morality to a place where there is none? Does it provide the means to transform a person's life or does it transform the whole community? Should we bring the arts in the same way others provide food? Or are they a vehicle for something else? Is theatre a prisoner's window to view and understand society or a means of personal reflection? Is theatre in prisons about bringing 'soul' and humanising the system, or is it to transform it? Does the very existence of theatre in prison mean that our society can be judged as civilised?

The contributors to this collection start the process of asking these questions, of interrogating the field. They find some answers, but they also stimulate further questioning. All have experienced the immense power of theatre or the arts in a secure institutional setting. They all approach the inquiry from different perspectives and with experience of different practice. Some are theatre artists,

---

5   See National Center on Institutions and Alternatives Press Release, 19 August 1996. This
      also notes that one in every 167 US residents was incarcerated, with approximately one in
      ten young African-American young men behind bars.

some are therapists, some are ex- or current prisoners and some contribute to structured rehabilitation programmes. All are struggling to define work at the borders, at the margins of arts practice and literally at the edge of society. At the core however this book deals with how theatre effects change. How by participating and performing a person can reflect upon their lives, their environment, their community and society and in so doing contribute to a process of personal, institutional and social change.

Is drama itself frowned upon – my opinion

Background

Whilst the practice of theatre and drama in the criminal justice system has certainly grown in recent years there has been little analysis of its real role, why it is becoming 'fashionable' or what link it has with traditional approaches to rehabilitation. Seldom have the questions outlined above been tackled. Even my view that it has perhaps become 'fashionable' might be dismissed by long-time staff working within the system who have neither heard of nor seen any theatre in their workplace. The practice has often been marginalised both by the institutions and agencies of criminal justice as well as by the practitioners and artists themselves. Rarely is there an adequate expression of why it is in the criminal justice system at all. Often explanation is based on a series of hunches, assumptions and anecdotes. It is as likely to be understood as an additional prison leisure activity, a novel way of presenting teaching materials, or a management attempt to keep inmates happy, as it is to be viewed as a serious part of the rehabilitation process or a major challenge to the politics of punishment. At worst it can be viewed with hostility – an 'absurd' privilege which may actually contribute to the crime problem (Bidinotto 1994). *– True?*

This book is an attempt to redress this balance by giving a forum for a number of practitioners to write about their work. It offers theory, description, guidance, history and analysis, without falling into one category. At this stage in the development of theatre in prisons it is more important to hear a telling of experience, than to start to construct an academic boundary around the field. Some writers do develop the discourse within a more academic frame, but it is not meant to be a book of one purpose. It aims to represent, as best it can, some of the different voices in the field. Of course all representations are in some ways selective and this is true of *Perspectives and Practices in Prison Theatre*. The disproportionate number of references to the Theatre in Prisons and Probation (TIPP) Centre is due to my allegiance to and familiarity with practitioners connected to that organisation. The nearly total reliance on UK experience is determined by my base in the North West of England. The emphasis I place on the American prison system in this introduction is due to my current residence in the US. Prison theatre as an interrogated field is relatively new and the importance of writing at this stage in its history is to start the debate.

Where did it all begin?

It would be wrong to try to create an over-neat chronological history of prison theatre. There are moments in the past which are significant, but also there are significant moments which are not yet known. The 'Acting for a Change – Theatre with Offenders' conference in 1992[6] brought together practitioners who had in many cases been doing ground-breaking work in near-total isolation. Their work and that of others like them should not be viewed as any less significant than the practice which is more familiar. One of the objectives in establishing the TIPP Centre was to offer a focus for theatre in prisons in the UK and a place which would try to ensure that good and remarkable experience was not forgotten. Although we have managed to gather information on much of the practice in the UK, there is a great deal still to be acknowledged. The documentation of all arts work in prisons has been painstakingly undertaken by the Unit for the Arts and Offenders with support from the Home Office and Arts Council (Peaker and Pratt 1996), but this can never be the complete picture. Taken beyond our national boundary, the history and practice of theatre in prisons is only starting to become visible. The work in France, Spain, Italy and other European countries is well developed but its precise detail is relatively unknown to us in the UK. There is startling educational theatre work with puppets in South African prisons, theatre for development in the prisons in Burkina Faso, major recreations of classic texts with the women prisoners in Massachusetts, work in Peru, Romania and Brazil. And more. History is so often selective, or dominated by western European or North American perspectives, that I do not want to continue that tradition by maintaining any special place for our collection of experiences. I hope these chapters trigger debate and a questioning of practice, but also an urge to write so that a future collection can offer greater historical insight to the field and be more dynamically international.

Significant moments?

There are, however, moments in the last years that do give clues as to how the practice has developed in the UK. The meeting of two women prisoners in HMP Askham Grange in 1979, leading to the setting up of Clean Break Theatre Company, is one such 'significant moment' and provides a key to the development of this field in the UK. The focus on working with ex-prisoners, also shared by Insight Arts Trust, has been a major force in shaping the interaction between theatre and criminal justice. Both these companies now work on the inside and on the outside and offer a sense of continuity between the two. The performance by

6   This conference took place in Manchester University and was run by what was to become the Theatre in Prisons and Probation Centre.

ex-prisoners or the performance of material created by ex-prisoners to a prison audience offers a powerful model for this work. Both the chapters by Pauline Gladstone and Angus McLewin and the one by Chris Johnston debate the difficulties and challenges presented by this. Pauline and Angus focus more on the crossover between therapy and theatre, whilst Chris Johnston creates an imaginary dialogue between a prison officer and a theatre director to illustrate the precarious role played by artists in institutions, especially when they are ex-prisoners themselves.

The concerns and questions in Chapter 3 are echoed in the chapter by Sally Stamp whose practice bridges the worlds of therapy and theatre. Having worked as both a drama teacher and dramatherapist in secure settings she offers here an analysis of the differences and confusions between the two fields. The questions arising here are also touched upon by other authors in this collection. For example Joe White queries whether the implicit therapeutic qualities of a theatre rehearsal process make it more powerful by default than an explicitly therapeutic alternative. Whilst none of these chapters present the final word in this debate, all demonstrate the need for further questioning of the relations between theatre and the world of dramatherapy.

The therapeutic and rehabilitative intention of theatre in prisons has been a major concern of Geese Theatre's work since Clark Baim arrived from Geese Theatre US to set up the UK company in 1987. The US company was set up by ex-patriate British director John Bergmann in 1980. This has a strong claim for inclusion in my 'significant moment' collection, as Geese have gone on to become the largest company in the field, now familiar to many practitioners both in the theatre and the criminal justice system. Alun Mountford and Mark Farrall's chapter here discusses their current work and also their continuing search for new and imaginative approaches to offender rehabilitation. The innovative fusion of rehabilitation theory and theatre methods as presented here and elsewhere (Bergman, Hewish and Ruding 1996) demonstrates that they are key practitioners of one of the major approaches to prison theatre. Although they still exist at the borders of the fields of theatre and therapy, they are very much at the centre of practice in specialised rehabilitation, particularly in the areas of violent and sexual offender treatment.

I have already mentioned the conference in 1992 which led to the TIPP Centre being established by myself and Paul Heritage. With no pretence to impartiality, this I believe was another 'significant moment'. Since then the Centre has gone on to develop numerous programmes for prison and probation services and also offer research and training opportunities in theatre and criminal justice. Its link with Manchester University Drama Department has meant that it has also directed undergraduate teaching in prison theatre, and it now delivers with the Department an MA in Applied Drama. Again as the Director of the Centre I cannot offer an objective view of TIPP's place in the field, but I do feel it has played a role in creating a higher profile for theatre in prisons. Hosting the book launch of Augusto Boal's *Rainbow of Desire* in 1995 (Boal 1995), the Centre demonstrated that it is also interested in linking in to wider debates on theatre and social change. At the same time its workshops at the 'What Works'[7] conferences indicate that it is involving itself with the current debates in offender rehabilitation. The interaction of Boal's Forum Theatre (Boal 1992) with approaches to cognitive behavioural offender intervention (McGuire and Priestley 1985) has led to TIPP creating programmes on offending behaviour (Blagg!), violence (The Pump!), bullying, employment and drug use. All combine the participative and transformative techniques of Theatre of the Oppressed with the effectiveness criterion and methodology of traditional rehabilitation programmes (Thompson 1995). All continue to be developed and practiced as TIPP now expands into the fields of crime prevention and early intervention.

The original momentum to establish the TIPP Centre was influenced greatly by the work of Robert Clare in HMP Manchester. By involving staff and students from Manchester University Drama Department, he set up a link with the prison that was to prove vital in the Centre's development. His chapter in this collection outlines vividly the dynamics of his approach to prison theatre. In concentrating exclusively on the artistic road from first meeting to performance, he demonstrates the profound impact this process can have. His group transform themselves from Strangeways prisoners to strong performers. In working with the participants as actors they become actors. Whilst Robert Clare clearly states that it is for others to assess the therapeutic value of his work, his structured creative process provides another link to the debates surrounding theatre and therapy.

Other 'significant moments' in this openly selective history have often been strong collaborative efforts. The TIPP Centre, Geese Theatre, Insight Arts Trust, Clean Break, Plan B Arts, Safe Ground, and the Unit for the Arts and Offenders make up the Standing Committee for Theatre in the Criminal Justice System which has been responsible for advocating theatre's involvement with criminal justice. The committee succeeded in getting the Association of Chief Officers of Probation to agree to a position paper on arts in probation settings in 1994. This paper has subsequently been used by Probation Services to support the development of theatre programmes. For example, the Projects Unit of Greater Manchester Probation Service used the paper to support its partnership with the TIPP Centre in creating an Anger Management Programme. In addition, the Committee is currently working with the Arts Council to create an arts founders' policy document for this area.

---

[7]   This international conference series is held at Salford University and is run in part by Greater Manchester Probation Service.

The most recent example of a willingness to collaborate and another 'significant moment' took place in 1996 when the TIPP Centre, Geese Theatre and the Unit for the Arts and Offenders hosted the Second European Conference on Theatre and Prisons at Manchester University. This event followed on from the first such conference in Milan in 1994. Attended by delegates from 11 countries, the event offered an opportunity to hear speakers, view work from around the world and engage in debate. The attendance of the Director General of the Prison Service, Richard Tilt, the ex-chief inspector of prisons, Steven Tumin, as well as artists, ex- and current prisoners made for a dynamic gathering. The conference celebrated the diversity of the field and the collaborative style signalled our desire to maintain an open definition for theatre in prison. The event led to the formation of an International Network for Theatre and Prisons and is due to be followed up with a third festival in 1998. Whilst at time of writing the venue is yet to be confirmed, it promises to further demonstrate prison theatre's vitality.

Defining the field – blurred edges

At all conferences there has been debate about how to frame the field and whether it is in fact a distinct area of practice. This becomes particularly acute in the naming of the events. It is perhaps strange that we define the practice by place (prison) rather than by community (prisoners). More often in the arena of community or social change theatre, a practice is defined by its constituent members – Black Theatre, Gay Theatre, Lesbian Theatre and so on. The identification of our work as theatre in prisons, rather than theatre with offenders, or theatre for rehabilitation, alters both its scope and how it is practised. It also affects what can and cannot be included as a legitimate part of the field. 'Theatre in Prisons' used here in the title suggests that the practice can be as wide and as inclusive as possible. Although it does set up a geographical boundary (successfully breached by some of the contributors!), it should not make exclusions based on who runs the project or what they do in practice. If I was only concerned about theatre *with* offenders, for example, it would not allow for proper discussion of theatre initiated *by* offenders, or practice by those on remand who should not have been labelled 'offender'. Whilst many contributors are debating what constitutes good practice, the important exercise at this stage is for all practices to be involved in that debate.

Ironically, one of the least familiar voices in this debate is that of the prisoners themselves. Knowledge and the creation of a history in any field is, I believe, selectively based on who has the power to get themselves heard. Theatre run by outside practitioners has become more known, whilst the work started and sustained by prisoners themselves is rarely documented. This book tries in a small way to reverse this with the contributions here of Joe White and Victor Hassine. Whilst Joe White talks eloquently about the personal benefits of theatre during

The defining of this field around where it takes place is further elaborated in the chapters by Anne Peaker and Murray Cox. The publication of *Shakespeare Comes to Broadmoor* (Cox 1992) represented the first time in English a whole publication was dedicated to theatre in a secure setting.[8] This book is 'brought up to date' by Murray Cox in this collection. Anne Peaker's chapter outlines the history of the TIPP Centre's work with HMP Manchester (Strangeways), demonstrating how it is very much a relationship with a whole institution with the practice changing over time. The space, and the political and ideological concerns governing that space, have directed and shaped how the TIPP Centre has operated and what has been achieved. Whilst TIPP has been running workshops with prisoners, it has also been training probation teams, and prison officers. It has been in the whole prison and not working with one constituent group. Similarly Murray Cox is not describing one form of practice but a wide variety of theatre practice within one institution. Whilst importantly this is a Special Hospital not a prison, it does indicate the varied, dynamic and complex way theatre can interact with an institution. Whilst a Shakespeare performance and a dramatherapy workshop are separate, they are both part of theatre *in* this space. What is significant is that because of this shared venue, the relationship between them starts to blur.

Those blurred edges are also there in the confusion and struggle to define theatre's wider role in working in prison and with prisoners. What are we doing and for whom do we do it? To return to the theme of my earlier questions, is theatre in prisons about bringing 'soul' and humanising the system, or is it to transform it? The Arts In Corrections programme in California uses data on reduced prison discipline problems to promote its work (Brewster 1983); Martin Glynn's chapter documents the conflicts created when a black community activist enters the restricted confines of a prison, and Paul Heritage's chapter 'Rebellion and Theatre in Brazilian Prisons' describes the history of a rebellion in a Brazilian prison blamed on theatre practitioners. Jenny Hughes in describing the challenges faced by practitioners working in women prisons, criticises the move of theatre practice to accommodation with current punishment ideology. All are demonstrating the problems posed by the role of an artist in a place of punishment. Jenny Hughes' chapter tackles these problems directly. Her review of the TIPP Centre's Blagg! workshop in HMP Styal women's prison, demonstrates her belief in the importance of maintaining a sound pedagogical practice and valuing prisoners as 'whole and equal people in the process' (p.60). She argues with justification that theatre practice, under the pressure of funding restrictions, is in danger of being submerged under current criminal justice ideologies. In a

8   This book represents, unless anyone can tell me otherwise, the third. Honours for number two (even if it is a translation!) go to Kuziakina (1995).

similar way Paul Heritage questions whether we have given up our radical past in order to get through and continue to get through the gates. Both Paul Heritage and Jenny Hughes demand that the critical edge to the work is not lost. In what could almost be a question to the use of the Californian data, Heritage asks 'do we seek to create…tranquillity or inspire rebellion?' Martin Glynn's experience clearly demonstrates the difficulties faced with balancing these roles and the uneasy relationship with an institution a practitioner can have once s/he is past those gates. What should we be doing? Are we playing part of the disciplining role of the prison, or are we inciting rebellion? Can we comfortably define and find a blurred edge between these two? Are we content to liberate a person's imagination because we cannot liberate their body?

Another blurred edge exists between the prison space and the outside. In my opening remarks I noted how prison is a metaphor through which you can examine the world, and that theatre can offer the means to conduct that examination. Paul Heritage's first chapter describes prison theatre in Brazil as part of this process with theatre used explicitly to engage a group in a debate about their society. This project concluded with a full breach in the institutional space when prisoners left the prison to perform to an outside audience. Although a different practice, Alun Mountford and Mark Farrall's chapter also examines the link between being in the system and moving out. The probationers here undergo a ritual which tests their readiness to enter society before they symbolically and in reality leave the room. Jenny Hughes in her chapter exemplifies this blurred space and the potential it offers for transformation in her description of a collaborative project between women prisoners and a group of learning-disabled people. The gym where they conducted the work almost became a world apart. The theatre space in these cases is neither part of the prison/probation world nor part of the outside world – it is a blurred, transitional space (Winnicott 1986),[9] between the two worlds. How that space relates to the prison environment and looks to the outside needs to be further researched. Does it provide the prison with a safety valve to contain prisoners' energies or does it provide a transformative haven? Does one necessarily contradict the other? Does the institution have to be breached as in the Brazilian example or can a theatre space offer this within the prison? I do not claim to offer the answers here but, for the field and the practice to mature, we must be tackling these questions.

More prison places, less theatre spaces?

The practice of theatre in prison, however, is changing and, particularly in the US, it is becoming much rarer. Geese Theatre in 1997 reduced the scope of its touring

9   Quoted in the chapter by Sally Stamp, see p.94.

company, which has, since the company started, performed interactive theatre pieces to audiences in prisons across the UK. Countless prison arts practitioners in the US have stopped their work in a political climate which is championing 'no frill' prisons (Johnson, Bennett and Flanagan 1997). Again in the US, artists have been forced to concentrate more on prevention work which, whilst not wrong in itself, has meant that there has been a steady abandonment of programmes in adult prisons. Although there is some powerful theatre continuing inside the UK and US systems,[10] many practitioners are struggling to maintain their work.

The backdrop to these changes is the rise in prison populations internationally (Christie 1993; Donziger 1996; Miller 1996), the increasing power of the industrial complex that supports this, and the increasing energy being spent on the creation and design of new punishment spectacles (Christie 1993). In visits to several US Boot Camps[11] I have watched the performance of young men running around in quasi-military training. These shows are extremely popular with the media and with politicians but there is no evidence that they have any positive effect on those that are put through them (Bourque *et al.* 1996; Cullen, Wright and Applegate 1996) The importance has been the performance of punishment to an eager audience. If prison theatre is to survive the reduction in spaces, the increasing number of prisoners, the move to prevention and the rise of the new punishment spectacles, it needs to make a strong and clear response.

There are two main areas in which this response can be made. First it is important for all arts practitioners in the field of criminal justice to heed the call made by Michael Balfour and Lindsey Poole in their chapter 'Evaluating Theatre in Prisons and Probation'. They outline the need for sound evaluation of all programmes and also offer valuable guidelines for practice. They argue that for the field to mature it needs to incorporate sound evaluation into all projects. I would emphasise that in order to survive it needs to do that. It also needs to disseminate the results. Evaluation is part of the resources we have in sustaining our practice and entering the wider debates on criminal justice. It should demonstrate that theatre based programmes can enhance the effectiveness of cognitive behavioural rehabilitation programmes, prison education programmes, and other criminal justice interventions. Evaluation is in a sense the tool we can use to advocate a standard of effectiveness in criminal justice against the increasingly popular but ineffective and destructive performance of retribution.

Second, and of course this is linked to the need for evaluation, we must challenge more explicitly the performative nature of punishment both in our

---

10   In the US the work of Tim Mitchell in New York, Buzz Alexander and Pilar Anadon in Michigan deserve mention in this respect.

11   During 1996/7 I was on a Harkness Fellowship examining intervention and prevention strategies with adjudicated and 'at risk' youth. I visited boot camps in Florida and Texas.

research and practice. As Paul Heritage notes in his chapter 'Theatre, Prisons and Citizenship' we must 'acknowledge the grander spectacle' if we are to make any ground in reversing 'the discourse by which such power is uttered and performed' (p.40). Performance theorists and theatre practitioners can interrogate how punishment is directed by the demands of the audience that witness it and also those that control the gaze of that audience. In our practice and research we should be struggling to shift the gaze, disturb the performance, and reframe the discourse. Our practice – whether it be part of therapeutic programming, prison education and cultural work, or projects that involve the prisoner in their wider community – can demonstrate humane, effective and transformative interventions that work with prisoners as subjects of a learning process, and not as performers in a political game.

The struggle to disturb the performance of retribution has been going on for many years by artists and by many other professionals, but the calamity that 'tough on crime' measures have brought about in the US in particular, now puts this into sharper focus. The process of 'shifting the gaze', was the major topic of a meeting of prison artists and activists at the Blue Mountain Centre, New York state in May 1997. There individuals from many different organisations discussed how their work can continue to be developed in a context of mass incarceration and how they should be active in breaking the silence that surrounds this policy. The devastating figure of one in three African-American young men either on parole, in prison or on probation was familiar to all those present (Miller 1994). The selling of prison labour to private businesses by the state of Michigan, outlined by Buzz Alexander from the University of Michigan, was to most new information. The connections between the history of the penitentiary and the history of slavery in America have always been strong, but they are now more striking than ever. For example, the Louisianan State Penitentiary Angola situated on an old slave plantation was exploited as a profitable enterprise by a private businessman for much of the last century, and the practice of needing to run at a profit continued well into the twentieth century. Although the UK has a different history, large-scale imprisonment as an end of century response to social problems seems to be the policy of choice. The response of the Blue Mountain group was that in these contexts we can not stand idly by 'contributing' to the criminal justice system, as though its growth was benign and unproblematic. What we as practitioners should do however was less clear.

At a seminar on prison theatre during the 1997 Festival of Theatre of the Oppressed in Toronto, an activist by implication stated that it was an irrelevance in the real struggle for change in the criminal justice system. My response to the question of what practitioners should be doing, how we should be practically responding to the changing context, is partly made in reply to this person's desire to sideline our work. Theatre and education work in prisons is not a fringe activity in a more critical reaction to these issues. Any response to further prison building, retributive policies, crime and mass incarceration, needs to have work with prisoners at its centre. The people most effected by the criminal justice system – the perpetrators and victims – are those who must have a voice in a struggle to change it. Those locked up in their millions in the US and in their thousands across Europe are perhaps the key to unlocking a destructive policy stalemate.

But what is that work with prisoners? How can they play a role in challenging this policy direction? The answers to these questions, I believe, are to be found through adapting existing creative, rehabilitation and education programmes. These programmes currently provide a space for personal reflection and exploration. They offer a chance to develop an individual's ability to deal with their thinking and emotions. However, in only existing at the level of personal change I question their long-term effectiveness. Many have an impact on reoffending for example that diminishes over time (see the evaluation of the 'Capital Offender Program' of the Texas Youth Commission (Howell *et al.* 1995)). It is important therefore to broaden the individual change emphasis of prison based programmes. The Texas Youth Commission (1995 p.2) admits itself that 'success…is dependent not only upon changes in the…youth, but also in the environment to which they return.' The fear that many prisoners have of the power of their home environment to damage their best intentions to change, needs to be reframed by offering them the skills and confidence to change that environment. Whilst this might seem a daunting task with social change being an unrealistic goal, I would propose that even an engagement with the process of social change would provide a context for personal change to be sustained. In addition, an engagement with that process will allow prisoners and ex-prisoners to become advocates for a more effective and less destructive criminal justice system. They could increasingly take – as some have in the past[12] – a more central role in the debates surrounding crime and punishment.

This I believe represents a more progressive form of rehabilitation that could turn an individual from introspection to exploration of the world outside. It would provide for a strong development of individual cognitive skills, as well as an opportunity for group and community building. It would allow a space for imagining the unimaginable. It would ask questions and start a dialogue. It would work with prisoners as citizens who can not only change themselves but could also play a vital role in the society to which they will (in the most part) return. Theatre through workshop, rehearsal and performance can make an important contribution to this. Along with other forms of dynamic and progressive rehabilitation and education, it has the potential to encourage active and critical

---

12   The Scottish ex-prisoner Jimmy Boyle is a famous example. Having left the new closed
      Special Unit at Barlinnie prison, he became an active campaigner for young people.

imagining the unimaginable. It would ask questions and start a dialogue. It would work with prisoners as citizens who can not only change themselves but could also play a vital role in the society to which they will (in the most part) return. Theatre through workshop, rehearsal and performance can make an important contribution to this. Along with other forms of dynamic and progressive rehabilitation and education, it has the potential to encourage active and critical citizenship (Giroux 1992, p.1). As Deborah Prothrow-Stith (the former Public Health Commissioner for Massachusetts) says in describing a violence prevention initiative:

> All our great black leaders, from Harriet Tubman to Martin Luther King to Nelson Mandela, have channeled their anger at injustice into a force to reshape the world. This is what the violence prevention curriculum is all about. It is not about passivity. It is about using anger not to hurt oneself or one's peers, but to change the world. (Prothrow-Stith 1991, p.183)

For real progress in the field of offender rehabilitation and in a wider sense crime prevention, this linkage of personal and social change is vital. It challenges the punitive model of criminal justice replacing it with what Elias calls a 'social action model of corrections' (Hartnett forthcoming, p.13) which places the prisoners as 'whole and equal people in the process' (Hughes, this collection, p.60). The practice of prison theatre – the vital collision of two litmus tests – is part of and not an aside in this. To paraphrase Arne and Churchill, without theatre and the arts the criminal justice system will continue as 'soulless', and this will be reflected in a wider society with no 'virtue'. The practice of bringing 'soul' to the system, of encouraging the arts and theatre, might make for more humane and effective criminal justice, and the more humane the system, by the logic of Churchill and Dostoyevski, the more civilised our society. Theatre, as the many examples in this book demonstrate, has a vital, dynamic and challenging role to play.

The organisation of the book

There are 13 chapters in this book representing a wide variety of practice and debate in the field of prison theatre. I have loosely collected these in different sections, but these boundaries are somewhat blurred and some chapters could easily have been placed in a number of areas.

Part 1: Questioning the Practice

The first two chapters by Paul Heritage and Jenny Hughes, whilst describing different experiences of prison theatre practice, start to ask some of the questions about why the work is done and importantly what we should be doing. They both tackle vital areas of pedagogy and how inmates should be involved in the theatrical process.

Part 2: Therapy and Rehabilitation

The next four chapters take this debate further, examining the relation between theatre, therapy and rehabilitation. They look at the differences between the two disciplines, the crossovers, and also describe practice where theatre is placed as a central part of the rehabilitative process.

Part 3: Working in the Institution

Chapters seven to eleven examine the processes, pressures and problems faced when working in an institution. Writers give different insights as to how arts work is created, maintained and sometimes undermined in a prison setting.

Part 4: Evaluation and History

I could not let these two chapters stand alone! One describes a revealing moment in the history of prison theatre in Brazil and the other discusses and offers guidance in the field of programme evaluation. They are linked in that one looks backwards in order to question the future, whilst the other provides a guide for how the field can mature in the future. Both act as a fitting way to conclude this collection.

References

Austin American Statesman (1996) 'State corrections proposal looks to the past.' 6 September, p.1.

Bergman, J., Hewish, S. and Ruding, S. (1996) 'The violent illusion: dramatherapy and the dangerous voyage to the heart of change.' In M. Liebmann (ed) *Arts Approaches to Conflict*. London: Jessica Kingsley Publishers.

Bidinotto, R.J. (1994) 'Must our prisons be resorts?' *Readers' Digest*, November, 65–71.

Boal, A. (1992) *Games for Actors and Non-Actors*. London: Routledge.

Boal, A. (1995) *Rainbow of Desire*. London: Routledge.

Bourque, B.B., Cronin, R.C., Pearson, F.R., Felker, D.B., Han, M. and Hill, S.M. (1996) *National Institute of Justice Research Report: Boot Camps for Juvenile Offenders: An Implementation Evaluation of Three Demonstration Programs*. US Department of Justice, Office of Justice Programs. NCJ 157316.

Brewster, L. (1983) *An Evaluation of the Arts-In-Corrections Program of the California Department of Corrections*. California: San Jose State University.

Christie, N. (1993) *Crime Control as Industry: Towards Gulags Western Style*. London: Routledge.

Cox, M. (ed) (1992) *Shakespeare Comes to Broadmoor: 'The Actors are Come Hither' The Performance of Tragedy in a Secure Psychiatric Hospital*. London: Jessica Kingsley Publishers.

Cullen, A.T., Wright, J.P. and Applegate, B.K. (1996) 'Control in the community: the limits of reform?' In A.T. Harland (ed) *Choosing Correctional Options that Work*. London: Sage.

Donziger, S.R. (1996) (ed) *The Real War on Crime: The Report of the National Criminal Justice Commission*, New York: Harper Perennial.

Freire, P. (1970) *Pedagogy of the Oppressed.* London: Penguin.

Garland, D. (1990) *Punishment and Modern Society: A Study in Social Theory.* Oxford: Clarendon Press.

Giroux, H. (1992) *Border Crossings: Cultural Workers and the Politics of Education.* London: Routledge.

Hartnett, S. (forthcoming) 'Combining progressive prison pedagogy and outreach projects: classrooms of possibility as workshops for democracy.' *Crime, Law and Social Change, High Performance Magazine* Spring, 75, p.2.

High Performance Magazine (1997) 'Prez, Guus plead more $$ for arts.'

Howell, J.C., Krisberg, B., Hawkins, J.D., and Wilson J.J. (eds) (1995) *A Sourcebook: Serious Violent, and Chronic Juvenile Offenders.* Thousand Oaks, California: Sage Publications.

Johnson, W.W., Bennett, K. and Flanagan, T.J. (1997) 'Getting tough on prisoners: results from the National Corrections Executive Survey, 1995.' *Crime and Delinquency 43*, 1, 24–41.

Kuziakina, N. (1995) *Theatre in the Solovki Prison Camp.* Trans: B.M. Meerovich. Luxembourg: Harvard Academic Publishers.

McGuire, J. and Priestley, P. (1985) *Offending Behaviour: Skills and Stratagems for Going Straight.* London: Batsford.

Miller, J. (1994) 'From social safety net to dragnet: African American males in the criminal justice system.' *Washington and Lee Law Review.* Spring, 479–490.

Miller, J. (1996) *Search and Destroy: African-American Males in the Criminal Justice System.* Cambridge: Cambridge University Press.

Peaker, A. and Pratt, B. (1996) *Arts Activities in Prisons: 1993–1995. A Directory.* London: HM Prison Service.

Prothrow-Stith, D. (1991) *Deadly Consequences.* New York: Harper Perennial.

Rideau, W. and Wikberg, R. (1992) *Life Sentences: Rage and Survival Behind Bars.* New York: Times Books.

Texas Youth Commission (1995) *The Resocialization Approach.* Austin, Texas: Texas Youth Commission.

The Times (1997) 'Reformer Straw is on Parole.' 12 July.

Thompson, J. (1995) 'Blagg! Rehearsing for change.' *Probation Journal 42*, 190–194.

Winnicott (1986) *Home is Where We Start From.* Harmondsworth: Penguin.

PART I

Questioning the Practice

Preface

Victor Hassine

When it was time to cast for my play, I was faced with a choice: I could have gone out and recruited either from the prison's brightest or from its less literate mainstream. If the actors were to be chosen from the brightest, the performance would probably end up being more articulate and true to the script. But these bright inmate actors would be hard to replace should they be unable to make the performance. On the other hand, if the actors were chosen from the mainstream, the play would have to be adjusted for easier reading and recollection, but finding understudies would not be a problem.

I anticipated that for a multitude of reasons, understood best by those who have dealt with prison bureaucracies, the inmates who participated in the play would be subject to close scrutiny by the prison guards. Anything new or different in a prison is always somehow resisted by staff, and I guessed that in this case resistance would take the form of harassing the actors by issuing them 'petty misconducts' in an attempt to disturb rehearsals. For this reason I chose to recruit the cast from the mainstream. In fact I asked some people who could barely read if they wanted to participate. In this way I felt protected from what I thought would be the guards' reaction to a prison play.

As it turned out, my instincts were right. It took over a year to get the play performed because so many of the actors were ending up in the 'hole' (solitary confinement). On several occasions even I was personally threatened by different guards because of my part in writing the play and getting permission to stage it. Nevertheless, after several cast changes and because of a strong desire to thwart the guards, the play was finally staged.

Because of my decision to recruit from the mainstream and the guards' acts of resistance and interference, what resulted was in fact a laboratory study on how inmates taken from the broad base of an inmate population were affected by their involvement in the performing arts. My revelation of the true power of theatre came when I saw with my own eyes how profoundly my friend Howard had been changed by his involvement in the production. Howard was the play's lead actor, but before that he was just another hyperactive drug addict, a convicted burglar who had a penchant for laziness and the misleading of others. He was a man in his early thirties who, though very articulate, had poor reading and writing abilities and tended to focus all of his talents on charming people out of their belongings.

His drug addiction was so acute that he had managed to convince himself to get committed to the mental health unit of the prison. In this way, he reasoned, he could get free medically prescribed drugs. In his drug-induced stupor, Howard did not do much more than eat, sleep, and take medication.

I never really thought Howard would or could see the play through. But I figured there would be no harm in getting him involved in just a bit part. And Howard himself at first did not seem to take the play seriously – he would miss rehearsals, not know his lines and he kept ending up in the hole.

About a month or two into rehearsals, the director decided that it was time to try out for parts. She had everyone read different parts and in the end, much to my surprise, she asked Howard to do the lead. And that is when Howard began to change.

Howard's change was not gradual, it was immediate. He would carry the script with him everywhere. He would follow me around, asking me to advise him on what I meant exactly at different parts in the script. I remember a few times while I was in the prison's gym, getting in some weightlifting, I would be pumping iron, while he would perform his part. Thinking back on it, we must have seemed quite the odd couple, but there was no shaking Howard. He was on a mission.

I remember the day when he finally shed his script and was able to recall his lines. Earlier he had been sent to the hole for another one of his petty misconduct situations and the guards had refused to let him take his script with him. For the two weeks he was in the hole, he had racked his brain to recall his part, and practised, in his solitary cell, the scenes he could remember. When he finally returned to the general population he immediately found me in the yard, and as we walked around the half-mile prison yard track, Howard recited almost all of his lines with few errors. I was impressed, but a little embarrassed by the animated gestures he had made as we walked around the yard.

There was more to my noticing Howard's transformation than just his determination to memorise his lines. After all he could have been doing nothing more than focusing his addictive personality on remembering his parts. But one day, in as serious a tone as I had ever remembered Howard addressing me, he said, 'You know what, Vic, every time I read my part and try to act it out, I can feel something different that you're trying to say. I mean, I can feel it inside – boy, that's really deep.' Coming from Howard this was an indication of profound change.

Within six months Howard had decided that he had to get off the 'nut block', get into the prison drug and alcohol recovery unit, go back to school, and give up drugs. And in fact, he eventually wound up doing all of those things.

I remember on the day of the performance I nervously watched Howard fill the stage with his character. He had a glazed 'I'm high' look on his face, as he worked the audience, probably in the same way that he used to hustle the victims of his petty con games. I could tell he understood the character, the play, the audience, and, now for the first time in a very long time, himself.

Howard was finally released. The Superintendent, as a reward for his fine performance and noticeable change in behaviour, recommended his parole despite his multiple misconduct situations and his recent stay on the mental health block. Before he went home, Howard and I talked together about him and the play, and I listened to Howard describe what he had felt during the performance. I am not talking about the vainglorious aspects of his brush with success, Howard told me about the character he had portrayed: a drug-addicted thief who had killed someone during a robbery and wound up getting executed in the electric chair.

'I saw myself in the character, Victor, I really did. I mean it was like it was really me killing the guy, and getting electrocuted. It was me raping Dude in prison and getting molested when I was young. I cried, Victor, cried when the mother was neglecting me. I'm not going to let what happened to that guy happen to me, Victor. No, that's it for me. I'm done doing that shit and letting my parents down. I'm going home, Vic – I mean I'm going home,' my friend Howard finally gushed out, with an air of determination that seemed in contrast to his whole prison existence until that moment.

And Howard did just that; he went home. I call him on the phone regularly. He is now engaged and working hard at a couple of labouring jobs to finance his new life. His success is how I know of the great influence theatre can have in prison. How people who cannot read and write can nevertheless learn important lessons in life, by way of their hearts and souls. Role-playing can bring to a whole prison population more understanding and wisdom than all the books in the world.

Let's face the facts, not all of us are lucky enough to possess the gifts of reading and writing, so instead of punishing people for their lack of ability, we need to give them what they truly need: a theatre to learn in, a play to learn from and a chance to feel proud of what they have learned.

CHAPTER 1

Theatre, Prisons and Citizenship

A South American Way

Paul Heritage

Punishment has always been performed. Foucault begins his analysis of penal systems in *Discipline and Punish* (1979) with an all too visual account of the staging of the punishment of the regicide Damiens in 1757. The account carries a detailed description of the tearing of the body as four horses – which have to be increased to six when the first four cannot manage the task – rip his limbs apart. The chroniclers are careful to record how late in this process the unfortunate Damiens was still to be heard crying out. The horror of the punishment was matched to the perceived horror of the crime and played out to an appreciative audience. It was not so much the effect on the offender that was at issue (although clearly that was considerable) but the spectacle of the retribution that was important.

The focus of the modern criminal justice system has shifted from the act of the crime to the nature of the criminal, and thus the spectacle of punishment has changed. What Foucault traces in his works on power within penal and psychiatric institutions is the transition from a time when criminal law consisted of only the offence and the penalty to the contemporary criminology which recognises the crime and the criminal. The offence is now less important in itself than it is as a signal for understanding the offender – a system in which legal justice 'has at least as much to do with criminals as with crimes' (Kritzman 1988, p.128). The performative function of punishment is all too evident in the execution of Damiens. How does this translate to the contemporary penal spectacle, and what role do theatre workers in prison assume or perform in the context of the transformed ideological intent of the process of incarceration? How do we participate in the mechanisms of repression, and is there any potential to operate outside such paradigms? We may not be tearing the flesh with red-hot pincers but what other functions have we found within the penal system? It is these questions that I want to make central to the enquiry of this article.

In order to ask these questions I shall be focusing on work that the TIPP Centre (the Theatre in Prisons and Probation Centre) at Manchester University has been developing in Brazil over the last five years. In Britain the TIPP Centre runs a variety of programmes which concentrate on offending behaviour, developed in a way that responds to the ideological and thus financial climate. Thus the Centre has devised and run programmes in response to the demands and perceived needs of the British criminal justice system. It is hard to disengage from the immediate site of production and resist the particular discourses that fashion the work on which the TIPP Centre has embarked. The Brazilian projects have given the opportunity to distance, re-examine and re-focus the work that the TIPP Centre is doing in Britain.

The first stages took place in the futuristic capital city of Brasília, at the federal penitential complex called *Papuda* – a word that Brazilian children use to indicate the noise a turkey makes. Britain hardly fares any better in the names it gives to prisons, with Wormwood Scrubs, Risley and Strangeways conjuring up gruesome images. The name was given to Papuda when it was being constructed next to a large turkey farm, which has now become a sprawling agrarian community in the scrub lands beyond the Brazilian capital. The prison may not have adequate funding but it certainly does not lack space, occupying a vast site which necessitates travel by car or on horseback between the various locations. There are three prisons in the one complex, where approximately 1400 male and 75 female inmates are held. These are divided between semi-open and maximum security buildings.

On entering the prison for the first time, the prisoner is given a booklet. It begins with a letter to the inmate from the head of the Federal Penitentiary system, Colonel Flávio Acauan Souto. Forty years in the Brazilian army, Colonel Souto is a formidable man and was my guide to Papuda when I first visited Brazil in 1991. So let him be yours.

Você/You

Who are you?

You are an inmate of this penal establishment. Society usually just calls it PRISON.

What is a PRISON? Ultimately, what are you?

You are someone that has committed an illicit act; you were judged and condemned to a sentence which restricts your liberty. You are someone that society, through the Justice system, resolved to isolate, temporarily, from your normal living.

Take note: temporarily.

What does society hope from you? The reply is simple and direct: that you should recuperate, re-educate yourself and if possible return to live a normal life in liberty, with your neighbours and those whom you love. However, above all else you are a human being, who is temporarily distant from society, but you have not left it. You are a human being, who thinks, speaks, acts and feels like any other. And also – recognise yourself – suffers like anyone else.

The State maintains, on its side, a weighty and expensive structure which seeks both your isolation and your recuperation. There are penitentiaries, prisons and jails spread throughout the whole country. This penal establishment in which you live is only a small part of a vast complex which sadly has to be maintained and paid for.

No-one denies that the Brazilian prison system is deficient, badly equipped – even cruel.

Our establishment is trying to transform itself into one of the exceptions of this sad regime. For this, a great effort is being made to bring about better conditions for the inmates and the administration. This begins with four fundamental points: DISCIPLINE/HYGIENE/WORK/STUDY (Cartilha do Interno:5)

There are various ideologies manifest in this writing, some of which we may recognise from the British situation, others which are resoundingly new. It is a personal address – a private interrogation, situating the reader (the inmate) in the context of a public system that is itself at fault. It is hard to imagine the British Home Office being able to write a letter to a new prisoner that includes the sentence: 'No-one denies the British prison system is deficient, badly equipped – even cruel'. Indeed, in past pronouncements we have seen the British government, in the face of all the evidence to the contrary, still believing that the prison system in Britain is working. The letter from Colonel Souto assumes the opposite. There is no talk here of evil or of wrongdoing by the individual. The illicit act is simply referred to as the reason for being in prison but there are no moral assumptions implicit in the writing, except with reference to the State's provisions. There is recourse to medical terminology but it is variant from British practice in that this is not the language of social hygiene – cleaning up the communal body by expelling the corrupted/diseased member. Nor is there invoked any outside agency that will be responsible for transforming the individual. The emphasis here is on self-healing – not something that will be done *to* the inmate but *by* the inmate. Thus the letter seeks to make the addressee the subject and not the object of a process.

But perhaps of greatest significance is the declaration of the continued status of the prisoner's citizenship. In common with most countries the Brazilian prison population has no voting rights. The Colonel, however, emphasises in this document that the prisoner is still a citizen. When I first met him in August 1991, the Colonel finished my guided tour of the prison in the pig farm. Amongst the noisy feeding rituals of these outsized animals, the Colonel explained his philosophy for Papuda: that every prisoner has a right to food, health care, education and work because these are the fundamental rights of all citizens, but that none of these have any meaning without culture because it is through culture that humans understand and define themselves.

The invitation to return to Papuda came from Colonel Souto, but the trip was paid for by the British Council and CNPq (a national Brazilian funding agency for research in education and science). The purpose was specific. The authorities at Papuda had already begun to implement the first four points of the Colonel's programme. FUNAP (the State Foundation for the Assistance of Prison Workers) began work seven years ago and already provides work or education for 60 per cent of the prison population. They are increasing this figure annually. Food and hygiene in Papuda are far superior to anything I experienced in other Brazilian prisons although it is important to see the physical circumstances of the Brazilian penal system within the context of wider social conditions.

As always, the physical conditions of incarceration can only be assessed in relation to the state of living for people in liberty. Ninety-five per cent of the Brazilian prison population comes from a situation of abject poverty, according to figures released by the Ministry of Justice in 1993. Few of them will have had regular food of any nutritional value, 89 per cent of them will never have had fixed work, and 76 per cent are unable to read or write when they enter the prison. Everything that the prison authorities are trying to implement must be taken against this scenario. It is also important to stress that this is a system under immense strain within a country that faces huge social and economic problems, many of them related to the debt crisis facing most Latin American countries. The consequences of this are most strikingly evident in the lack of resources available to the prison authorities when 32 million Brazilians live in total poverty – a state better rendered in Portuguese as *miséria*. The low priority of the penal system and the abysmal salaries paid to the military and civil police combine to create a situation of vulnerability both for those who work in the prisons and those who are incarcerated in them. Although Papuda prides itself on the low level of violent incidences within the prison, death is a constant measure of the lives of Brazilian prisoners. During my time in Brazil the military police killed 120 inmates in two hours in a São Paulo prison.[1] This is an extreme example of a brutality that can affect the relationships between the inmates. During one of the initial drama workshops a bloodied knife flew through the bars of the window onto the cell

1   Casa de Detenção, São Paulo (Carandiru) 2 October 1992. For an account of the massacre see *Veja* 14 October 1992.

floor as a fight in the yard outside culminated in the death of a prisoner. The achievements by the Federal prison authorities over the past few years in Papuda are a testament to the vision and faith of some remarkable people.

Although FUNAP had begun to transform the material conditions and educational provision in Papuda, there was by 1992 still no cultural programme and thus I was invited to attempt the establishment of theatre work in the prison. This began in January 1993 with two groups of inmates, one in CIR (a maximum security unit) and the other in the *Núcleo de Custodia* (a semi-open unit). Both of these are male institutions but seven women were brought in each day to the Núcleo from the women's prison to create the first mixed gender group. This was important for the work from the outset, and although initially resistant the administration has used the success of this project to provide an increase in joint programmes between the Núcleo and the women's penitentiary. Every day during the project the women would be collected from their cells and we would then march in formation with an armed escort along a yellow line to the rehearsal rooms across the yard of the men's prison. I have nothing but admiration for the bravery of these women, and nothing but respect for the men on the yard who never once shouted obscenities or commented negatively as we crossed their territory. I could not guarantee the same decency in Britain, and for all the supposed *machismo* of Brazilian society I was surprised daily by the generosity and understanding between the sexes in the prison compound. Perhaps the fact that families are allowed to visit their relatives and spend the day with them in the yard and that all inmates have the right to one conjugal visit per week ameliorates in some way the inhuman nature of incarceration. Those who have visited British prisons will know that the single-gender, officially de-sexualised identity of the establishments contributes in no small way to the brutality of the confinement.

The two initial projects were similar in format to the ones run by the TIPP Centre in Britain. Beginning with games and simple acting exercises, Image Theatre was used to discover subject matter for the plays that the groups went on to create for performance. Rooted in the techniques of Boal's Theatre of the Oppressed, the process is designed to sensitise the group to working with each other and to discovering ways of debating their lives through theatre. There were some notable characterising features of the work. The ideas and images expressed a clear commentary on Brazilian society. The groups had a great facility to demonstrate the oppressions they experienced and make connections between the different mechanisms of repression. Thus the CIR group produced a play about slavery in Brazil, which began by showing the arrival of the Africans through to the abolition of slavery in 1893. They followed this opening with three scenes demonstrating slavery in contemporary Brazil: in the *fazendas* of the Northeast, in the soap opera domination of television, and in the racist slavery of the criminal justice system where the vast majority of the prison population is black or *mulato*. The presentation in the Núcleo was based on a poem that questioned why Brazil with all its richness should keep its people in such abject misery. Such themes running through all the projects demonstrate the determination of all the participants to engage in a debate about their country. The process of the theatre work was constantly focused on the most effective ways to achieve an impact. The theatrical forms that evolved were cooked from foreign and native ingredients, but the techniques originated from the writings of two Brazilians, Augusto Boal and Paulo Freire. Thus the groups worked towards final presentations using a process which began with practices developed in British prisons but became peculiarly Brazilian. Using an eclectic style that drew from *capoeira*,[2] carnival and soap opera, the plays presented the individual trajectory of a particular protagonist within a framework of the structure of oppression.

The poem *Porque ó Brasil*, that formed the basis for one of the projects, was written by one of the inmates from words and images that had been created by the group in a drama workshop. Moisés was 21 when he wrote the poem and was two months away from completing a two year sentence. Like 60 per cent of the prisoners he was an ex-street child, but within Papuda he had achieved a certain level of respect. Unable to afford teachers from outside to work in the prison, FUNAP (with the help of the Education Foundation) trains inmates to teach the other inmates. Each monitor, as they are known, teaches one or two disciplines within the Education Sector that is run by one of the guards. Moisés, for example, was the maths teacher. This innovatory system provides opportunities for inmates to take their first and second grades in the prison (which are roughly equivalent to British GCSE and 'A' levels), and has even seen some of them pass the university entrance exam, the *vestibulário*. One of the members of the other project, Francisco, had entered Papuda unable to read or write and had just passed the vestibulário when I arrived. Thus the inmates do, in a very real sense, educate themselves in the prison. By placing the inmate in a position of authority and responsibility in front of a room of 30 prisoners, Papuda is creating a pedagogy that enables both pupil and teacher to improve themselves and earn respect. The inmate becomes both subject of the teaching and of the learning, rather than being the fixed object of the pedagogical process. It abandons both the barriers of conventional education and the procedures of authority that supposedly stabilise prison life.

This made the theatre project so much more viable within Papuda because it functioned on the established principle of passing on techniques and processes that others could continue. In Britain most of the work we generate is controlled

2   *Capoeira* is a folkloric dance that was practised by slaves as a means of disguising their training in martial arts. Capoeira academies exist in most towns throughout Brazil and displays range from the frankly tourist to the quasi-religious.

by the authorities in such a way that little is left but a memory when we leave. Here in Brazil the theatre projects benefited from a system that already valued the ability of the prisoners to organise and facilitate their own work. Hence after my departure the groups were able to undertake further performances on other wings of the prison and for their families on a Sunday. Undoubtedly this has been made easier by the support that the project has received from the authorities at the top of the administrative structure. Colonel Souto is responsible for the general co-ordination of the Federal penitentiaries, not the day-to-day running of the prisons. However, with his encouragement and the active support of Dr Angelo Roncalli de Ramos Barros (the Director of FUNAP) the theatre work has been embedded into the life of Papuda. The complex and diverse reasons why this has been possible undoubtedly include the supposed prestige of the international links, the funding of the British Council and the establishment of a project that linked Papuda with the Drama Department at the University of Brasília. But despite the contradictory agendas that can be located in the decisions to support the theatre work, its development within a system of such limited resources represents an extraordinary commitment by the authorities, and a real achievement for the men and women involved.

Although as ever the process of the drama workshops provided the strength of the project as a whole, it was the theatre performances themselves that finally brought about the tangible successes and, for me, a significant re-evaluation of the appropriate focus for theatre in prisons. In the past it has become a common feature of prison theatre (and perhaps of other similar projects) that the most important moments for theatre practitioners are in the workshops and rehearsals, and that the process not the product is central to the achievement of the project. Often this is expressed more in terms of a healing than a learning process, focusing on the individual working within a group environment in order to learn supposedly quantifiable social skills. It moulds itself very comfortably into the ideological framework of a punishment system that concentrates on reforming an individual whose presence is considered both a danger and a disease within the social body. The performance is often seen merely as an affirmative adjunct of the *real* work that happens in the workshops. In Brazil, however, the performance was seen as fulfilling a more vital function. In the first place it advocated the work and thus allowed the development of the project. Thus at the first showing of the play about slavery, there were special guests from the Department of Justice, the University of Brasília, and the British Council who were funding the project. The prison administration staff present at the performance also included the Minister of Security, Colonel Brochard, watching the play amongst the inmate audience. The direct consequence of this performance was the invitations to continue the work. The proof of what had been achieved had to have its demonstration in the performance. This was, however, more than just a bizarre mixture of people brought together under armed guard to witness a play about the oppressions of the Brazilian justice system. What the occasion made manifest was the extraordinary power of theatre to facilitate a dialogue that could never happen in other circumstances. As yet that dialogue was one-way, but at least the production had reversed the normal direction and it had highlighted the centrality of the actual performance event.

Theatre Workshop, Papuda Prison, Brazil
Picture by Ricardo Padue

When I returned to Papuda in July 1993 it was with the specific intention to explore and extend this performance function within the projects. We set about working in much the same way but with a clear objective to establish Forum Theatre performances for each of the productions. The groups, consisting of about 15 members from before and 25 new performers, devised pieces over a three-week period dealing with a range of oppressions: racism; migration; HIV/AIDS; drugs; domestic violence; the assassination of street children. Those who had participated in the previous project helped train the new arrivals, matching the pedagogical ideals of the Education Sector in general. The plays presented the problems using a range of styles, with non-verbal Image Theatre framing naturalistic scenes that projected a protagonist's individual story. At the end of the performance the audience was asked to question the actors about their actions and suggest alternatives which the actors or the audience member would implement. Very pure and basic Forum Theatre as described by Boal. The potency of it within the prison was enormous, because suddenly a project that had previously reached only a handful of people was now incorporating between 150 and 200 at each performance. The level of the debate at each of the performances was impressive, focusing not only on the immediate problems to be solved for the protagonist but also on the complex issues that society itself needed to address. The concentration had shifted from healing the individual to changing society.

The dialogic powers of this theatrical discourse are well theorised by Augusto Boal. There is however an important departure from the norm in this model, in that at Papuda each performance involved the presence of the oppressor and the oppressed. The play about the street children thus showed the assassinations carried out by the police to an audience that included members of that force and their commanders as well as many who had lived their lives on the street. Each person had the opportunity to join the debate – to intervene, to stop and control the action. We also invited members of the Citizens' Action Campaign Against Hunger and Poverty to witness the plays and participate as appropriate. This significant political movement, established by the sociologist Herbert deSouza (Betinho), has formed committees in banks, schools, hospitals, factories and workplaces across the country. The purpose of the campaign is to create alternative ways for citizens to take an active and practical part in the solution of Brazil's problems. The committees not only organise the collection and distribution of food and the construction of new facilities, but are also instrumental in establishing a national debate that is outside of the normal political structures. In a society with such inequality as Brazil, with a political élite taken from a conspicuously narrow base, there is a special urgency to any movement which seeks to broaden the involvement of those who are disempowered and essentially disenfranchised. The Citizen's Action Campaign Against Hunger and Poverty is largely middle-class in its organisation, but here within the walls of Papuda there was a real opportunity to involve those members of society that had experienced and witnessed the miseries of poverty. Through theatre the inmates were brought into a debate and became a part of a struggle to search for the solutions that Brazil must find if it is to emerge from its continuing crisis. This was reinforced when the project culminated in a performance by the prisoners outside of the jail at the Palace of Justice in the centre of Brasília to an invited audience of the judiciary and 300 deputies from the Senate. A unique occurrence, the dangers posed to the inmates and other personnel were not inconsiderable (the original presentation had to be cancelled when the military police threatened to bomb the building), but the determination with which the group faced this audience and talked openly on the stage about their plight was an effective testimony to how far they had travelled during the project.

Since then, and largely as a result of this performance, Papuda has constructed a Studio Theatre inside the prison where a regular theatre group meets five days a week. There is now a waiting list of over 60 people to go on the training courses, which are run mainly by the inmates themselves. Where possible, visiting artists come in to run workshops on theatre techniques. I returned twice the following year, once with actors from the Royal Shakespeare Company and the National Theatre, and once to make a film about the work with the BBC. The original plan to provide a cultural centre within Papuda is now beginning to be realised with five theatre groups working on a daily basis within a whole wing of the prison which is dedicated to drama, music, visual arts and craft work.

The wider issues of the operation and function of cultural activity within a prison are being addressed in more complex ways than was initially imagined. By reactivating the inmate as citizen, theatre in prison can start to resist the formations that it too often adopts within the ideological frameworks imposed by the penal system. To ensure that the inmate remains subject and not object of the theatre process is a powerful and necessary directive if we are to claim any radical purpose to this work. How far this can be true is always questionable when the inmates themselves are rarely able to organise or control the structure of their activities, even when they acquire the techniques to develop their own work within sessions. Nor are theatre practitioners themselves free agents within the system that permits or prohibits such work around the margins of the greater performance of incarceration. The central characters are fixed, the dominant narratives inscribed and the main stage designed to perform a more powerful and affective ritual with the inmate's body than can ever be staged on the fringes where this work is contained. To acknowledge the grander spectacle initiates the attempt to reverse the discourse by which such power is uttered and performed. It is to begin a process that invokes the transformative powers of theatre in ways that concentrate not on the individual criminal but potentially on the society in which we all play a part, and thus to move away from the deeply reactionary notion that punishment has any significant determining effect on crime.

At a lecture in London,[3] the Brazilian educationalist Paulo Freire emphasised the essential need for dreams in human existence. What he reminded his audience was that our dreams, though individual by their nature, all exist within a social and historical dimension. Theatre in prison can be a powerful place to realise those dreams – to reinvent the present and to imagine a new future. I want to dedicate this article to Moisés who wrote the poem that inspired the first project. His story is an important reminder of a more complex reality than I have managed to describe. Two weeks after the March project, Moisés contracted meningitis. He

---

3   *The Educational Theory of Paulo Freire* with Professor Paulo Freire, Institute of Education, London, October 25/26 1993.

was 15 days in the prison before he was moved to a hospital where he died that same day. This was not the negligence of the prison authorities but the refusal of any hospital in the city to give a bed to a prisoner: the ultimate exclusion of the inmate from the social body – the ultimate denial of the citizen. The performance at the Palace of Justice finished with Moisés' poem about Brazil, which included the following words:

> Land of such riches and fantasies
> Betrayed by the touch of such conspicuous hands –
> While misery and poverty
> Break the citizen.
> Brazil, you have magic and culture
> Faith and adventure;
> What we need now is only a push.
>
> Oh why Brazil, such illusion?
> Oh why Brazil, such lamentation?
> I am only a citizen who is missing a piece of bread.

References

Kritzman, L.D. (ed) (1988) *Michel Foucault: Politics, Philosophy, Culture: Interviews and Other Writings, 1977–1984*. London: Routledge.

Further Reading

Boal, A. (1979) *Theatre of the Oppressed*. London: Pluto.
Foucault, M. (1979) *Discipline and Punish*. London: Peregrine.
Freire, P. (1972) *Pedagogy of the Oppressed*. London: Penguin.

CHAPTER 2

Resistance and Expression

Working with Women Prisoners and Drama

Jenny Hughes

I have worked in the field of drama and theatre with offenders for three years, initially as a student and subsequently as a freelance drama worker and part-time teacher. Approximately half of this work has been with women prisoners in HMP Styal. The aim of this paper is to explore the experience of working with women prisoners and drama. Discussions of this experience usually include a variety of questions and these form the stimulus of this chapter. Should drama with women prisoners be different in objective? How can we adapt drama models developed to confront male offending to address the different issues and experiences of women? Should we adapt those models or should we start anew? Is it a difference in nature or emphasis? Why are women in prison generally more resistant to drama than men? Is it possible to provide an adequate theatre and drama resource for women within prisons considering the extreme discrimination and oppression women face throughout the criminal justice system?

I have approached the exploration of these questions in two parts. In order to understand and usefully practise drama with women prisoners it is vital that the material context of the work is taken into account. Without an awareness of the pressures and frustrations of women's lives in prison it is impossible to work usefully or understand them. The first part of the chapter will therefore discuss the specific setting of a women's prison and the experiences of women prisoners. This first section is written from the perspective of a worker within the institution. It is drawn from the experiences I have had and observed as well as those that were related to me by the women with whom I worked. I have tried to add weight to these subjective reflections by including information and arguments from other research and related experience of women's prisons and women prisoners.

In the second part of the paper I will give a detailed description and analysis of drama work with women prisoners, again, drawing on my personal experience, though backed up by the observations of co-workers and the evaluations of the women that were involved in the various projects. The body of work that I will discuss ranges from offence and behaviour-focused workshops to issue and creative skills projects. Specifically, this will include: the experience of facilitating a six-day drama course with young offenders as part of their minimum statutory requirement of education; the Blagg! offence-focused workshop developed by the Theatre in Prisons and Probation Centre at Manchester University (run with young offenders and other groups throughout the prison); and finally, a four week long special drama project integrating women prisoners with adults with learning disabilities.

At present most drama and theatre initiatives within the criminal justice system are delivered as one-off ventures or packages without co-ordination or long-term development. This is true at least for the work in Styal and, I would argue, relates to the field as a whole. It happens this way because of the lack of money available to support the field of work. Drama and theatre work with offenders, however, is a rapidly maturing field. Its roots are in radical community theatre; a political theatre that sought to make theatre more accessible and relevant to the working class through a content and medium that was more relevant to the real pressures of living and aimed to raise a consciousness of an unjust system. Much of our work with offenders has now become accepted and comfortable within prison regimes that are ineffective, discriminatory and oppressive.

The assimilation of drama and theatre into such a system and the need to hold on to the little financial support there is for the work has meant in many instances that the aim of political challenge has been neutralised. There is much pressure on practitioners to survive by conforming within this system, for example, through devising offending behaviour packages that have the single aim of confronting offending behaviour and reinforcing the idea of the individual's responsibility. This aim fits very well within a right wing government that does not want to address the real roots of crime in poverty, unemployment, lack of opportunity and the emotional and social devastation that material deprivation causes in individuals and working-class communities. The reactionary trends in current practice are the ones that have been assigned the funding to develop into more than one-off ventures and have become, in my view, dangerously close to acting as nothing more than a new tool in the system of exploitation and oppression.

The drama work with women prisoners I have been involved in has led to a questioning of dominant practice. It is my intention through this paper to describe a process that has provided an opportunity to think about an alternative trend in the field. The development of a practice that is relevant and useful to women prisoners has, in my view, fundamental and far-reaching implications for the field as a whole.

Women prisoners...

> The prison service does not cater for women's experience, it does not even acknowledge women's offending. There's no infrastructure within the system to support initiatives that take women's experience seriously. There is a desperate need for a co-ordinated and fully resourced approach...[1]

Throughout the 1990s the prison population in Great Britain has grown by 25 per cent to a record level of 56,000 (*Socialist Worker* 1996). This is a result of a right-wing government's policy that insists that more prisons and harsher punishment are the answer to the problem of crime. In 1996, with a general election approaching, came a reiteration of 'prison works' campaigns and the announcement of further costly new prison-building schemes. This was blatant electioneering on behalf of a desperate and unpopular Conservative Party. The Labour Party in Britain are offering no alternative to the right's supposed solution to rising crime. The record increase in the prison population is therefore set to continue for the foreseeable future.

Right-wing governments insist that prison works. This is a strange dream. Again and again serious research and even Home Office commissioned reports prove the opposite: <u>prison does nothing but increase crime rates.</u> Experiences of custody increase the likelihood threefold that a prisoner will reoffend on release (*Socialist Worker* 1996). Prisons brutalise and degrade offenders; they shatter self-esteem and good intentions. The rate of reoffending after custody increases with young offenders: recent statistics show that four out of five young people will be reconvicted within two years of custody (*Socialist Worker* 1996). As the government moves further right in their policies towards offenders the function of prisons of ignoring social problems and keeping the rest of society quiet is becoming more sharp in focus. The overwhelming majority of people in prison are working-class. Unemployment, the disintegration of the health and education services, rising poverty and homelessness affect working-class people most harshly and are the real causes of crime. In one of the richest countries in the world they are also a sign of an inept and ruthless government. The real causes of crime continue to be disregarded in favour of more scapegoating policies and increases in the prison population.

The number of women in prison has increased by over 100 per cent since 1970 (John Crace in *The Guardian*, 1996). The overwhelming majority of women in prison are young working-class women, either unemployed or in part-time or low-paid jobs. Thirty seven per cent of women imprisoned in 1993 received a custodial sentence for default of fine payments. The crimes most often committed

---

1   Rose Dickinson, Instructional Officer and Drama Co-ordinator at HMP Styal, in interview with the writer, August 1996.

by women are the relatively minor offences of theft, handling and forgery. Theft typically means shoplifting for clothes and food and other items necessary for basic subsistence – many of the women that fit into this category are single parents providing for children. A minority are drug addicts supporting a habit and very few women in prison are involved in major crime rackets in an organised or systematic way. Approximately 10 per cent of women in prison are there for offences involving violence (John Crace in *The Guardian* 1996).

Pat Carlen states that one factor contributing to the population increase of women's prisons is public expenditure cuts in the 1980s, continuing in harshness in the 1990s (O'Dwyer, Wilson and Carlen 1987). Cuts have increased the chances of women struggling to provide for themselves and their children being caught in a poverty trap that may result in crime. Cuts have hit welfare and health agencies hardest: the lack of access to facilities on the outside has meant that many women that are capable of living safe lives outside now face custody. The attacks on services has also led to a rise in the numbers of vulnerable women in prison. A sizeable and growing proportion of women in prison therefore are suffering from serious mental health problems.

What is the experience of prison by women? There has been some excellent research on the discriminatory treatment of women both within the criminal justice system as a whole and within prison. They describe a general experience of prison by women that is frustrating, isolating, dangerous, mind-numbing, depressing, mystifying and humiliating. Women's prisons are less well resourced, especially in terms of education and training opportunities. Education and training tend to focus on domestic subjects such as cookery and craftwork rather than being linked in any real way to the experiences or needs of women prisoners. Evidence also suggests that regimes in women's prisons are more disciplinary than men's. There is, for example, consistently twice as many punishments delivered for offences against prison discipline (O'Dwyer *et al.* 1987). The figure is suggestive of the higher incidence of violence in women's prisons – a symptom of the extraordinary powerlessness women experience throughout the system.

My experience whilst working in HMP Styal was that women would routinely arrive in the education department for drama sessions tired from lack of exercise or sleep, wound up by officers on the house, angry, depressed, lethargic from prescribed drugs or bad food or out of their mind with anxiety about their cases, children outside and other worries. It never ceased to amaze me how much havoc an institution based on order and control could wreak on the lives of these women, from a relatively minor and petty level of making mistakes in wages (received for work in prison) to a serious level concerning the care of children outside and parole decisions. This contradiction is the subject of Elaine Genders' and Elaine Player's essay, 'Women in prison: the treatment, the control and the experience' (Genders and Player 1987). They state that the isolating function and lack of autonomy and control over their lives that women in prison experience undermines any attempt on their part to take responsibility for their lives outside or access help in any real way.

The criminal justice system is riddled with sexist assumptions that create a blind spot in terms of the reality of women's lives. Pat Carlen has summarised this sexist tendency in looking at sentencing policy for women:

> [T]he majority of British women prisoners have not been gaoled because of the seriousness of their crimes but because of either their aberrant domestic circumstances or less than conventional lifestyles; the failure of the non-penal welfare or health institutions to cope with their problems; or their own refusal to comply with culturally conditioned female gender stereotype requirements...these practices have resulted in it being denied that they are 'real' women... (O'Dwyer et al. 1987)

A woman, once in court, is likely to be sentenced because she is wearing trousers and has short hair or because she is a single mother without a stable male partner, because she has no money or because she lives a particular lifestyle. Magistrates, prison governors, prison officers and politicians consistently misunderstand, condemn, abuse and disempower women offenders.

HMP Styal has not fared well in serious publications describing the experience of women prisoners. In fact, Styal has been the focus of various public outcries over the last few years. Two of these received attention from the national press: the manacling of a woman prisoner whilst she was giving birth in an outside hospital and the high incidence of illegal drug taking amongst young offenders in the prison, some of whom became addicted to hard drugs during their sentences. The stories that escaped the cloud of secrecy that surround closed institutions in Britain are just the tip of the iceberg in terms of horrifying practices and abuses of power that occur routinely within prisons.

New management since the early 1990s has improved aspects of Styal – the destruction of Bleak House in 1995, the punishment block that has been the sight of much criticism from ex-prisoners for example, can only be described as a positive reform. In 1996, however, because of the overcrowding problems in the prison there was talk of reopening Bleak House. Also, in 1995 came the introduction of mandatory drug testing within the prison service as a whole: inmates, randomly picked, are directed to give a urine sample which is subsequently tested for illegal drugs. If tested positive the inmate is likely to be charged and face an addition to her sentence. Those who refuse to take the test are charged for an offence against prison discipline and may also face an addition to their sentence. The practice of mandatory drug testing in prison, apart from being degrading, is ineffective and very expensive. Many women that I met in Styal took some form of illegal drug during their sentence – to alleviate boredom or tension or to maintain a habit from the outside. Illegal drugs are still being taken in Styal well after the introduction of mandatory drug testing. The policy could even be seen to encourage the use of hard drugs as inmates know that traces of drugs like heroin disappear from the body more quickly than a soft drug like cannabis.

I want to end this section with a comment about the attempts of some workers to implement initiatives that begin to effect changes within the system. Many of the workers in Styal attempt to work in a meaningful and supportive way with women prisoners though the regime tends to frustrate these aspirations. For example, whilst spending massive sums on making mandatory drug testing operational the prison regime gave no financial assistance to the 'User Friendly' drugs rehabilitation group: a fully confidential and voluntary programme, supported by the women and run by a prison nurse voluntarily and in her own time. After running a successful programme with women for several years this group has collapsed as a result of the lack of support it received from the regime.

This discussion of women's prisons and aspects of the regime at Styal highlight how prisons continue to function more on a punitive model than in a rehabilitative or needs-focused way. A punitive ideology permeates the system from top to bottom and ensures that reforms within prisons remain of a transient nature. Andrew Rutherford in his essay 'Penal reform and prison realities' states, '...the most striking aspect of prison reform over the last two centuries is how little of it there has been. In most instances the gains have been modest, tenuous and short-lived...for every step forward, the institution often seems to slip back two steps' (Rutherford 1991, pp.2–3). Rutherford describes the pioneering work of individual governors and workers within prison in effecting reforms but adds the proviso:

> [T]he prison and the system of which it is a part tend to resist internal reform initiatives. Occasional collective efforts by prisoners to improve their lot have mostly been sharply put down...the authoritarian and mechanistic character of the prison system also ensures that the staff reformer is vulnerable to being co-opted, marginalised or driven out. (Rutherford 1991, p.8)

Rutherford calls for a co-ordinated approach from professionals working across the criminal justice system to attempt to reduce the prison population: a reduction of prisoners is for him the only realistic avenue for reform. Feminists like Carlen and Worrall (1987) also call for a co-ordinated approach. They aim to generate an awareness of the current contradictions in the treatment of women offenders and to assert the need for women's voices to be heard by those with power. But is this enough – and are such proposals realistic considering the state of the system in the 1990s?

The next section shows how drama work with offenders can be placed in amongst these debates through a description of the development of drama projects in Styal.

...and drama

> Yet their [women offenders] attempts to cope with it [the criminal justice system] were characterised by neither total acceptance nor outright rejection of the treatment they received...their attempts were characterised by accommodation – by a mixture of self – blame and suppressed anger, translated into a variety of petty resistances and rituals... (Worral 1990, p.160)

There is a general belief amongst theatre practitioners working within the criminal justice system that women offenders are a more resistant, volatile and less predictable group to work with than men. An honest look at my experience of working with both male and female offenders supports this belief. Some groups of women I have encountered respond with ease, enthusiasm and confidence to drama work. However, the general, at least initial, response of groups to an unfamiliar medium and member of staff has been one of hostility, suspicion, anxiety and occasionally ridicule. I see this resistance as a logical and understandable response to the contradictory and oppressive treatment women are subject to. Rose Dickinson, Instructional Officer and Drama Co-ordinator in Styal, adds that, 'all the people that come in to work here from male establishments are surprised at how reticent the women are...it comes from their social conditioning, women are told to sit down and be quiet and tend to feel so guilty about who they actually are, they want to hide themselves and their feelings.'[2]

Many women, particularly working-class women, lack confidence in expressing themselves in formal, group or public settings. With drama there is the added pressure of being required to be physically expressive; to move around and do imaginative and bizarre things with your body in front of peers, colleagues or even perfect strangers can be an extremely intimidating prospect. The dangers in prison are intensified. Looking a fool can lead to scapegoating and bullying by other prisoners and even by staff. Maintaining a strong or 'tough' image in prison is therefore very important and participation in a drama session can threaten this. Drama exercises depend on close physical, mental and emotional co-operation and contact. Not being taken seriously or being misunderstood can create feelings of extreme vulnerability. If a woman is working on a theme or issue that relates to experiences in her past, criticism or laughter can re-stimulate painful feelings. The general deadening routine and intrusiveness of prison life discussed above can all work to de-motivate, shut down and shut off women from themselves, others and their environment. Drama can suffer as a result of this environment as well as potentially undermine the alienating effect of the institution and open up participants physiologically and emotionally.

2   Rose Dickinson in interview with the writer, August 1996.

Rose Dickinson was crucially important in getting the first drama projects in Styal off the ground and remains to co-ordinate and develop new projects. She expresses a desire to, 'get them to do something, get them up off their bottoms, wake them up, see them start to react to something from the outside world, show them that there was something with which they could connect, encourage them to believe in themselves and gain some confidence.'[3] Initial projects, taking the form of residencies run by students from both Chester College and Manchester University, did meet with success of this nature. Drama disrupted the routine of the prison for the women, offered the opportunity to mix with people from outside, put their point of view, explore issues of relevance, have a laugh, try something different and gain confidence. Feedback from women who participated in residencies would often focus on the fact that the projects offered the opportunity of feeling 'normal' and being listened to and treated 'equally'.

These initial projects were difficult, not only as a result of working with the resistance and unpredictability of the women but also because of the hostility of prison staff and the fears of governors higher up in the regime. Drama projects were seen as an inappropriate luxury by some staff and outsiders coming into the prison to work with the women were regarded as a security risk. My first project in Styal in 1992, a two-week residency with young offenders led to a direct confrontation with the regime. Officers made complaints to the governor about noise, video and photography work, paper being stuck on the walls and over the window in the door. This resulted in the memorable occasion of myself, student colleagues and our supervisor being called up in front of the governor who gave us a telling off and forbade the use of a video camera for the remainder of the project (though we had cleared the use of the camera with the security department before the project began). Those were the days!

The picture is quite different today: student residencies are now a regular and normal part of the regime. Clean Break theatre company visit the prison with performances for the women and drama has become an accepted part of the young offender education programme. In 1995, new management bought Blagg!, the drama-based offending-behaviour workshop designed by the Theatre in Prisons and Probation Department at Manchester University (TIPP). Together with the Blagg! set came a three-day training event run by James Thompson from TIPP with a selection of prison officers and representatives from the psychiatric, education and health departments in the prison. The object was to train prison staff to deliver the workshop themselves with groups of women inside the prison. This was a significant development in the provision of drama to women prisoners: it introduced the uses and benefits of drama to a cross-disciplinary section of staff, therefore creating potential for a co-ordinated approach within the system. It was

3   Interview with the writer, August 1996.

also, to my knowledge, the first attempt to deliver a structured offending-behaviour programme specifically to groups of women within the prison service. The challenge to the staff was to find a way to make this programme appropriate to women's experiences of offending.

The workshop revolves around the character of Jo Blaggs, a woman prisoner. The group create this character, giving her a biography and an offence for which she has been sentenced. Volunteers from the group enact this offence and its consequence for Jo and her victim, exploring the thoughts and feelings of the characters involved. The group then creates the series of events that led to Jo committing the offence: events that could have taken place from five minutes to up to ten or fifteen years before. Interventions are made by the group as each scene is enacted, taking the form of Jo's attempts to change the course of events. The group suggest and rehearse alternative routes Jo could have taken out of situations. The workshop can be a powerful tool assisting individuals in looking at their lives, acknowledging the pressures that they are under, and devising and testing for themselves potentially more positive ways of responding to those pressures. It can provoke honest, personal and profound discussions with offenders around a variety of issues. Working with a fictional character created by the group makes the focus of the workshop both representative of the group's experience and distanced enough to function as a safe context through which to discuss personal issues and experiences.

I will discuss two implementations of the Blagg! workshop. The first with a group of eight young offenders was facilitated by myself, with assistance from a prison officer and a prison nurse, both of whom attended the training event. The second, facilitated by Rose Dickinson, assisted by two prison psychologists who had also attended the training, was run with women from Howard House, the Vulnerable Prisoners unit. Both days encountered difficulties. First, the staff members involved contradicted each other in their style of delivery and their reactions to the input and behaviour of the women. Second, the process was hindered by the resistance of the women.

Resistance was not the biggest issue in the first Blagg! — with young offenders. I had been working with young offenders on a weekly basis and generally achieved some level of positive participation. What was more obstructive was the responses of the participating prison officer. Throughout the day the officer interrupted, blocked and contradicted the suggestions of the women: in one discussion about how Jo had started taking drugs her response was, 'no, that's just not real, she can't possibly have been on the streets taking drugs when she was only 12'. Her comment in the evaluation at the end of the day was that she did not think I had gone far enough to emphasise the consequences of Jo's offence on the victim. The victim in this case was a man who had picked up Jo as a prostitute and physically attacked her. She had stabbed him in self-defence. I thought that there were more important issues than victim empathy to be explored here. It was clear from this experience that a co-ordinated approach that involves the regime at such close quarters would take a long time to develop: officers are trained to distrust, discipline and punish prisoners. In this instance they found the business of listening to and understanding women an alien and forbidden practice.

Rose had found the same difficulty in the workshop that she had facilitated with co-workers that had attended the training. She comments, 'there is a desire for the workshop being used to whip the women, you slam them with what they've done and the consequences bit, the message is "we have the answers, you have to change your way", this denies their experience and shuts doors...'[4] This comment and the experience related highlights the dangers of drama work being assimilated into the punitive ideology and practice of prison regimes. The objective becomes to confront women with what they have done and force them into taking responsibility for their actions. The assumption behind this is that women are irresponsible and thoughtless; the object is to make individuals change. It is clear that this is a very real danger: the officer's obstructive comments in the Blagg! described above were responded to by the women with a mixture of acceptance and humility: her status as a uniformed officer accorded her a power over the women that, at least within this workshop, they accepted. I am absolutely certain that if I had come out with a similar response (as a young teacher who had been working with the group for several weeks on a relatively equal footing) I would immediately have been challenged by them.

Beneath this specific example of the involvement of the regime in drama work lies an even more suspect operation. There is a desire to address offending behaviour within the criminal justice system and this becomes part of the veneer of a prison in presenting itself as an agency of crime prevention. In the prison service statement of aims the following is written, 'it is our duty to look after them with humanity and help them lead law-abiding and useful lives in custody and after release'. Through investing in programmes like Blagg! the institution can be seen to be fulfilling its responsibilities. Women can be processed through the workshop and a tick put on their files showing that the system has done its job. If a woman offends again then she must take full responsibility and what other solution is there left but confinement and punishment? Trendy alternatives have been tried, 'there are just some people that are too Inadequate or evil to be allowed into society, a criminal by name, a criminal by nature'.

Another interesting aspect of this second workshop was the group's insistence on presenting Jo as a victim. This is echoed in the first workshop – where the Jo created committed her crime in self-defence. For some women this presentation may clearly correlate with aspects of their offending: the options at the point of

4   Interview with the writer, August 1996.

the offence are so narrow that committing the crime is the only viable way out. For example, again in the story created above: Jo began taking drugs at 12 to block out the abuse suffered at the hands of her father; on being thrown out of home at 16 she goes to live with her drug dealer boyfriend who pressures her into prostitution to pay for both their habits. The crime here was tied up in a complex web of relationships and pressures within which the woman experiences herself as powerless. The alternative is clouded and would involve reversing twenty years or so of history and breaking relationships upon which emotional and physical survival is dependent. The line between who is victim and who is offender tends not to be so clear with a woman's offending because her experience is rooted in this material and emotional experience of powerlessness.

In addition to this realisation, it was clear from the second workshop that there was a need to acknowledge that self-denial was a very significant factor in women's presentation of their offending. Rose comments, 'women have amazing skill in manipulating and denying their experience…it is denial, self denial, "this isn't really me", it is a coping mechanism…'[5] The experience or person women present to the world can be far from what is really going on and effectively shuts away obvious discomfort and pain. Rose sees this is the result of the debilitating guilt and shame that women tend to feel about their offences, in turn caused by the higher standards of behaviour society as a whole expects of women. Self-denial can be seen as a symptom of women's powerlessness and resistance. Women who do offend are likely to suffer to the degree that an alienation from themselves becomes a means of survival. The high incidence of self-harm amongst women offenders supports this argument: self-harm can be a way of coping with extreme pain and as well as an expression of powerlessness.

Patricia Holmes, an independent counsellor who has worked in Styal for five years responds to these facts of women's experience when she says, 'Why do people want women to take responsibility for what they've done? Usually they feel so much guilt about what they have done and who they are that they can't move on any further.'[6] The prison regime and the criminal justice system as a whole is a reinforcing agent of this debilitating self-blame and powerlessness through its refusal to address reality and its manner of condemning women. Rose Dickenson sees shame as the primary reason for women's resistance and reticence: 'they have so much to hide that they do not accept other people on face value, they cannot understand why you're doing what you're doing…they have to feel a trust and respect for the people they are working with, and this can take a long time to develop…'[7] I would add that power is another significant contributing factor to

5   Interview with the writer, August 1996.
6   Patricia Holmes, Independent Counsellor, in interview with the writer, November 1995.
7   Interview with the writer, August 1996.

resistance: a common reaction to being systematically misunderstood, ignored and stereotyped. Anyone who has worked in women's prisons will be familiar with resistance and a feeling of continually shifting ground and unpredictability within groups: the 'one step forwards, two steps back' process of establishing trust and a balance of power with groups.

For Blagg! to work at all within Styal it was crucially important for the worker to remain supportive and committed to participants, accepting their presentations of experience before tentatively and skilfully beginning to challenge and highlight links and contradictions in the material that was being offered. The intention to 'confront' women with their behaviour was potentially damaging, demeaning and restrictive. Rose sees that a very different use for Blagg! could be beneficial: 'I want to see an offending-behaviour programme that makes the links between what they've done, where they are today, to help them recognise the truth of their lives and start a process that can be worked on long term, a kind of diagnostic thing...'[8] What Rose hints at here is a long-term and person-centred therapeutic programme that trusts, accepts and refuses to judge the woman, works with her at her own pace to look at difficulties in her life, enabling her to gain a clearer and stronger self-awareness with her self-esteem remaining intact and reinforced.

After the learning experiences of the first trial runs of Blagg! in Styal this is exactly what we attempted, with Patricia Holmes and Alice Brodbeck, the two independent counsellors working regularly in the prison. We worked with groups of young offenders because I was teaching them regularly at the time. My work with them over a year had already led me to working in a more person-centred way. The drama course on the young-offender programme had developed into quite a positive intervention into the regime. Drama-wise the emphasis was open-ended role play stimulating candid and informal discussions within groups about common experiences.

The open-ended and loosely drama-based sessions seemed gave the women an opportunity to relate to each other, share problems and advice, ask questions, develop trust, work out opinions, discuss issues and enjoy themselves. Some groups would arrive at sessions with the request for a group 'chat'. Common themes and experiences recurred within groups: prison, bullying and violence, crime, drugs, friendship, families, relationships, sexuality, feelings, image. Ground rules for these sessions were set by the women as part of the group's organic development, 'I'll say this but it's not to go further than this room, right?' It was during these sessions that I was allowed a glimpse of the real experiences, thoughts and feelings of the women. I was shocked into an understanding of how much awareness of themselves the women had and could develop in the right,

8   Interview with the writer, August 1996.

supportive environment, of how many questions they had about themselves and how they relished the opportunity to ask and explore.

The Blagg! sessions run with either Alice or Patricia breathed new life into this process. They began to work with the women around aspects of their lives and produced a more profound contact with and understanding of themselves than I was able to with little therapeutic training or awareness. The workshop began to change: the offence receded in importance as the focus became the developing of Jo's story from her early life and exploring thoughts and feelings around traumatic experiences. The border between fiction and reality disappeared for some participants as groups became fully engaged with the content and began talking and playing out scenes openly from their own lives. We began to schedule the Blagg! early on in the six-week course to allow the women to continue the group work if they wished, or simply to use me and the group as a support in processing thoughts and feelings triggered by Blagg!.

Some women would continue working on their own issues with Alice or Patricia in one to one counselling sessions. As Patricia states, 'I think the sessions are extremely useful as a safe way for women to introduce concerns that can be discussed in more detail later. The work undertaken so far has been able to explore with women the reasons behind their crimes and the subsequent feelings of loss, fear and abandonment.'[9] The feedback received from the women that participated in Blagg! was very positive: 'I learnt to talk about myself in front of others without getting embarrassed...', 'I am less confused than I was...', 'it's good because you know nothing will go any further...', 'you know you're taking part and you have to use your brains before speaking...', 'it's useful as you learn new things every time...', 'it makes me understand my life, I had to do this to see how I was living...'[10]

I have given the development of Blagg! at Styal so much space as it has relevance to the central exploration of this chapter: the different experience of working with women prisoners and drama. The development of Blagg! at Styal relates to how offending-behaviour drama programmes work with women. The discussion is specific to my experience in Styal but important generalisations can be made. Underneath all this development lies a conflict in practice between a person-centred and a 'challenging offending behaviour' approach. In practice the latter leads to a focus on technique and strategy delivered in affordable 'programmes' and 'packages' that are open to manipulation by the system and susceptible to the pressures within the system that compound women's experience of powerlessness. The approach that we developed in Styal requires a

9   Patricia Holmes, in internal monitoring of the Blagg! Workshop, HMP Styal, September 1995.
10   Participants of the Blagg! Workshop, throughout 1995, from the writer's own archives.

long-term commitment from the prison and a tangible ideological shift away from the sole obsession with individual's taking responsibility for their behaviour.

In the meantime, work continues in Styal simply because of the extraordinary commitment of individual workers like Rose Dickinson and through the continuing involvement of independent agencies like Alice and Patricia and TIPP. This involvement is unstable, however, and depends upon the integrity of the governor and the limits of the prison's budget, at present under greater and greater pressure because of the policies of the Home Office.

The essence of the approach developed in Styal and what I have argued so far is the need to put the material conditions in which women prisoners find themselves and the experiences and relationships that they stimulate at the heart of our explanation and understanding of them and our planning. If we want to talk about rehabilitation in any real way we need to extend real opportunities to prisoners to try different ways of being through offering activities and relationships that significantly change the ideological and material conditions that exist in prison. In Styal this happened through the support and involvement of independent agencies, each of whom brought a set of practices and an agenda that contradicted the punitive approach. The project discussed in the following section came closer in practice than any other in my experience to achieving this ideal of working with women prisoners and drama.

The special project

> Well, my point of view is when we come in here, I block off that I'm in prison. I'm on the normal outside world with normal people and I'm communicating. I'm not in prison. When I step into this gym, that's it. I'm in a different world. When I step out them doors I'm back in prison.

> It gives you a lot of confidence and that. I didn't think I'd be able to do it, but now I've got close to them…it's given me an insight into what they're feeling and how they feel about us.[11]

The special project was an integrated venture taken by Contact Theatre in Manchester, Wythenshawe Day Resource Centre for adults with learning disabilities and HMP Styal. Contact Theatre is a major theatre venue in Manchester. Staff from the Community and Education Department at Contact Theatre did the fund-raising and administration for the project and offered artistic supervision. The project ran for four weeks between May and June 1995: beginning with a preparation week with for the participants from each institution. It culminated in a two-week integration period where a group of nine service

11   Two participants of the special project, in interview with Greater Manchester Radio, June 1995.

users from Wythenshawe came into the prison daily to work with eight women offenders on a variety of drama exercises and activities. The project attracted quite a lot of attention from the local press as a ground breaking initiative. It was unique in terms of its specific structure and the forms of drama that we attempted to work with, though a similar 'integrated' initiative between inmates and people with learning disabilities has been successfully attempted at HMP Nottingham, a male prison.

The project was sponsored by Contact Theatre and involved a year-long process of fund – raising and negotiation between all of the participating institutions. Funds were eventually raised from private trusts: neither the prison or social services were able to contribute much financially because of budget restraints. Myself and Dave Calvert, a drama worker specialising in work with adults with learning disabilities devised and facilitated the workshops. Of the eight women that volunteered to take part four were young offenders and four were of mixed age. Their sentence length varied from life to three months.

The project had three broad aims: to produce theatre work through the exploration of a theme and ways of working common to both groups; to offer both groups a constructive break in routine and a practical experience of drama and groupwork; to offer access to new environments and working relationships and thus the opportunity to develop personal and social skills in a stimulating setting. In describing and analysing the project I will take each week in turn and summarise at the end of the section the connection of this work to the overall theme of working with drama and women prisoners and the associated arguments of the ideology and practice developed so far.

As mentioned above, in their first encounter with drama groups of women in Styal generally responded with most ease to naturalistic improvisation exercises dealing with themes close or identical to their own life experience. This was the case during the first 'preparation' week in Styal. This way of working fitted group's expectations of what drama 'is' and is 'for' – an opportunity to present their own issues, a platform upon which they could be represented and respected fairly and realistically. The challenge of the whole project, from the perspective of the Styal group, was to make the leap from this form of drama work to the fantasy and physically based exercises that the group from Wythenshawe were familiar with and able to engage in freely. This was the focus, in artistic terms, of the process of integration; the success of the project would be measured against the degree to which we could facilitate this process.

This artistic focus, of course, would necessitate multiple other changes from the Styal group; in ways of relating and communicating, in frames of reference, in openness, confidence, motivation, co-operation, understanding and empathy. They would have to leap from one world (of prison) to another (the 'normal outside world' as quoted above) and back again in the space of each day of the integrated two weeks. I went into this project with a mixture of great trepidation and anticipation. I knew that the women could be unpredictable, resistant, volatile, unmotivated, frequently wound up by the petty rules and regulations of the regime. They would have to block out the effects of this environment and exhibit patience, awareness, willingness and a non-aggressive front if they were to work successfully with the Wythenshawe group. I wondered if we were mad in attempting to achieve this with women whose offending histories could arguably be said to prove that empathy for others and self-awareness was beyond their personal capacity. None of my fears of this nature were in any way realised.

Exercises and activities prepared for the first week with the Styal group were aimed at raising a consciousness of this artistic and social leap. The women participated in role play sessions where they were asked to play themselves attempting to communicate with or help to achieve various tasks someone who could not speak, or hear, or had lost the use of their legs, or who constantly misunderstood them. Sessions like these led into long discussions about prejudice and discrimination in which some women would offer instances from their own experience as well as examples that they imagined that the Wythenhsawe group might have been subjected to. We used scenarios from these discussions as a basis for forum theatre pieces performed with small audiences within the education block. Also, during the first week the women drew up a list of group skills (including have patience, listening, show respect, treat equally, co-operation) that they wanted to employ in the following weeks. These formed the ground rules and an informal contract that the women had devised and agreed to for the duration of the project.

My attempt to lead the women in fantasy or non-naturalistic based exercises failed in this first week, partly because the room in which we were working was very small and often disturbed by other inmates wandering in and out, and partly as a result of the resistance of the women. The group would invariably want to return to developing an improvisation from the previous session dealing with the familiar themes of prison life, drugs, relationships, family and so on. I tried to challenge the preoccupation with the themes of prison 'culture' with questions as to how they thought the Wythenshawe group would understand or respond to various scenes or characters they wanted to portray. I began to intervene and challenge references to drugs, crime and even the women's use of prison lingo in talking to each other. The response was generally one of astonishment and anxiety: 'well, how can we speak to them, what are we supposed to do?'. The group gradually came to an intensified awareness of the role they played in prison and the fronts or masks they employed as survival strategies within their daily environment.

The two week long 'integration' period of the project was spent in the prison gym and this allowed extra space for physical exercises and free flow fantasy work. We planned paired work for the beginning of this period, one member from the prison group working with one of the Wythenshawe group to complete physical, imaginative and problem-solving tasks using props, costumes, masks and musical instruments. Many of the exercises were those that the women had resisted the week before. In this context, however, they engaged quite freely. The group from Wythenshawe were very responsive to direction from the leaders, and, in contrast to the Styal group, very free in a physical sense, and less concrete in an imaginative sense. Working one to one with individuals that were prepared to let go in this way freed the women up in their approach to drama work. The speed and the ease with which they overcame their nerves and inhibitions astonished me. I had rarely achieved this degree of creativity with groups: the move to the gym and the stimulus provided by the visitors had provided the necessary conditions to produce startling changes in the prison group. These changes continued and were reinforced as the project developed.

As the group became accustomed to the way of working and familiar with each other it was clear that some new stimulus was required. At the beginning of the second week of the integration period we introduced a metallic frame of a large cube and several lengths of colourful sari material. The group could interpret the cube in whatever way they chose and different uses were explored and enacted (the cube was large enough for scenes to be created within it). It also had enough flexibility as an idea to accommodate the variety of abilities in the group and lent itself as a tool to structure the process, define the acting space and function as a set for the final performance piece that was recorded on video.

The decision to work towards a performance piece tested the success of the integration between the groups. The women had formed supportive, communicative and creative relationships with the Wythenshawe group throughout the first week. Each day before the Wythenshawe group had arrived and after they left I had an opportunity to warm up and wind down with the Styal group. These sessions were one of the safety valves that we had planned into the project and were intended to be a space for the women to resolve any difficulties that might have arisen before the next day of the project. The sessions functioned to ease the integration of the women back into the prison environment after each day. They also provided the women with a space to share their own thoughts, feelings and perceptions of the process and a chance for me to give feedback about how well the women were working with the visiting group.

It was through these sessions that I got a real sense of the personal impact of the project on the women. Their assessment of each day generally expressed how seriously they took their role in the project, how at ease they felt with the visitors, how aware they were of not dominating the process and how delighted they felt at the achievements of the group. I felt as though I was working with an altered group of women than those I had met on the education block a week before: many individuals had become more expressive, aware, creative, alert and sensitive. These changes in manner were accompanied by a change in appearance in some of the women which I can only describe as more relaxed and open.

A crucial component in facilitating these changes was the attitudes of the Wythenshawe group. They approached the women without value judgements or preconceptions and accepted each woman as she presented herself in the workshops. The pressure to live up to a prison image was eliminated and fears about being seen as criminals were dissipated: the women could relax. This theme of acceptance was touchingly reinforced for the women when one morning a member of the Wythenshawe group brought a note from her mother saying, 'May I thank you on behalf of my daughter, for giving her a nice time as she has enjoyed it very much, and may I wish all the very best for the future to all the inmates, may God bless you all, Cheers.'

I have presented this project as the closest of any that I have been involved in to achieving my ideal of drama work with women prisoners. Several factors contributed to the success: the women were trusted to behave responsibly and safely with a vulnerable group; they were valued as whole and equal people in the process rather than exhibitors of offending behaviour; the drama activities established both the different-ness of the space from the regular prison environment and a culture of openness, experimentation, expression and creativity within safe limits. The combination of an artistic and social focus gave the project a therapeutic as well as an educational impact.

Conclusion

[I]t is exceptionally difficult to distinguish between those [emergent elements in cultural production] which are really some new phase of the dominant culture, and those which are substantially alternative or oppositional to it – emergent in the strictest sense, rather than merely novel... (Williams 1977, p.123)

The close-down period of the special project included a feedback or checking out session with both groups. We received some extremely positive feedback from all the participants and staff involved in the process. The Styal women were particularly keen to follow up the experience with more drama projects and to continue the link with the Wythenshawe centre. Some provisional plans for further initiatives were drawn up with Contact Theatre but the project has not yet been repeated because of lack of funds.

One of the participants from the prison group described the project as a 'total new era for Styal prison'. Her comment underlines for me the potential that this initiative and the other projects described in this paper illuminate in terms of the role of arts practice within the criminal justice system. Each initiative shows the power of drama and theatre work to transform women offenders' experience of prison and perception of herself as well as to challenge the dominant punitive ideology and practice of custody. Drama as an arts medium works with, illuminates and makes public the whole person and the whole experience in all its complexity and contradiction, strength and weakness. My experience of doing drama with women in Styal shows again and again the waste inherent in a system that locks people up, and then abuses, mystifies, and forgets them. By thriving on the cusp of this contradiction drama work within closed and oppressive institutions can exist and continue to reinvent itself as a potent and transformative force, both on a personal and political level.

I have argued that offence-focused projects based on a cognitive behavioural model are not appropriate for use with women. I have questioned the whole premise of a practice that fits so comfortably with a system that exploits and oppresses. Such practice assimilates the values and ideas of a reactionary system. I have suggested that a person-centred approach, because it puts the individual at the heart of the work and places fundamental value on their experiences and perceptions, can succeed. It makes the creation of a blind spot in terms of the real conditions of life for individuals impossible and allows for a fully respectful and accurate approach to those that we work with. This was found to work in Styal. Such an approach poses more challenges to the system as it values the human individual and is committed to their potential and growth.

However, there is for me a more important argument to be had than a debate between two methodologies, both of which have their own shortcomings. The fundamental dilemma facing the practitioner is an economic one and relates to how he or she can make a living doing this sort of work. The economic pressure of having to make the work attractive within the current system will, perhaps, continually neutralise the radical impact of the work. This is a fundamental dilemma for any practitioner who both chooses to work within the criminal justice system and has a real concern for delivering a service that will be relevant and beneficial to offenders. My secondary intention through this chapter has been to continue to highlight this dilemma through openly addressing the political and ideological implications of the work in this field.

In the introduction to this paper I stated my contention that drama work with women prisoners has a vital role to play in the development and strengthening of an oppositional trend in the field of work. Because the experience of drama with women prisoners is different, because women generally do not accept or benefit from the traditional offending behaviour models and approaches to work (based on confronting behaviour) developed so far, the practice of successful drama work with women prisoners highlights important issues. Many elements of the argument I have presented have direct relevance to, are similar or identical to work with male offenders. The importance of the work with women, therefore, relates to how current practice as a whole can fulfil its potential as a challenge, however transient this may be, to the system. If we can substantially address this problem then we can begin to talk about an arts practice that, rather than being assimilated into an oppressive culture, can oppose it and present an alternative.

References

Carlen, P. and Worrall, A. (eds) (1987) *Gender, Crime and Justice*. London: Open University Press.

Crace, J. (1996) Inside the news: Behind bars: Women in prison.' *The Guardian*, 23 January, p.8.

Genders, E. and Player, E. (1987) 'Women in prison: The treatment, the control and the experience.' In P. Carlen and A. Worrall (eds) (1987) *Gender, Crime and Justice*. London: Open University Press.

O'Dwyer, Wilson and Carlen, P. (1987) 'Women's imprisonment in England, Wales and Scotland: recurring issues.' In P. Carlen and A. Worrall (eds) *Gender, Crime and Justice*. London: Open University Press.

Rutherford, A. (1991) 'Prison reform and penal realities.' In D. Whitfield (ed) *The State of British Prisons 200 Years On*. London: Routledge.

Socialist Worker (1996) 'Now Tories "get tough" with kids.' 24 August, p.7.

Williams, R. (1977) *Marxism and Literature*. Oxford: Oxford University Press.

Worrall, A. (1990) *Offending Women*. London: Routledge.

Further Reading

Whitfield, D. (ed) (1991) *The State of British Prisons 200 Years On*. London: Routledge.

PART II

Therapy and Rehabilitation

Preface

Victor Hassine

What I learned from my prison theatre experience was that while a novel or short story might project a point of view or even direct one, a play can not only project and persuade, but it can also exist inside a viewer. It allows the viewer of drama to actually feel within themselves portions of the play that he/she can identify with.

I believe this is so, because reading a short story only involves the brain through the optical nerves, whilst watching a play stimulates the brain through at least two of the body's senses; sight and sound. This means that the perceptions you receive when reading are like listening to a record in monotone while watching a play is like hearing in stereo.

So when a person watches a drama unfold and listens to the words in synch with the actions of a skilled actor, the experience becomes deeply etched into consciousness. In fact, subsequent recall or recollection of that performance may be confused by the viewer as an actual experience.

This is important to know because in a prison most inmates are functionally illiterate. Reading and reading comprehension are torturous ordeals for most of them and an impossibility for many. Such men become visual learners out of necessity. Their collective experiences are limited to what they have seen with their eyes or heard with their ears. Because of this, a theatre performance in prison is much more than entertainment; it is a point of view or an important lesson that can be learned by the many who cannot read or write.

The only more effective way to convey new thoughts and ideas in a prison is to have inmates perform them. If watching a play doubles sensory perception when compared to reading, then performing in a play more than quadruples that perception, because all five sense are used by an actor during a performance.

This being the case, all of his senses must first understand the lesson, before he can try to act it out. So what I learned from prison theatre is that the best way to communicate with inmates is to stage a performance and involve as many in the performance as possible.

CHAPTER 3

Treading on Tales

Telling all Stories

Pauline Gladstone and Angus McLewin

This chapter is a space for Clean Break women to speak about what it means to devise theatre based on their own life experiences. It is also a space to share an ongoing dialogue with another organisation, 4 ARTS, that has a more explicit brief of exploring the boundaries between drama and dramatherapy. 4 ARTS have become involved in developing long-term arts projects for people with mental health problems in community settings as part of the implementation of the Care in the Community programme. This involvement has made them question their community arts practice. Angus McLewin, Dramatherapist at 4 ARTS, and Pauline Gladstone, the Education Co-ordinator of Clean Break, are jointly exploring what is really going on when you transform this kind of raw material into a piece of theatre that can be communicated to an audience. Of the many issues that have arisen through this dialogue, certain key concerns have been identified.

Through work at Clean Break these emerge as:

- Just how safe is the 'as if' of drama in a context where an arts product, such as a piece of theatre, is being created?

- Can you ever really claim to be *just* working with an arts process when you are working with vulnerable groups?

- Can an arts process really be rehabilitative or therapeutic and, if so, are there any particular or extra features it would need to have in order to achieve this?

From 4 ARTS' perspective they centre on:

- Comparing drama methods with dramatherapeutic and psychodramatic processes to better inform this field of work.

- Identifying the potential for developing new models for theatre, therapy and social action.

Clean Break: the background

Clean Break Theatre Company was formed in 1979 by two women serving time in HMP Askham Grange, in order to communicate their experiences of imprisonment to others. When they left, it was formalised into a small-scale touring company. To this day the company continues to tour professional shows that deal with issues around women and the criminal justice system to arts and prison venues.

A 'writer in residence' is commissioned to write these plays, working closely with women in prison and on probation. For example, the 1996 production *Mules* was written by Winsome Pinnock and explored the plight of women foreign nationals serving time in England for drugs trafficking offences. It was researched with women in Jamaica, in HMP Holloway and with creative writing students on Clean Break's Theatre Education and Training Programme.

'See, Her, Hear, Speak' (1995)
Clean Break Theatre Company rehearsing '...sometimes I feel like a motherless child.'
Picture by Anette Hang

For the past five years, Clean Break has offered a Theatre Education and Training Programme to all women ex-offenders and ex-prisoners. This is a free service, including travel, child care and lunch. Sixty women currently study with us each year on courses that are accredited by the London Open College Federation. The aim is to provide a safe environment in which women can explore life by working creatively and co-operatively as a member of a group in the medium of drama and related arts. We seek to enhance their life opportunities in a culture in which they are clearly disadvantaged. The reasons why women join our Clean Break courses are as individual as the people themselves: a spectrum from wanting to gain some self-confidence to wanting to be a professional actor. Women can come in to try out introductory courses which run for six weeks, one day per week, such as 'Acting For Life 1', 'Basic Video Skills', 'Creative Writing', or 'Singing and Dance'. They can then go on to do 'Acting For Life 2', followed by 'Acting For Life 3', which both run for twelve weeks and 'Advanced Creative Writing' which is an ongoing group. In their second year, students can opt to take an access course: 'Theatre In The Community'. This course is designed to prepare students both for university entrance and further training within the field of community drama.

We also try to create as solid a bridge as possible to professional production – as part of their training, students can take a 'Professional Development Course' which looks at the reality of small-scale touring from the perspectives of the director, writer and stage management team, as well as covering auditioning and the unique world of Equity.

Another strand of the company's work is National Outreach. This involves current and ex-students alongside education and training staff in giving talks, presentations, workshops, training events and performances. Our aim is to educate the wider public and relevant professionals on the role that theatre can play in examining the issues around women and the criminal justice system. It brings our particular experience of working with women ex-offenders to targeted audiences and demonstrates how others working in this field could learn from our positive experience of using theatre as part of a rehabilitative process to help break the cycle of criminality.

Events vary from international conferences to after-dinner entertainment. Sometimes performances are devised in response to a particular brief. This was the case with *Normal Location* which was produced by three current students in response to a request from Surrey Probation Service who wanted to present Voluntary Associates with what female ex-offenders themselves considered to be the key issues around the imprisonment of women. It was the same for *See Her Hear Speak*, which was produced for a Campaign Against Domestic Violence conference.

On other occasions, a piece of work being devised as part of a course coincides with the theme of an outside event. This is how *Brainstorming*, produced by the Community Theatre group came to be performed at Keele University for an Institute for the Study and Treatment of Delinquency conference 'Tackling

Drugs, One Year On', as well as at a Women With Special Needs conference in Northampton, organised by the International Institute For Special Offender Services. The piece happened to concern drugs in prison and featured CI Wing (psychiatric) at HMP Holloway!

The dialogue

Pauline: I suggest that it would be helpful for us now to look at what was actually going on in devising the three pieces of work outlined above, namely:

Normal Location (1994)

See Her Hear Speak (1995)

Brainstorming (1996).

Angus: For me, it would be useful to take one step further back and look at the fact that there are four different parties involved here: you as a theatre company, the funders, the commissioners of the plays and the students. Their aims, in emphasis at least, are all likely to be different. Some will be complementary and some may be in conflict. That is the dynamic with which you are working. For example, will the aims of the commissioner of the play fulfil those of your students, without compromising them or putting them in a vulnerable position? It puts us, as arts practitioners, very much in the position of having to struggle with the role of being the honest broker.

There are also different criteria involved in the exploring and devising process compared with the criteria for the performance product. Are your aims therapeutic, rehabilitative or educational, in either or both aspects? Also there is a difference between the sharing and enacting of life stories to fellow students, which is more akin to what goes on in a closed dramatherapy group, and a public performance based on very personal stories.

Pauline: The role of the honest broker has proved to be a difficult one for me: I admit that it is very hard to keep my own agenda out of the picture, or even to be clear about when my own needs and wants are active in the directorial decisions that I am making. For example, it is easy to become infatuated with someone's life story.

Angus: That's interesting, because in dramatherapy training, you have to address those issues all the time. You have to ask what is my stuff, what am I projecting and wanting from the situation and what are group members projecting onto it and wanting from me? In psychotherapeutic terms this is working with the concepts of transference and countertransference and you need to be aware that this is happening, particularly when working with people in vulnerable situations.

Pauline: Let us go on to look more closely at the first of these plays: *Normal Location.*

The brief from Surrey Probation Service was to highlight three or four key areas of concern facing women prisoners, in a piece of theatre running for 30 minutes. Three current students studying Community Theatre agreed to undertake this project. The initial 'trawling' began slowly, painfully and anecdotally. Common areas of concern were noted and then experimented with by using some 'Pressure Circles', where each issue was personified and could walk towards each woman in turn. The women then had the power to halt its approach at a distance that symbolically represented its relative power and influence in their own experience.

Angus: Straight away, I find myself asking where the theatre is and where the therapy is in this initial 'trawling' process. If you are sitting talking in a group about something so directly personal, this is already into groupwork: a bit like running a therapy group. It is not like actors exploring and researching issues that concern or interest them, but are not theirs.

The pressure circles are straight from Moreno's social atom, which is used in group work, group therapy and of course psychodrama. By doing this, you are using very direct techniques, for example, using doubling and role reversal, which are very accessible and also very alluring. A dramatherapeutic approach, by contrast, would tend to use indirect approaches, such as metaphor and dramatic projection, to trawl for the same direct stories.

Pauline: From this 'trawling' stage, the common threads that emerged were: being separated from children; the taking of drugs to numb a sentence out of existence; and the unreality of the prison environment which leads to women splitting off parts of themselves to present a protective 'front' and to the stripping of any normal sense of day-to-day responsibility to the point where small events can get blown out of all proportion.

As a group, the students explored what it meant to adopt a 'front', beginning with memories from the playground and leading to the physicalisation of a posturing and protective body mask. This eventually distilled into an opening sequence in which the actors played the game, 'Chin, Chan, Changa', (commonly known as Paper, Scissors, Stone). They faced out from a tight circle and after each refrain, 'Chin, Chan, Changa', turned in to face the others with a set attitude which shifted each time as a multiplicity of possible stances that might see them through a prison sentence. The actors used internal monologues to communicate their assessments of each other as 'hard' or 'someone I could have it out with'.

Angus: Here you are using games to trawl for ideas, then using the re-playing of a game from childhood as a metaphor for those that had to be played as an adult in prison. Keeping that particular game structure in the devising process and then transposing it into the final performance – that's an interesting journey of re-living, then representing direct experiences, and it stays more within the framework of drama.

Pauline: The memories came thick and fast about the pettiness that is cultivated in this unreal world: fighting over whether someone 'has nicked my mug', when they 'are all blue, all plastic and all belong to Her Majesty'; arguing over how many inches a window should be open; accusing someone of taking your dog-end out of an ashtray and so on. These were naturalistically explored and represented as bite-sized views from a typical day, punctuated by reminders to the audience from the cast of the precise time: a sentence being served minute by minute.

When it came to looking at the issues around coping with the separation from children, they had to use many more distancing approaches in both trawling for and portraying significant material. There was a tangible empathy and solidarity between the three actors, but the fundamental problem was how to find and work with a process that genuinely protected the individual in the shared ownership of personal material, whereby the following statements would be true:

You can portray my experience: I, yours.

I can speak your words: you can show my pain.

And I suppose the biggest question is: *Is* it possible to protect people fully in the devising process, particularly when the subject matter is directly personal and particularly painful?

There were the tears of recollection and these tears touched that invisible and tenuous border between working within an arts process and stepping over into something that might feel closer to a psychodramatic/therapeutic process, without acknowledging that that is what is going on. At Clean Break, we profess to be working within an art form but with therapeutic aims, yet what is happening in the drama space often does not feel that clear or that safe.

Angus: I find myself asking, what kind of distancing can you use when you are working with a group of people in a drama context, talking about their own direct experiences and having to portray themselves or their children, or witness their fellow students enact their story for them. The answer for me is that you cannot. Therefore you need to be able to create ways in which people can step slowly and safely in and out of the roles and situations they have developed in the drama. In dramatherapy this is the clearly recognised structure of en-roling and de-roling. Put simply, it is a series of manageable stepping stones, facilitated by the dramatherapist, to get closer and closer to re-experiencing a moment, engaging with the emotions, and then being able to step back out slowly to clarify, reflect and assimilate that experience.

Pauline: In *Normal Location*, it often felt very close to Playback Theatre, which is used in dramatherapy and psychodrama, whereby a significant event from a person's life can be reconstructed by that individual by choosing other people in the group to represent who was there (including any relevant objects) and by giving enough information for them to be able to re-enact what was going on. For example Noorghana instructed Susan on how to perform for her exactly the way that she had to prise her daughter's fingers from her blouse at the end of a visit and how she actually sat when she was forced to communicate with her own child through a wall of glass.

Susan wanted to communicate what it felt like to stand in court having recently given birth to her third child and hear the judge pronounce a custodial sentence. She wanted her children to be represented as 'presently absent' in the scenario, so they were represented by the other two actors, looking into the court through an imaginary door.

Looking back on the whole experience now, Susan says:

> It was hard to do it – hardest to devise. I wanted to block it all out and after I went back home after rehearsals, it brought back all those feelings and I had to go back and shut it all down again. I'd

wake up in the morning and there'd be something there because I'd dug those feelings up.

So, you can see from this comment why I am worried about the effects of this work on my students.

Angus: Referring to the original aims: if the aim is for rehabilitation, this will involve some degree of reconciliation and integration of unresolved experiences. To do this you have to revisit and therefore re-experience them and this is emotionally disturbing, but it can be positive if put within a therapeutic framework. Again from a dramatherapeutic point of view, one of the criteria for success is the drama to life connection, and from what Susan is saying, the connections were very direct, conscious and overt.

Pauline: Susan goes on to say:

> But going through the performance has made me stronger – made me accept it a bit more – not blocking it off like before, but putting it to one side – I used to feel guilty for my son, really guilty, but I don't any more because I've expressed it to a few people, let them know where I'm coming from – I needed to go back to understand a bit more about myself, know how it really felt.

Clearly other more obviously therapeutic processes work with reflection and the kind of repetition that can bring new insights, but is there something different and valuable about producing theatre to communicate an understanding of an experience?

Is there something unique about a recipe that goes...

1. Take a raw slice of your own life and explore it in as many ways as you can with others using drama processes.

2. Travel all the way through naturalism to the fantastic and the absurd and then return again.

3. Pass it back and forth with others like a ball with a heartbeat.

4. Shape it to say what you want it to say.

5. Give it a style that suits your purpose.

6. Rehearse it – hearing, touching, seeing, speaking it over and over again with fresh insights on each repetition.

7. Finally, perform it on a number of occasions to different audiences – to bodies of anonymous people with whom you

are communicating simultaneously and in an art form that allows for individual interpretation.

Susan goes on to say:

> The whole process was painful but not when we were performing. Sometimes it was – where I was in court, hoping and doubting at the same time, the anxiety, the panic came back. It brought up different feelings every time I performed it – I even felt like stopping once because I didn't want to go back, but I'm glad I did. New feelings came up that weren't there at the time – vulnerability, wide open, I hadn't tuned into that before, when I was in court. I felt the same anger but not so intense. I wouldn't want to do any more on my life – yeah, I don't need to tell people any more about my life and me – because this is me now – it's made me want to move on.

Angus: So now maybe it's useful just to make the distinction between what goes on in the devising process and what can happen in the performance. The performance element in dramatherapy is called enactment. The enactment allows for spontaneity in much the same way as in an improvised drama. It also enables a spontaneous connection with the emotions involved in revisiting a particular time and place, and therefore has very little emotional distance, whereas acting would be about recreating or representing a situation, not about directly feeling it at the time. A scale that is used in dramatherapy relates the levels of empathy, that is, identification, and the levels of distance involved and these can be compared to the contrast between Stanislavski and Brecht's theories and methods in theatre. It sounds as if Susan was back in that courtroom every time she performed it – therefore it was likely to be emotional enactment rather than acting.

Pauline: For Noorghana, the audience was so important:

> It gave me the opportunity to say: this is real – this really happened, and someone would listen, unlike a magazine article, I was there to get the reactions and to bring them in emotionally.

Noorghana particularly wanted to communicate the point of view of a child whose mother was imprisoned and who therefore served a life sentence herself, only being reunited with her just before she died. This was the story of Noorghana's life.

> Nobody had ever asked me what it was like to grow up without a mother – there was a lot of freedom in the play – I could devise it

fresh every time – my personal monologue gave me a chance to be myself.

Noorghana chose to address the audience directly at the end of the play with a personal monologue. This was improvised at each performance. It was incredible to witness and hear which language changed or stayed the same.

> There was some fear that people would not believe it or that they would just pity me – you want people to understand and you get new understanding yourself, e.g. I suddenly realised that the people who brought me up were paid workers, no different to a bus driver. It takes you back in time; past, future and present are there and you perceive it different every day – mentally you go back into that space. Emotionally it was healthy for me to do it because I wanted the world to know what it had been like and it was emotional – I wanted to tell my story to relieve something in me and I wanted to get to judges and magistrates.

It is interesting to consider the relevance of the audience and the context. This in a sense is the politics of this kind of work. Here it mattered very much that Noorghana reached the people who represented those that she blamed for her life.

> I had gone on blaming them – they were a handful of individuals who had power over my life. I had mixed feelings – on the one hand I wanted to say: 'Fuck you, you're going to hear this whether you like it or not', but on the other hand, if there was one person in the audience who took me seriously and believed in it, it might influence their decisions in the future in their working career.

Angus: For me, there are lots of things going on here at once and they are all powerful and fascinating. In Noorghana's personal monologue, she was being herself, talking directly to the audience that she wanted to reach. From what she was saying, there was a strong need for, on the one hand, some level of emotional catharsis as in 'you go back in time; past, future and present are there and you perceive it different every day', and on the other, a desire for what might be called social action – effecting change in the real world, such as where Noorghana hopes that her performance 'might influence their decisions in the future'.

Pauline: Performing to a different audience, drama students, was a completely different experience:

It was very exposing for me – I took a risk and on this occasionit was really worth it – people who hadn't parents could connect with my story.

At the end of a performance, the formal recognition that communication has taken place is the applause. Something has been witnessed and acknowledged in a public way. For Noorghana:

> The clapping is a recognition that I'm not used to. I don't take it personally, I think it's for something they've seen. It's an acknowledgement that you're real, that someone's taken notice of you. But it can also be confusing and seemingly contradictory when you have an investment in the material.

For Susan:

> The clapping, it's crazy; how can you clap someone's experience, I would have preferred them to be more emotional, more of an impact, rather than having enjoyed it.

Angus: So for me, there is now the whole concept of personal, emotional and inner change, compared and related to the notions of social change and social action – in other words, how the inner and outer experiences relate to the role of the audience. In a closed dramatherapy group, the role of the audience can be that of witnessing and acknowledging a person's enactment. It is a public performance for and in a closed group and allows for and can contain levels of emotional catharsis for both performers and audience – it is less likely to involve any kind of applause and it sounds like that was what Susan was wanting for her very personal and moving story.

Whereas for Noorghana, the applause is not only an acknowledgement, but also a recognition of how effective the drama has been in communicating to her chosen audience. As she experimented with the different levels of emotional distance each time she improvised her monologue, it appears from what she is saying that she was making a journey from individual, personal change to instigating and effecting a form of direct social action. Because of this she wanted the conventional acknowledgement of applause which is associated with a public performance.

Pauline: Noorghana concludes about the whole experience:

> For so many years it didn't come out in a healthy way – through relationships breaking down, drugs – now I can cope with what

my life has been and I can move on. Drama is really good for people with dysfunctional backgrounds; you can re-enact things without it taking you over and eating you up. It is therapeutic – otherwise you get stuck – drama gives you the belief that you can be creative and it's been a really positive thing in my life.

See Her Hear Speak was about domestic violence. It differed from *Normal Location* in several respects. It expressed a collective view rather than communicating individual stories. It needed to be extremely distanced and explored through abstraction and meta-phor because of the nature of the subject matter. It was devised by six women over a period of eight weeks. They began by using Image Theatre techniques (Boal 1992) to construct sculpted images of the meaning of domestic violence to each individual; they then further explored the commonality of this kind of life experience by creating an image of the images, drawing on Augusto Boal's meth-ods which they were currently studying. It became more abstract through this process of distillation.

Based on the principles of recognition and resonance, they then worked with the final image; women replaced each other within the sculpt if something rang true for them and then spoke aloud their internal monologues, beginning with just one line each. They then 'doubled' each image so that several views of these inner thoughts could speak alongside each other, the convention being to stand behind or next to the figure and 'speak think' for them. It was an additive process; no thoughts were judged or rejected and there could never be too many people contributing. They then explored the ways in which reality is masked and hidden by vic-tims of domestic violence by stretching this even further into the fantastic and the absurd. Excuses and cover-ups for bruises were taken to the extreme: 'I was eating a marshmallow and my teeth cracked'. The show opened with some of the original sculpts melt-ing slowly from one to the other on the stage, punctuated by these absurd explanations spoken from frozen moments.

There was an unanimous decision to avoid portraying violence directly. The key scene in the piece, that tried to convey the vic-tim's perspective in terms of the complex emotional base for staying in such an abusive relationship, was represented through the personification of the objects that inhabited the same physical space, so it was the teapot, the clock, the table, the chair and the cupboard in the kitchen that spoke to the audience. The table said: 'My back is scorched when they forget the mats. She wipes me clean; sometimes there are flowers; or fists.' The cupboard observed: 'Sometimes I'm full of surprises; sometimes they are.'

The furniture was physicalised by each performer and they experimented extensively with this, including using the voice to create appropriate sounds for each piece.

During the devising process, they also worked with the question: 'Why do you stay with him?' again, taking this to its limits, long

'Brainstorming' (1996)
Clean Break Theatre Company rehearsing '...home insurance is free.'
Picture by Angus McLewin

after they thought they had expressed every possible reason. They discovered that it is at the point when they thought that they had run out that another layer of truthfulness was revealed and spoken aloud. In the play, it was the furniture that relentlessly asked the central character this question, and she peeled away layers of explanation in her replies until she reached: 'I don't want to be alone'.

The students had been studying some of Boal's introspective approaches (Boal 1995), and they found them invaluable in devising this piece of theatre. They continued to explore why individuals stay in situations that are clearly doing them a lot of harm, by physicalising all the people who 'lived' in their heads and influenced their actions. Drawing on Boal's 'Cop In The Head' (Boal 1995, p.40), they created sculpts and gave them identities. For example, one became the mother-in-law 'who believes marriage is for life'. The sculpts found a way of moving that expressed their point of view and one or two lines that could be repeated over and over again. The victim was surrounded by this cast of internal characters who nagged at her simultaneously: 'If you come home, I won't have my room any more.' 'Forgive and forget; turn the other cheek.' 'I'm strong if you are weak; you're too weak to fight him.' She could not remove them from her head: the acting arena. She tried to position them physically further away but they shuffled back until they were right in her face and reached a crescendo of admonitions.

To continue with this part of their analysis of domestic violence, they decided to try out another of Boal's processes: the series of techniques called 'The Rainbow Of Desire' (Boal 1995). This time, every actor was sculpted by everyone in turn to represent a desire of the victim in this context. Again, this was a collective process, exploring the full range of needs and wants that one might have if faced with this life situation. These were shared and then refined on the basis of recognition or a shared identification with each desire.

It is interesting that the students turned to Boal's processes in this work and I think it is no coincidence that he is a practitioner who seems to be grappling himself with the boundaries between theatre as an art form and theatre as a forum for understanding the collective psyche.

Angus: It sounds an interesting piece of performance, using most of Boal's techniques from his Image Theatre and some of the more psychodramatic structures from 'The Rainbow of Desire', but, although distancing and abstraction techniques were used, I wonder how easy it is to keep within them? If you are framed as an 'actor', working on devising and rehearsing for a performance, the discipline and the 'role' of actor force you to control an emotional distance and take responsibility for yourself, and that is after years of training.

I also wonder about the time factors involved in creating performance work of this kind. If you are exploring an issue which may touch your participants' life experiences directly, and are using these explorations as part of a devising process to create, rehearse and perform a piece when you may only be working one day a week for six to eight weeks, how can you give enough time to that process of journey from emotional identification to aesthetic distance? I am afraid it leaves me thinking who was the piece really for – the women, the director, the theatre company or the commissioners?

Brainstorming was different again. It began life as a piece of original writing by a student on a Clean Break Creative Writing course. Its theme was the relationship between the official 'misuse' of drugs in women's prisons and the unofficial culture of drug use and dealing. It was based on this student's own experiences. It then became the starting point for a show devised by a Community Theatre group as a final examination piece.

It was fraught with problems from the beginning, particularly over the ownership of the material and the decision-making process. This was entirely my own fault since I did not anticipate the complexity of working with independently generated writing and the particular problems of honouring everybody's perspective in this kind of situation. On reflection, I should have worked to create clear boundaries of responsibility and role between that of a writer and that of an actor.

I have not got the answers, but again I find it useful to ask myself questions about what was really going on for the people taking part in this, and what kind of performance piece it was finally going to be. It is the old process and product dilemma.

It is one person's story being developed into a piece of drama by a group who also share similar experiences. Inevitably, the others in the group are going to say – where is my story? – I want and need to tell my story. Then, when it becomes a collective group story, the person who wrote the original story may also ask, 'Where is

my story now?' So, when working in this way, it is worth noting
that while the techniques and structures you used stayed very much
within the conventions of drama, we can throw some more light on
the problems you faced in the devising process by looking both at
the way dramatherapists work with individual stories in a group
context and at the way a psychodramatist chooses to work with
only one protagonist's story.

Pauline: The setting for this piece of theatre was a women's prison so there
were no metaphors at work here. This necessitated a different
approach to protect the experience for the cast: they used songs
and game-like structures within the conventions of physical theatre
to achieve this. Physical theatre, for Clean Break, is taken to mean
theatre that explores and expresses the essence of a situation or
relationship through playing with and stretching the physicality of
its reality. It has proved invaluable in this kind of work and women
at Clean Break hugely enjoy its freedoms and its potential for
expressing the inexpressible. It also leads students into the realms
of dark comedy which is itself a powerful protection that in no
way diminishes what is being communicated.

The final set comprised of five life-sized 'cell doors', complete with
opening hatches, that could be moved freely around the stage, as
well as two benches constructed out of four more of these grey
doors. There was plenty of time given to playing with the set and
'dancing' a prison into existence. This evolved into a movement
sequence that opened the play, establishing where they were and
the relationship between prisoner and officer.

The writer's story touched many of the cast's own experiences. The
person who portrayed the writer commented:

> Our life experiences were very similar – the only difference was I
> went into care and mental institutions.

At one point in the play this character, played by Michelle, was
told by the prison doctor that she was going onto C Wing (psychiatric).

> It took me back to my childhood when I was at boarding school
> and when I was told I wasn't fit to be in school and they took me
> away to an adolescent secure unit – it gave me a flashback to that
> time, almost the same words. The first time I said them, I was
> angry, I didn't want to be touched, I wanted to block it off, but it's
> got to come out; it's poison. The more you say it, it becomes an

everyday thing, you're having to visit it more often; it's a kind of healing.

At the beginning of the play, Michelle portrayed the writer as a child, giving her mother medication in the evenings and then waiting for her to begin to drift off, before leading her to bed.

> When I said the lines, I was literally back in time. I was there. Reflecting on *my* mother hit me more than any other bit. I saw my own mother traumatised when I was seven, from taking an overdose. It touched my mother: it touched my own past.

There were several occasions in *Brainstorming* when Michelle sailed close to her own winds. She has since reflected a great deal on this time:

> All my experiences are there for a reason – it's a circle and I'm going to give out, communicate what's gone down for me and get some humility and give it back in a gentle way, in the right context. Drama is a form of therapy for me; it brings out extensions of my personality; you're playing that part again, how it was then. If you can touch someone else portraying someone on the stage, you've done something constructive in this life.

Michelle also wrote many of the songs that featured in the play.

> It's easier to sing about other things than play a part I haven't experienced. It's easier to play parts I've been through, all you have to do is call on your memory.

Michelle made several comparisons with her experience of therapy:

> Sometimes it was difficult to work on ideas with others; sometimes I lost my temper; it was like being in group therapy. I feel I've grown a lot, I'm blossoming.

For Sharon too it was close to home:

> I based my character on what it was like before; some of it took me back; how I dealt with people in the play was like how I dealt with people inside. It was based on my memories – it's reborn – relived – refreshing my memory; but you can cope better because you're not really there; you're just acting out what went down.

At one point, Sharon's character slammed a hatch open and shouted for attention; she wanted some music in the day room. This was based on a real incident that the writer remembered, where she pleaded for some music on C Wing and got an old record player, complete with some of the officers' unwanted discs;

she then proceeded to teach sedated women to dance her own
invention: the Largactyl Shuffle! Sharon comments:

> Looking through the hatch, it was a chance to be angry and I
> thought back to when I was behind a door and how angry I was.
> Drama is a good way to communicate things. Drama is good for
> people who are frightened to speak out, to find another way to
> get it out; it's change, full stop. It gives out that little message of
> change: we're here.

The play was outrageously funny at times. For example Sharon
tried to train Michelle not to take her swig of 'knock-out mixture'
so that they could trade with it later. This was pure slapstick that
tickled the audience every time, yet it also clearly highlighted the
complexities of controlling drug use in prisons.

The laughter was important for the performers, it had its own particular rehabilitative potential. They found themselves comparing
the 'rush' from doing 'hooky' things with that of making people
laugh in a performance and finding that the 'buzz' from the latter
actually stronger and better. It was described as if performing in
comedy was a drug in its own right!

The writer shared many of the same feelings about the play as the
actors:

> I didn't find it hard to put things down; it brought up lots of
> feelings – frustration, sadness, laughter, all sorts of things. It was
> like yesterday – you can see it in your head and you can hear the
> keys; you're back there when you really think about it, which you
> have to do for writing.

As in the devising process, writing can reveal new feelings:

> I feel guilty about some of the girls I didn't give much attention to
> when I was there – that was because the writing made me think
> about it all over again.

When she watched the play there were a mixture of feelings:

> When I saw it, I was trying to take it all in but I was on Cloud
> Nine. I was watching my mate all the time for her reaction. I was
> embarrassed but in a good way and I was proud.

> When I was watching my mum being led across the stage, it was
> like butterflies and a knot in my stomach. I turned to my mate:

'Do you know who that is?' – of course she did; she's the only one who knows me from way back.

In conclusion, she adds:

> The second time I watched it, I was looking at people's reactions and I was excited by their faces as they reacted and laughed. It was brilliant to hear the laughter – it was more exciting watching them laugh at the show, a hundred times more than if I'd just told them a story. The experience made me feel really important, it made me feel for the first time that it wasn't a pub, it was reaching different people from different walks of life. It helped me to start believing in myself because the same reactions were coming from such different faces. I can trust that more because they are independent of each other.

So, another play came to an end for another cast, but the research and development of an appropriate methodology continues.

Concluding the dialogue

Angus: In debating the ways we use drama with vulnerable and disadvantaged groups, especially when we are working with their direct and personal experiences, I find it more and more useful to look at how other therapies use and incorporate techniques and processes from the performing arts. In addition it is important to examine how the performing arts use techniques from a range of creative therapies, group work and group psychotherapy. For example, when we think about the fundamental elements we use in drama and compare them to the five instruments in the psychodrama technique; the Stage, the Protagonist, the Director, the Auxiliaries and the Audience, it helps me to focus on what I am doing and why.

- The Stage – the dramatic space: how do we define it and how do we use it?
- The Protagonist – is the person a participant, an actor or an enactor?
- The Director – are you a facilitator, a director, a counsellor, a therapist or adviser on skills and techniques?
- The Auxiliaries – the other members of the group: are they performers, witnesses, friends or rivals?
- The Audience – witnesses or part of the drama; closed or public performances?

Realistically, we may be in any combination of those roles and we are nearly always working in complex and complicated situations, trying to honour a range of aims. For these reasons I find it useful to have a therapeutic framework to evaluate what kind of drama is being developed.

Pauline: Casting a dramatherapeutic eye on this work has proved to be illuminating and has gone a long way towards addressing my three concerns at the beginning of the chapter. It does feel as if the extra features that this kind of arts work would need to have in order to be able to claim to be safe, therapeutic and rehabilitative, could be identified by studying dramatherapy structures and principles and thereby evolving what may turn out to be a kind of hybrid between theatre and therapy.

Angus: On reflection, I found it useful to create some distance myself, to step back and try and make sense of the range of ways that people are working with vulnerable and volatile groups. For theatre practitioners, there is a range of ways of working with drama that can fulfil therapeutic, rehabilitative and educational aims. They encompass aspects of different therapy and group work models and practice. There is also a long history of Theatre Therapies, from Evreinov in post-revolutionary Russia, Moreno in America, through to the range of current practitioners working with the notion and concepts of Therapeutic Theatre. For example, John Bergman (Bergman and Hewish 1996, p.102), in describing Geese Theatre's work with the Violent Illusion trilogy, openly describes it as a form of dramatherapy which uses, 'dramatic metaphors to mimic and induce dangerous behaviours, feelings and thoughts in the framework of learning.' Dramatherapist Pete Holloway (Holloway 1996, p.139), describes his work in acute intervention within a psychiatric hospital context as 'the invitation to become the active agents within our own dramas'. Boal's theatre therapy methods as exemplified in *The Rainbow of Desire* (Boal 1995), draw on and use the psychodramatic techniques of doubling, sculpting and role reversal, which, as I suggested earlier, are very seductive and easy to use. These 'theatric therapies' (*ibid.*) and techniques are also used by many other professionals.

In my recent experiences of training probation officers, I encountered tales of the frequent and sometimes misunderstood use of role play to effect 'quick fix' catharsis. Role play was being used by professionals feeling under increasing pressure to obtain results and get people through rehabilitation and re-education programmes. I am concerned about a reliance on such quick fixes when compared to theatre's potential for sustainable inner change and the opportunities it presents for social change.

In the TIPP Centre's development of drama-based programmes for Manchester Probation Service, they found they were reversing their practice of 'drama workshops that do some groupwork', towards the notion of 'groupwork that uses drama' (Thompson 1996, p?). With the understanding of their particular influences – 'Augusto Boal, Psychodrama, Improvisational Theatre and Dramatherapy' (Thompson 1996, p.78) – they focused on developing longer-term aims in relation to short-term rehabilitation programmes for offending behaviour and anger management, by trying to enable individuals to 'undo that script, re-write it, practise alternatives, and develop the potential for positive outcomes' (Thompson 1996, p.70).

As many of us continue to develop these hybrid arts processes which aim to be safe, therapeutic and rehabilitative, what can this actually mean in terms of social change for individuals and groups, and social activism for minority and disadvantaged groups?

Social change? Are we looking for a change of behaviour, brought about by taking part in a creative rehabilitation programme?

Social action? Is it people repositioning themselves in relation to society? For example ex-offenders and ex-mental health system users enrolling as university students, treating themselves as equals and being treated with equality and respect?

Social activism? Is it people, empowered by their experiences of the arts and now having access, confidence and control, effecting change in current corrective and rehabilitative policies? Within this complex creative, social and political spectrum, the biggest question I am left with is – are we truly opening doors or sometimes, just closing books?

Postscript

This collaborative research will continue under the title of The Scene Through Project. It will provide an academic base for others to explore the same issues by offering a short course as part of the postgraduate programme at Central School of Speech and Drama in London from Summer 1998. This will be open to all professionals and postgraduate students wishing to specialise in this field.

References

Bergman, J. and Hewish, S. (1996) 'The violent illusion: dramatherapy and the dangerous voyage to the heart of change.' In M. Liebmann (ed) *Arts Approaches To Conflict*. London: Jessica Kingsley Publishers.

Boal, A. (1992) *Games For Actors and Non-Actors*. London: Routledge.

Boal, A. (1995) *The Rainbow of Desire*. London: Routledge.

Holloway, P. (1996) 'Dramatherapy in acute intervention.' In S.M. Mitchell (ed) *Dramatherapy Clinical Studies*. London: Jessica Kingsley Publishers.

Thompson, J. (1996) 'Stage fights: violence, anger and drama.' In M. Liebmann (ed) *Arts Approaches To Conflict*. London: Jessica Kingsley Publishers.

Further Reading

Blatner, A. (1973) *Acting In*. New York: Springer.

Emunah, R. (1994) *Acting For Real: Drama Therapy; Process, Technique, and Performance*. New York: Brunner Mazel.

Jones, P. (1996) *Drama As Therapy, Theatre As Living*. London: Routledge.

Schutzman. M. and Cohen-Cruz, J. (1994) *Playing Boal – Theatre, Therapy and Activism*. London: Routledge.

CHAPTER 4

Holding On

Dramatherapy with Offenders

Sally Stamp

Background

In this chapter I plan to deal with the complicated issue of where drama ends and dramatherapy begins, in reference to working with offenders. I will be looking particularly at the difference between drama teaching and dramatherapy. This is of especial interest to me as I have worked as both a drama teacher and a dramatherapist in prisons and this chapter is also an exploration of how and why I changed from one task to the other. I began teaching drama and Basic Education in Brixton prison and, over five years, worked five days a week there and in other London prisons. Like many other people using drama in prisons I was struck by how powerful it was as a medium. It touched on all sorts of areas of the prisoners' lives and led them from being suspicious and defensive, to being able to trust each other and share their experiences. There were times when it could have been easy to allow them to talk about their lives and problems but this did not feel comfortable. My task was teaching drama. During this time I came across a prisoner who was guilty of the hideous murder of his girlfriend. He said he was desperate to get help while he was in prison because he knew he would do the same thing again when he got out. I knew about the therapeutic work going on at Grendon Underwood, but that was only one prison. There seemed to be a need for something that combined drama and therapy and this led to me train as a dramatherapist.

I am interested in what it was in my experience of working in prisons that led to me becoming a dramatherapist. There is such a pressure to do something with offenders, to prevent them from re-offending, get them to look at themselves, that the solutions to these problems can distract people from their real jobs. Boundaries and containment are very concrete in secure settings but those that cover professional roles can become very blurred. It is possible to become caught up in grandiose and evangelical ideas about saving or changing people, either individually or as a representative of a profession, or as a facilitator of a particular programme. It can be hard to resist the feeling that you are the one person with the answer and this needs a constant watchfulness. It is this that makes the issue of drama or dramatherapy so important: not because one is the right answer and the other is not, but because you can set out doing one thing and be drawn into doing the other. If your aims change, do the people you are working with know? Do they agree? Do other staff involved with them know? Does your manager know and, as importantly, do they support you? Does your training cover this change in working? All these questions are important, but the most crucial ones to consider are:

Why do you want to do it?

and:

Are you safe?

I made my decision to train as a dramatherapist in isolation: I wanted to fill what I saw was a need in the prison where I was working. I had a secure role as a teacher, and was supported by the Education department. It was only when I began to work as a dramatherapist that these questions became so important. I find myself repeatedly coming back to them, especially when I begin in a new institution. I began to think more about how I related to other professionals: what on earth did they make of a dramatherapist? The reactions from staff and the development of working relations with them has made me think about what happens to anyone employed in secure settings, especially prisons. The point is that anyone working in a secure institution is affected by this pressure to do something with the prisoners. Prisons are increasingly offering programmes on specific issues which can lead to prison staff running specialist groups with minimal training, inadequate supervision, and on subjects, like sexual offending, which they may find deeply disturbing. There are also a lot of effective and good staff doing this work. But how do they feel about changing their role? And how is this seen by the rest of the population in the prison? How does this affect the relationship between me and other staff? Am I seem as competition, as a threat, or as a resource and someone useful?

I want to use my professional development as a way of looking at the connection between drama and dramatherapy. I will compare work that I did as a drama teacher with examples from my experiences as a dramatherapist, and also at how my approach as a dramatherapist has changed as I have been influenced by the work and by the ideas of people writing about offenders.

I have titled the chapter 'Holding On' for various reasons. It reflects both my experience of trying to persevere with the work despite institutional difficulties, and against the anxiety and fear of the prisoners. It seems to mirror the experience of the prisoners trying to see their sentence through, and also the struggle to continue the work. Finally, I hope it says something about the institutions' ability to have faith in the work and support it.

Names and places

Since training I have worked solely in secure institutions: prisons, adolescent secure units, and now a Regional Secure Unit, all in and around London. The settings and people have varied. The prisons were large, high-security male prisons, where the men had committed a range of crimes, and the turnover was high. The adolescent secure units were Local Authority institutions where I worked in the closed secure sections with Section 53 young men, between 14 and 18. Those held under Section 53 are children who are charged with serious offences which, if an adult were charged with the same offences, would lead to lengthy custodial sentences. These were offences like rape, arson and murder. Some were serving sentences of up to two years, some were awaiting trial and some were being assessed. The Regional Secure Unit is for psychiatric offenders, men or women, who all have a diagnosis of mental illness, as well as having committed offences. It is a hospital setting so the emphasis is on treatment rather than merely custody. It is staffed by nurses rather than officers. Although not all the people I have worked with have been sentenced, and may have subsequently been found not guilty, they have all been imprisoned. I shall therefore refer to them as prisoners. I will concentrate as far as possible on dramatherapy in prisons; if I refer to my work in other settings I will make this clear.

What is dramatherapy?

A definition of dramatherapy is a slippery thing: it can be too broad or too clumsy. The British Association of Dramatherapists publishes an information pack which gives two accounts. Johnson states:

> Dramatherapy, like other arts therapies (art, music and dance), is the application of a creative medium to psychotherapy. (Johnson 1980, p.159–160)

This gives a clear idea of the intentions of the work but does not help to understand what this might mean in practice. What can happen then is that non-dramatherapists listen to descriptions of clinical work and say 'But I do that'. So why can they not be called dramatherapists? This is where the psychotherapy part of the statement needs to be thought about, and the training involved needs to be considered. The Whitley Council says that a dramatherapist is:

> a person who is responsible for organizing appropriate programmes of drama activities of a therapeutic application with patients, individually or in groups, and possesses a degree or qualification considered equivalent for entry to an accepted post-graduate training course and also a qualification in dramatherapy following

the completion of an accepted course at a recognized institution for higher or further education. (DHSS 1991)

This emphasises a specific dramatherapy training as the main factor in identifying a dramatherapist, but it is not just the qualification itself that is important. It is also the experiencing of the dramatherapy process so the therapist will have some knowledge themselves of what their clients will experience. Through this the therapist becomes aware of how their own difficulties and anxieties come into the work. It is strongly recommended that they receive psychotherapy (some advocate dramatherapy) throughout the course. As well as deepening their knowledge of the therapeutic process, it also focuses on issues that arise in their lives so that they become aware of their own vulnerable areas. The training emphasises where the therapist's material and the client's material meets, rather than focusing solely on the client's issues. The dramatherapist uses thoughts and feelings about the work and the client to understand what is happening with the client. I had been working with a prisoner who had been looking at incidents in his early life that he had never told anyone. In one session he talked about feeling very angry, and sat with hands clenched, unable to look at me. Sitting with him I felt afraid, then helpless, and then very sad. I realised that I might be feeling something of the sadness he could not allow himself to feel, and which he blocked out with anger. I was then able to use this awareness to approach the work in a different way. Otherwise it could have easily led to him walking out, and to me and other staff thinking he was not able to do the work.

This is where it is important that there is a contract, an agreement between the prisoners or patients and the dramatherapist that the work is therapeutic, that they do not begin doing drama and find themselves involved in therapy. This might seem a technical issue but there is a noticeable difference in the attitude of prisoners to a drama class and a dramatherapy session. It is crucial to the work: if someone does not know this they are not going to feel safe. While working as a drama teacher I remember a prisoner saying that he did not want to come to the class any more because he did not want to talk about himself. This followed an exercise we had done where pairs were asked to find three things in common with each other. He did not feel safe talking about himself even at this level.

To elaborate further on dramatherapy as the 'therapeutic application of drama', Jones (1996) says:

A connection is created between the client's inner world, problematic situation or life experience and the activity in the Dramatherapy session. (Jones 1996, p.6)

The importance here is the conscious attempts of the therapist to help the client make this connection; this is the focus of the work. The purpose is to help the client to see their problem in a new way, and through this to allow them to change. A dramatherapist might choose to work cognitively or in any number of ways, but the main point is that the emphasis is on the individual or individuals in the room and the issues that they are concerned with. So it is not a working through of a set agenda but a working through of what emerges, including not wanting to do the work. It seems that it is this flexibility, and the therapist's ability to manage the boredom, apathy, idealisation, neediness and rage that the prisoner is likely to exhibit, that marks a clear difference.

Why do dramatherapy in prisons?

Deciding that there was a need for dramatherapy in prisons was straightforward but arguing a case for it with prison authorities was more complicated. I had come from a background of teaching drama in prison where this was an acceptable activity. It clearly came under the area of education and so there was a place for drama classes. However, much as I might feel that dramatherapy was useful, why should the prison authorities, and even the prisoners themselves agree? Prisons are not therapeutic places; staff and prisoners are unlikely to understand why you should want to work as a sort of therapist in a place for people who are not mad. When working with prisoners with a diagnosis of psychiatric illness it could be more acceptable. However, with these people there are instead concerns about whether the prisoners are well enough to be able to do the work and the fear that dramatherapy may make them more vulnerable and increase the risk of suicide. So it could be a case of we do not need a dramatherapist because the prisoners are not ill, or because they are too ill and need to be treated with drugs. And yet I knew that there were prisoners who did not have a psychiatric label who were asking for help.

I became more and more concerned with the question of whether prisoners could use therapy or not. I also wondered if there was a link between the offence and the offenders early history. I was particularly interested in the psychoanalytic viewpoint because it seemed to make sense of my thoughts. This led me to take a diploma in Forensic Psychotherapy at the Portman Clinic in London. Through this I came across Felicity de Zulueta's research (1993) into the early history of violent offenders. She is a psychiatrist, psychoanalytical psychotherapist and biologist and has found that there is a link between particular child and mother relationships and those who commit violent crimes. This suggested that therapy could help these people make connections between their childhood lives and their offences. If this could happen then perhaps they would be less likely to offend.

I have been struck that several times prisoners have told me they are relieved to be in prison. There seem to be a number of reasons for this. Some have a huge problem controlling their violence. They feel safe in a secure setting because they know they stand far less chance of being able to carry through their murderous thoughts there than they do outside. Similarly others have felt at the mercy of drugs and alcohol when free. They describe having their lowest self-esteem while using substances. Outside it is up to them how much they take, but inside prison their intake is, largely, controlled by the institution. Having said this, drugs are often more available in secure settings. However, perhaps the presence of staff, and the sense that they are in a system that is trying to prevent their use of substances in some way prevents extreme excess. At least there is someone who might notice and care, someone who cannot be easily avoided. Also, people can enjoy being looked after, and having everything provided.

My experience bears out the paediatrician and psychoanalyst D.W. Winnicott that:

> While under strong management an antisocial child may seem to be all right; but give him freedom and he soon feels the threat of madness. So he offends against society (without knowing what he is doing) in order to re-establish control from outside. (Winnicott 1964, p.229)

He sees the criminal act as a way for the offender to avoid facing extremely painful early experiences, and prison is seen as a way of having the control and stability that was lacking in infancy.

Having actions restricted can mean that a prisoner has an opportunity to reflect on their life. I have been struck by how chaotic most prisoners' lives seem to be when they have talked about what they do outside. Contained in a secure setting they can have time to think, so that long-term anxieties and problems may surface. This can be very difficult and they may become depressed and suicidal. It also means that they might want to do something about this, and look out for help. Prisoners have often talked about using their incarceration as a time to think things through and plan for the future.

So 'being inside' can be very useful, and can be seen as a time of change; participating in dramatherapy in prison can be a medium for this. It can help towards rehabilitation, looking at the change between life inside and life outside. It can be a way of looking at the issues that might be leading to the repetition of offending. It can be an opportunity to explore personal issues and anxieties that stem from early life. It can be particularly useful because it does not have to tackle these issues directly; they can be worked with indirectly, through techniques such as role play.

How drama and dramatherapy are similar

I want to look more closely at the two disciplines and to tease them apart. Some of the similarities are:

- structures: drama and theatre techniques are familiar to both; and the organisation of sessions in both disciplines can be alike

- use of personal experience: in each case work can be based on elements of the prisoners' lives
- membership: who attends and the requirements for attending can be similar.

Structures

In dramatherapy, as in drama, the building blocks of the work may include role play, improvisation, hot-seating, story-building, voice and movement. Both will be expanding an individual's dramatic repertoire so that people are more flexible in the use of their bodies. This involves being both spontaneous and free, and at the same time more in control. In each situation people will be moving between the imaginary world of acting, story-telling, performing, and the real world of their lives. The management of the session time will similarly involve a process of warm-up, main activity and ending. The function of the warm-up will be to engage the group or the individual: to introduce drama skills relevant to the session and raise particular themes and make some links between these and the individuals' lives. It will also address the dynamics of the individual or group, helping them to feel safe with the work. For example, the session might start with pair work before leading into whole group activities. The main activity will be the focus of the session, chosen either by the facilitator, the group, or the teacher/therapist.

Contract

People may decide to join a drama class or take part in a performance. This could be called a contract. In dramatherapy however this is more explicit, and the prisoner is given as much information as possible to enable them to make a clear choice about whether they want to attend or not. They need to know what it will involve, how long it will run for, where it will take place and when. Staff should be consulted and informed.

Focus

In discussing the contract people need to be aware that they will be looking at personal material.

Process

In dramatherapy the process is different. Initially the work is about establishing a group, or partnership, and then developing a relationship with the therapist. Gradually personal material is shared and worked with and, as the sessions progress, group members might be discussing more difficult feelings or situations.

The therapist is likely to be tested or challenged. A vital part of the work will be the ending. Often offenders will have avoided endings by getting rid of people first, by minimising that person's importance, by going from one relationship to another, and so on. To have committed themselves to a person or group of people for a period, and to have seen the contract through from beginning to end can be valuable in itself.

Relationship with teacher / therapist

The relationship between prisoners and the therapist is very different to that of prisoners and teacher. The dramatherapist may be idealised as the only person to understand them. Group members might want the therapist to speak for them, to become some sort of advocate. This can fluctuate with the therapist also being denigrated and seen as useless. It can be very hard for the prisoners to be ambivalent about people in general, that is to see them in a balanced way, and this is more extreme with the therapist. The danger is that they split staff, so you are seen as good and officers as bad, or vice versa. This needs managing carefully to try and bring both views together. Also the therapist might be experienced as key people from their lives. For example, as someone who has let them down or betrayed them. They may feel angry and destructive towards the therapist, or see him or her as someone very powerful who can save them. The therapist uses these feelings from the group and his or her own feelings about the prisoners to understand what is going on, and this is why training is essential. For example, the therapist might be working with someone who has just been bereaved. If they have not worked through their own experiences of death it can be very frightening, or even dangerous for both of them. A dramatherapist needs to be able to manage very strong feelings in him or herself, and in the prisoners. The therapist cannot simply hand over the work to another teacher or worker if it does become too difficult for him or her, because the fantasy of the group or individual will be that they have damaged or destroyed that therapist, and that he or she could not cope with the prisoners or the feelings aroused. If you have put yourself in a position saying that you will listen to feelings the prisoners find difficult and help the group or individual to understand them and then you leave, the message is that you find them difficult too.

Autobiography – fact or fiction?

I want to show two ways of drawing upon autobiographical material in my work: one as a drama teacher, and one as a dramatherapist. Autobiography is used in many ways in drama and dramatherapy. It is used both directly and indirectly (for example through fictional characters). In using autobiography with any group there are issues of disclosure, dealing with distressing material, safety and trust.

With offenders these issues are magnified because they have committed a crime, so they will be more anxious about how much they reveal about themselves, and to whom. Anyone's life story is by definition subjective: decisions have to be made on what is left in or taken out, and the audience or listener will influence these decisions. With prisoners the questions of how fictional the real story is and how close to reality the fictional account is, become more acute. In the background are issues of innocence and guilt, accountability and responsibility, denial and ownership.

Autobiography in drama

This is how I used autobiographical material as a drama teacher; at the same time I was training as a dramatherapist. Myself and two other drama teachers planned to stage a performance in the prison where we were working. It was primarily a remand prison, with a huge turnover, and the only performance space available was the chapel. These problems had previously made such a project seem impossible, but recently an outside organisation had led workshops and rehearsals, culminating in a performance. This proved that such a thing was possible, with the help of the prison. The event had been successful, but the prisoners had been kept in peripheral roles, while professionals took the leads. We felt that the men could carry a performance on their own, and also felt that they should devise a piece themselves rather than use an existing script.

I took the story of the film *It's A Wonderful Life* as a framework to base the story on. The performance was set for Christmas so the show had to have some seasonal connection. I did not want to do a pantomime as that seemed quite limited in scope. Also Christmas was always a difficult time in prisons, and many of the men wanted to forget what time of year it was, rather than celebrate it. So it had to fit with the season without being unbearably festive. The film was set at Christmas so that was the link. But it also has a structure which was readily accessible, and perhaps especially to prisoners: a man is about to kill himself because his life seems unbearable, a figure appears and shows him the good things that have happened in his life, and then what awful things would happen if he died, the hero then realises that his life is worth living and his problems are resolved. This was the outline which we were to fill in.

Because the prison population was moving through so fast we set the structure that whoever turned up for the class developed the story, so whether there were two or twenty, the work would continue, and each person would contribute to it. We began by streamlining the classes into one, enlisted the current students and recruited more throughout the writing, as people moved on. The first session was selling the idea, in the second we showed the film. This was tricky as the men's responses were mixed: some felt that it was too Hollywood, others that it was too white, too middle-class, or they could not see how it had anything to do with them. At the same time some were moved by the story and joked about this. It seemed that this was a defence against feeling sad or upset. We suggested that we began with the main character in prison, and developed the story from there, with this they very quickly developed ideas for the main character and what his dilemma was. One idea which was strongly supported was that the hero was a pimp and drug dealer: they wanted the story to portray prostitution, violence and drug addiction. They wanted it to be realistic and adult.

This was an interesting situation: within dramatherapy I would have accepted the outline and used it to work through the themes that emerged in the story. Within the scope of drama we could have used the idea, but we also had to be aware of the rest of the institution and message we were presenting to others. We discussed this with them and they accepted the point, although the main instigator of the idea was unhappy. It seemed that a part of the group wanted to test out what of themselves was acceptable: were they allowed to be violent and abusive or did they have to be different, middle-class, and white? Also involved was the degree to which the project belonged to them, and how much they were being used by the drama staff and the prison. Again, this was not the forum to explore their feelings about this. There had been some discussion, a clear decision had been made by the group and we moved on to devising the piece.

The main character was in prison, having been framed by a corrupt businessman for a theft which he did not commit. He had lost his girlfriend because he refused to give up the job which he loved, running a youth centre, for one with more money and shorter hours. The youth centre was going to be demolished for development and his ex-girlfriend was now with the businessman. The person who shows his past and future was a friend he had known since childhood who had a lengthy criminal history. So they chose to create a story about a man who faced several personal difficulties, who had to make hard decisions, and contrast him with a figure who had chosen to break the law.

Once the basic theme was established I suggested that we created scenes at key points in his life, based on the notion of seven-year stages. So the first scene happened when he was seven, and described the beginning of the friendship. The second scene was set at the age of 14, and showed the hero making a choice between breaking the law or not, and so on. To write the play each scene was improvised until the group was satisfied with the result, it was audio-taped, typed up, then re-read and refined, if necessary. Their commitment was striking. A core group emerged who attended every session. There was intense debate about each scene, and they were fiercely protective about the project. Although the process was a difficult one, and they often found it hard to tolerate indecision, they stuck with it and respected each other's views. They were also able to accept criticism about scenes, because the story belonged to the group, and they wanted it to be as good as possible. Even though some people maybe came to four, two, or only one session, they were still as involved as if they had participated since the beginning, and accepted that they had contributed to something that was being continued by others.

It was obvious that the group were strongly identifying with the story, because of their commitment, but this was underlined when another professional sat in on a session and said that the scene we were working on had actually happened to one of the group. As we began rehearsing for the performance one of the cast talked of how hard it was to act the part of being depressed in several of the scenes because he was afraid of being stuck like that. He said that it reminded him of his own depression. In the context of the play it was only possible to talk about leaving his role behind, and having somewhere outside the play where he could talk about the feelings that came up. The audience's response to the performance was also interesting. Several prisoners spoke of seeing their lives up there. Many thanked us for allowing fellow prisoners to do something 'for us, about us, by us': the work had given the audience a sense of power and self-esteem. The men involved in the performance talked of feeling good about themselves. One said this was the first time in his life he had done so. Also, they described feeling part of something. This was brought into focus by one of them who said that it had been almost like being part of a family.

Although the story was not explicitly autobiographical, it obviously told aspects of the men's lives. In a later production with a looser structure where each person had to create their own character, the men more obviously developed characters based on themselves. Each one had a past history of crime, and often a drug problem, and they were nearly all trying to begin a new life. Part of the value for them in the performance was in having their lives recognised and recognised behind the fictional characters. Using autobiographical material in drama allowed them to be both themselves and not themselves at the same time. They were acting a version of themselves which was modified by the needs of the story, the other characters and the performance. Their responses within role were affected by a critical process: what should their character do in that situation? As well as this being affected by aesthetics, it also opened up individuals to societal and moral pressures. In their version of *It's A Wonderful Life*, why did the main character have to choose not to follow his friend into crime? Because we had decided that the script said so.

Autobiography in dramatherapy

Within dramatherapy I have used autobiography in a variety of ways with individuals and groups. I have used a similar structure to the one described above in a men's prison and an adolescent secure unit with young men who had committed very serious offences. In both cases I used it as a way to begin working with them, so that we could work with material without them feeling vulnerable. What was striking was that in each case they distanced the characters from themselves. They did this by choosing extreme situations, they gave the characters bizarre names, and they laughed and joked about the story they had developed. In the prison this was instigated by one of the group who seemed to be trying to sabotage the session. At the end they said that they would be serious next time. Similarly, the young men felt their ideas had not been any good and decided to work in a different way the following week. They later came back to the story and did complete it.

Although the stories in each case were extreme, there were fundamental connections. It seemed as if they were testing out whether or not I could accept their extremes. They also wanted to see if they could be taken seriously. By choosing to work with rather stereotypical story lines everything was kept at a distance, which was very important as this was the very beginning of the group's life. They were anxious as to whether their ideas were good enough. This was especially noticeable when working with groups of adolescents and it was common for them to feel that their story was bad and not worth continuing with. The men seemed to feel that if they were taking the sessions seriously, they should talk directly about themselves, and that this had been inhibited by the group member they felt was letting them down. In fact, problems faced by the character they had created were ones that they brought to the group over time: difficulties accepting authority; substance abuse; concerns about relationships with woman; infidelity and promiscuity; struggling with the responsibility of fatherhood and self-esteem.

It had been a similar response to the first story idea for *It's A Wonderful Life*, except that there was no future audience to hold in mind; the only people they could offend or please were themselves and me. It seems that this was part of the process of them finding out what they thought was acceptable or not acceptable as a group. At the end of the sessions they identified that the most important part of the group had been the permission to speak as equals, and set their own agenda. The exercise had been the first step in that process.

I attempted to use autobiography more directly with another group of prisoners, with whom I worked for a limited amount of time looking at self-esteem. It was my first dramatherapy project and I was running the group in the prison where I worked as a drama teacher. Some of the people in the group were people who had been in *It's A Wonderful Life*. We met for two sessions a week, with one focusing on the central theme of self-esteem. In the other I asked them to work on telling their life story, using other people in the group as actors. Each life story was then to be presented in the penultimate session. My idea was that these autobiographies would allow them to tell their stories in their own way, presenting themselves as they wanted to be seen. Most of them were acquainted with each other. I used different structures to facilitate this, such as life-lines and Moreno's social atom (Jones 1996). It soon became apparent how difficult and painful telling the story of their own lives was.

The first exercise was drawing a life-line to represent events in their lives. There was no writing, just a symbolic line. I then asked them to map on the line either a point of celebration, crisis or a turning point. This incident was then told and enacted. This was the basis of the 'script'. To decide on the 'actors' I used Moreno's social atom. This is a way of mapping the significant elements in someone's life, and the relationships between them. It can be done on paper, or using people or objects arranged spatially. The person chooses a mark or object/person to represent themselves, then does the same for family members, friends, colleagues etc. Other important aspects of life, like work, drink, drugs, and so on are included. They are placed in relation to the person, so that the most important are nearest. The end result is a visual map of the person's emotional attachments.

All of them saw their lives as normal and uneventful, apart from a wobble which resulted in their current sentence. Most chose celebration as point of focus, though one chose a turning point. What was striking was that, in each case, the offenders found it very difficult to separate out individuals. They either grouped a range of people together in one group, for example family, or they placed all their important people equally close to themselves. An exception to this was someone who was so hated that they were either placed as far away as possible, or were not included in the mapping at all. Also in contrast someone, frequently the mother, was idealised as loving and understanding. Where they were seemingly given equal importance, the individual undermined this by describing them as OK or all right. It seemed hard for them to think about people unless they could refer to specific incidents; to think about them in the abstract was too much. It can be useful to have these recordings for people to look back on and compare different attitudes. The exercises can be a way of beginning work, but I have also felt that people found them intrusive. Even when using these structures as obliquely as possible – for example, by not naming any of the characters in the social atom – people could find them too revealing. It was as though they gave themselves away by putting something out in the open.

The group of prisoners who had been working on their autobiographies were disappointed at the end of the project because they had expected to act out their problems and find different solutions. They had wanted to use their life stories, but in a very focused way that looked at problematic but manageable pieces. I had expected them to give up too much of themselves to scrutiny; it was what I wanted, not what they wanted. I thought that it would be liberating for them to tell their story in their own way. But what had happened was too painful to tell: drug and alcohol abuse, abandonment, physical abuse. They wanted to make light of it, to think of the future. It was also difficult to share this with a middle-class woman. What seemed important is that the prisoners could work from a safe distance so that they could get close up and say, 'I did this', or stand from further back and say 'Someone like me did this', or say 'I only did this in role but wouldn't do this for real'. For people to be able to reveal themselves they need to be safe. Secure institutions do not encourage trust between people, public use is made of personal information and sometimes this can be dangerous. There needs to be a no man's land between the fact and the fiction where people can move, so that two things, or more, can be true at the same time. In this sort of transitional space (Winnicott 1986) they can be both themselves and themselves in a role: they can be depressed and pretending to be depressed, for example. And in this zone the group or the individual and therapist can explore, say, depression, without having to be on one side or the other.

Yet, as I have described above, the group of prisoners wanted to work cognitively: this is a problem, how do we solve it? Within this there is the area of playing, of trying out different approaches. In later groups I have worked more eclectically, using whatever approach seems appropriate for the group or individual at any time. So a theme or issue arises and I offer a way of working with it. As well as what is said or done I am aware of the importance of what is unspoken, the dynamics of the group and myself in relation to them. Who decides what happens in the session? How am I made to feel? What do I perceive others feeling? How does this get communicated back to the group? This is a major difference between drama and dramatherapy: the focus in drama is on a product or performance rather than on relationships. I will describe a specific exercise that I have used in both drama and dramatherapy sessions.

From drama to therapy

The structure is to divide a group into observers and players, with a minimum of three players. They are each given a number between one and the number of players. So, if there are five of them they would be given a number between one and five. They are then given a type of person they are playing, on a continuum of most successful to least. For example, this could be actors, from superstar to struggling fringe performer. They are questioned in turn by the observers who have to guess what number they are playing. The performers have to speak in character giving appropriate answers to their part. The skill is in taking the role convincingly, but suggesting that you are another status. The observers have to work out the status level behind the fiction.

I have often used this as an exercise leading into building characters and taking on roles. In one particular case in a prison with a high turnover I used it in a class where there was a mixture of prisoners who had attended for months and some who were new to the group. The situation was a dating agency interviewing men as potential dates. They were presenting themselves to the agency, not a specific woman, although I was aware that I was the only woman in the room and they were thinking of my judgement as well. The performers played their roles convincingly and they each presented themselves as ideal dates. The differences were mainly to do with money and possessions, but also what their characters offered as what a woman wanted on a date. There was a great deal of hilarity as they recognised things they or friends had said or done. There was also an understanding that there was a gap between what they did to get a woman and what they did normally. So a possible winner was the man who had a house, good job, expensive car who would give his date roses and take her for a romantic meal for two. There was a lot of debate about what a woman wanted in a man. Generally they felt that women were most interested in money and possessions, but some argued for care and understanding. In this debate they cited personal experience but it was possible to contain this within the exercise. There could have easily been prolonged discussion about relationships between men and women, and the exercise was very revealing about their attitudes and experiences, but it could also be one element of a session plan.

I have used the same structure with a young offender I worked with individually. He was shy, withdrawn, and dramatherapy was seen as a way for him to express himself. He was not able to talk about his anxieties and problems, apart from saying that he wanted to go home. Each of the young men I worked with there did a life-line and a social atom. His social atom had all his family grouped around him as one mass, all being equally important. His life-line revealed that he wanted to have lots of children. He attended his sessions regularly and over six months he became able to communicate more easily; as he began to trust me more he would bring things that bothered him and we explored them in a range of ways. He found it very hard to talk about his family, especially his mother, apart from to say that she was OK. He gave the impression that their lives were quite separate. A consistent theme was his interest in life stages, particularly birth and aging. He would ask me direct questions to try and understand what happened as people grew older. I suggested that we looked at this using board games as a base. We drew up a grid on paper with 80 squares: one for each year of someone's life. Each square was to have a picture or symbol to represent something that was likely to happen at that time of life. We would then translate this into a tableau or a scene which we enacted.

About two months before he was due to be released he was excited and quite anxious. We had been talking about our ending. He was looking at being with his family again, and thinking of his new girlfriend. Over the sessions there had been several mothers in his different stories, we began talking about good and bad mothers. I adapted the structure above to explore this. I suggested that we imagined he was four different women applying to an agency to adopt a child. I played someone from the agency, and asked each 'mother' the same questions. To mark the change from one character to the next, we set the framework of him 'knocking' on the door, being greeted by the person from the agency, giving a different name for every character, being interviewed and then leaving the 'office'. At the end we de-roled and I tried to guess which number each had been. We then discussed how he had found this, and looked at the differences between them. One of the questions was: why do you want a baby? He found this hard to answer in character, three of the characters said they did not know why, the fourth, the least ideal, said she wanted to have a child because she was bored. The main criteria for the best mother seemed to be money and material comforts. Another question had been what could they offer the child. Number one mother wanted to give the child a life and said she would spoil it. Mother number two said that what she could offer the child was money. The characters that he had created did not mention love or affection, but money. I felt that this reflected his difficulty in expressing a need for love, and also his experience of his relationship with his own mother.

In reflection I asked him what he thought a child wanted from a mother. This was difficult to answer. I asked him what he wanted from a mother. Poignantly, he said he wanted her to look after him, teach him things, to make him go to school and to take him to football classes. For the first time he was able to say that he wanted things from a mother: to be cared for and controlled. I felt that I had allowed him to learn things in the sessions, and that he had both developed a relationship with me, and had allowed himself to question relationships. People were no longer one mass surrounding him, but individuals separate from him that he had different feelings for. This exercise had allowed him to think about mothers without him feeling disloyal.

It was striking that throughout the work he would resist talking directly about his family, particularly his mother, but brought up issues about his family through talking about imaginary characters. Initially he created stories about what seemed to be fictional people, later he was able to admit that they were based on real people. But we had had the freedom to play each of the characters and speak about each of them from each characters' point of view, for example: what did the mother think of her daughter and her daughter's boyfriend. Then we also were able to speak about them as ourselves. In this way we were able to explore relationships and alternative interactions without focusing on specific people in his life.

The structure of the life grid was also used to create distance between the concerns he was bringing to the session and his life. The grid allowed him to ask questions about life stages and to explore them from different positions. The first stage was to draw an image to illustrate that particular age. Then he developed a scene, story or tableau based on this image which we would enact, or he would describe. We could then discuss them on different levels:

- as characters within the story
- as a character reflecting on the characters in the story
- as himself talking about the characters
- as myself talking about the character.

So we could move closer to or further away from our own direct opinions and it gave us room to play with ideas rather than be restricted to one view. Through this he could explore difficult and troubling thoughts and develop his own thoughts.

What I attempt to do in dramatherapy is to create a space to think about what issues come to the session. What happens is a function of my experience, knowledge and analysis of the situation, the offender's dramatic range and skills, the emotional intensity of the material, the level of engagement between us, and the amount of support provided by the institution. It is a complex and subtle process which might mean that I offer several structures which are rejected before one can be made use of. It also involves me trying to tune into that individual or those individuals so that I pick up any threads of ideas and use them to think what to offer. The prisoners themselves might have ideas of what they would like to do in the session, and this will be used as well.

Problems

There are problems which are specific to working in prisons and some are different for dramatherapists compared to drama workers. This is an exploration of the primary problems and how they relate to each discipline.

Fear of disclosure

Prisoners may be afraid of others knowing their offence because it will arouse strong feelings. Sex offences would be a major example of this. They also might be afraid of jeopardising a case that has not yet come to court, or that they may admit to a previous offence. Personal information can be used against them, and make them open to exploitation and bullying. There will be family and friendship loyalties they will not want to betray. They may be ashamed or embarrassed by some of their material. This fear is more extreme in dramatherapy because of the expectation that the work will involve discussing personal information. To protect themselves they may rubbish the work and test out the therapist by questioning the therapist's training, experience and understanding of them.

In drama one can focus on the 'as if' so that prisoners talk as a character not themselves. The focus can be kept away from the personal. The work can be kept within the boundary of drama, and discussion about their lives discouraged. In dramatherapy a contract of confidentiality can be discussed, and what people feel about disclosure. It is possible to work at a distance from the personal, through role or stories, for example.

Fear of building trust

In each discipline some trust is important in order to be able to work. But prisoners have many reasons to be distrustful. Some will have been informed on by co-defendants, friends or family. Often they will have had difficult family experiences and many will have been in care. Part of the work will be in developing the capacity to trust. As this happens people feel vulnerable and consequently may distance themselves, not attend, or leave the group. In both fields exercises can be used to build trust. In dramatherapy it could be useful to acknowledge this fear, and accept it. Again, setting group rules and establishing a contract of confidentiality can help the group feel safe.

Confidentiality

This is crucial in dramatherapy but also delicate: at what point does confidentiality become collusion? Prison staff may well be concerned that the therapist is colluding with the prisoners if they do not have access to information revealed in sessions. The prisoners themselves will be concerned about where this information goes, expecting it to go on their records. As a dramatherapist you need to be clear what your boundaries are, and then this has to be understood and agreed by both the staff involved and the prisoners.

It is important that the work here is properly prepared. If the staff are to understand dramatherapy and the need for confidentiality then time will be needed to give them information through a range of channels. I have sent proposals for dramatherapy to key members of staff and then met with them to discuss issues. I have found it very useful to run experiential workshops so that they have a clearer idea of why confidentiality is so essential. In this way I have raised some of the fears they might have about someone having information to which that they would not have access. Finally we have agreed situations when confidentiality would not hold. Usually this is if one of the group or the individual threatens to damage himself, someone else or property. However even this can be difficult. One of the prisoners I worked with talked of killing himself. I reported this to the staff at the end of the session and the prisoner was then angry with me for doing so. Although it was hard dealing with his anger it was vital that he knew he could be looked after by the prison staff and that I was not solely responsible for him.

Acting out

After a drama class or a performance prisoners might be elated and excited – the effect of dramatherapy can vary. At times they might be more confident, more open, more co-operative. However, there are also times when someone might be dealing with distressing material and become angry to avoid the sadness and depression this triggers. They may become suicidal. This is very difficult to manage, and can jeopardise the work if the prison staff are not aware of why this is happening. There needs to be thorough preparation before beginning the work and staff need to be informed of the process. They should not be put at risk by the work. This is where the referral process is important, so that staff are involved and take some responsibility for the treatment. Professional liaison needs to be clear, with a commitment to the work.

Attitudes of staff

Drama tends to have a bad reputation in prisons. It is seen as something that stirs the prisoners up. Drama workers are seen as difficult and demanding, with no understanding of why security is important. This is not always true, but this is often the picture. Dramatherapy is looked at even more questioningly. There may also be professional jealousy from people who see themselves providing this service already. It is important to spend time in advance getting staff involved, listening to their viewpoint and taking it into account. The referral system needs to be planned with staff so that it works for both parties.

Fitting into the structure

As a drama teacher there was an established structure for me to fit into. As a dramatherapist I have mostly been an outsider linked tangentially with a psychology department, an education department, or a specific wing. It is very difficult working in this isolated way, and ideally I would work in a team. There should at least be a recognised member of staff to take on some of the management difficulties.

Hidden agendas

With dramatherapy there is more scope for hidden agendas. Prisoners may think that if they get involved they will get benefits, they may think it will affect their home leave. Staff may want it to enhance a new regime or programme, or they may want to target a particular prisoner group which they have not yet been able to reach. To try and combat this it is important to establish the aims of the work and draw up a contract which can be referred to. It will be necessary to be clear about why the purchaser wants to buy the service. It is useful to ask a range of staff what they think the purpose of the work is and to have some discussion about this.

Conclusion

I have explored some of the similarities and differences between the practice of dramatherapy and drama in secure settings. I have attempted to discuss the complexity of this issue and the possible dangers of blurring the role of the two disciplines. I hope I have also given some indication of how important both approaches can be for those who are in secure settings. I feel that dramatherapy can be very useful as a therapy with offenders because it allows a safe distance for them to work on material, and it harnesses the energy of acting while developing the capacity for thinking. I think that my experience has shown that it has been most valuable when the work has been led by the offenders themselves, rather than to an agenda set by me. A major consideration has been the need for good communication with everyone involved in the work. It is essential that the dramatherapist and the work are understood by the institution and that the dramatherapist is recognised as a member of staff in the same way as a prison officer or nurse, rather than existing in a no man's land, outside the responsibility of the prison, Adolescent Secure Unit, Special Hospital, or Regional Secure Unit. If this happens, the powerful and difficult feelings prisoners or patients experience can be contained through a process of them understanding and thinking about these experiences rather than by reacting to them with violence or further offending.

References

de Zulueta, F. (1993) *From Pain to Violence: The Traumatic Roots of Destructiveness.* London: Whurr Publishers.

DHSS (1991) *Professions Allied to Medicine and Related Grades of Staff* (PTA Council), 2/98 App. B, (Dec.) London: DHSS.

Johnson, D. R. (1980) 'Drama therapy.' In R. Herink (ed) *The Psychotherapy Handbook: The A–Z Guide to More than 250 Different Therapies in Use Today.* Massachusetts: Meridian.

Jones, P. (1996) *Drama As Therapy.* London: Routledge.

Winnicott, D.W. (1964) *The Child, The Family, and The Outside World.* Harmondsworth: Penguin.

Winnicott, D.W. (1986) *Home Is Where We Start From.* Harmondsworth: Penguin.

CHAPTER 5

The House of Four Rooms

Theatre, Violence and the Cycle of Change

Alun Mountford and Mark Farrall

Introduction

For the past 16 years Geese Theatre Company (US and UK)[1] have pioneered the use of theatre and drama in the rehabilitation of offenders both in this country and in the United States. Founded in 1980 by expatriate British director, John Bergman, and influenced by a wide variety of theatre styles and practitioners, the US and UK companies have specialised in the use of mask and improvisational techniques to create interactive pieces that challenge offenders to confront their destructive behaviours. Over the years both companies' work has moved on to become an integral part of offender rehabilitation programmes in prisons and probation services throughout the US and the UK.

This chapter sets out to explore the development of the UK Company's work with violent offenders and in particular focuses on 'The House of Four Rooms', a theatrical structure used within the Company's two-week violent-offender programmes designed for prisons and probation services. Based in part on the Company's five-day intensive prison residency, 'The Violent Illusion', the structure aims to provide an interactive experience, tailored for each participant, which enhances and underlines the process of change an offender must go through in order to leave their violent past behind.

A question of violence

But first of all, what are the origins of violence? Is it an integral part of human behaviour? Of masculine make-up? Or is it a product of social conditioning?

These questions and many more besides have to be answered in order to inform our theatre work. It has been said that violence has always been with us. In

1   Geese Theatre Company (UK) was founded in 1987 by US Company member Clark Baim.

the early exploration of Man's origins, paleontologists and anthropologists, like Professor Raymond Dart (1953), popularised the still prevalent view of Man's brutal history, his domination of those weaker than himself, and his inherent, biological blood lust. Freud (1923) wrote on the power of the Id, the 'aggressive drive' bursting forth to wreak havoc in the conscious world, whilst behaviourists like Dollard et al. (1939) claimed that aggression was an inevitable response to frustration. Wars are waged throughout the world as one group endeavours to gain power over another: the Lebanon, the Gulf, Rwanda, Bosnia, Chechnya – the list goes on with one war finishing and another starting up in a seemingly endless conveyor belt of carnage.

Yet if humanity's primary predilection was only towards violence, then the society we live in would not exist. We would all be hacking to death our next-door neighbour, Saturday morning shopping would be a battleground, a package holiday would be an open invitation to invade the country of your choice. Clearly, people live reasonably well together most of the time; where there are disagreements, they very rarely end in violence.

There is a popular perception that we are surrounded by violence and violent individuals and that the modern world is a dangerous place to live in. There are obvious advantages for politicians in placing responsibility for social problems solely within the individual and whilst the ethic of personal responsibility and control of one's behaviour is absolutely at the core of Geese practice, an awareness of the sociopolitical issues must also inform our work.

Each person brings to their environment a unique package of inherent potentials which may be shaped, elicited or suppressed, by their surroundings. There appears to be a common agreement amongst the various schools of psychology regarding the origins of violence. Where a child has experienced psychological, physical or sexual abuse it is likely that in later life they will display violent and abusive behaviour (Miedzian 1992). The proposition seems simple and is supported by a mass of empirical evidence (Berkowitz 1978; Gelles 1983).

The truth is that of course there is no one explanation; people do contribute to their own downfall by acting in ways which shape and select the environment they experience, which then feeds into shaping their behaviour in response to that environment. They are immersed in their culture, defined to some degree by their socioeconomic position, perhaps living in a subculture outside of, or at a tangent to, the mainstream culture, while sharing many of that mainstream culture's values. Decades ago Cloward and Ohlin (1960) and Hirschi (1969) pointed out the gap between what is desired and what is achievable for such people, mainly young men, of working-class origins, who may well have low educational attainment, just as their parents may do.

Past experience of victimisation or trauma may feed the aggressive behaviours consciously or unconsciously (Hodge 1992), and the doing of the behaviours provide a great and enjoyable thrill. Physical or genetic factors, the 'hard wiring' of the brain, may mediate this response but not predetermine it. The offender may genuinely believe that their interpretation of interpersonal events and experience of the social world is accurate. For them people are hostile and aggressive for little reason, making violence an everyday occurrence, wholly understandable and justifiable.

In brief then, taking in all of the aspects above, a general Geese model would be that violence and aggression are in essence learnt behaviours serving a functional purpose of problem solving or gaining of goals for people who often lack other, more pro-social skills or tactics. The behaviours can be transmitted inter-generationally and culturally, in a social milieu that may be characterised by low educational attainment, poor work records, bad housing and a host of other factors.

Overall, this lack of attainment is set against a wider culture which measures success in terms of material goods and provides an 'iron cage' of masculinity (Sim 1993) where conflict resolution, mediation and non-aggressive behaviours are underrated and denigrated as somehow unmanly.

So what has drama and theatre got to do with all this?

Violence in the community; theatre and violent offenders

Geese Theatre Company (UK) spent the first 18 months of its life touring to prisons throughout the country, gradually building a reputation for a clear and incisive understanding of offenders and offender issues. As the Company's reputation grew, they were asked to become involved in community sentence programmes for Probation Services. In 1989, the Company were first invited to provide an input into Hereford and Worcester Probation Service's new offending behaviour course – the Programme for Achievement, Challenge and Training (PACT).

This area of the Company's work has now expanded to 14 counties throughout the country, providing input into offending-behaviour, sex-offender and violent-offender programmes. This required the recruitment of project workers, drawn mostly from the touring performance company, who would now specialise in theatre-based group work.

Probation Services are obliged to provide alternatives to custody, or Community Sentence Programmes. These are not voluntary, but are part of an order that an offender must complete as part of their probation requirements. It is possible for an offender to volunteer for a programme, but very few do.

The 'front' to the outside world – masks and Death Bird

Since the early days of the Company, masks have been a central metaphor. John Bergman and Geese (US) endeavoured to develop a style of theatre that in some way reflected the offenders' world. A number of workshops in various state penitentiaries took place in the developmental process of 'The Plague Game', an interactive performance that looks at maintaining relationships whilst in prison. In one such workshop an inmate provided the metaphor by relating how, when he had a visit from his mother or his partner, he always wore a mask. This mask would enable him to con money to pay off debts, buy drugs and generally survive. He would tell his mother how tough it was for him inside, or intimidate his partner into giving him whatever he wanted.

Drawing on the concept and usage developed by the Russian director Meyerhold in the 1920s (see Braun 1969), Geese (US) began to work with simple half-masks intended to represent the 'front' that an offender might use to keep harsh reality at bay. With the mask down, the character can lie, cheat, manipulate or do whatever he needs to do to maintain his self-image. When characters on stage wish, or are requested by the audience, to say what they really think and feel in a given situation, they lift their masks. However, the lifting of the mask does not necessarily mean that with the mask down a lie has been told, it simply suggests that a deeper truth may exist. Theatrically, the mask allows the actor to represent dynamically the 'inner voice' (the thought process), emphasising thoughts, beliefs, rules and values and their effect on behaviour.

Some masks are positive, others destructive and are connected to the idea that we play different roles in different situations. This idea of the 'playing of roles' is of importance in the Company's work as it refers to the 'flexibility', or the self-constructed aspect of personality. If being a violent offender is in part a particular role or mask in a particular situation, it should be possible for the offender to change masks, change their behaviours and thus change themselves (Gergen 1972).

We seek to identify those masks which are the most destructive and facilitate an awareness of the situations that provoke their appearance. Only with a clear understanding of how these destructive masks operate, and of when we are most likely to adopt them, can we heighten our awareness to our 'high-risk' situations. In isolating these masks clients can choose to make more informed decisions as to whether they wish to control them.

Whilst researching and developing the show *King Con*,[2] Bergman and the US Company began to explore the use of masks in more detail. Inspired in part by Yochelson and Samanow's seminal work *The Criminal Personality* (1976), they

---

2   *King Con* was the third piece developed by Bergman and Geese (US) and explored the structure of the 'criminal personality'.

created a series of masks that endeavoured to reflect the behaviours and manipulations that Yochelson and Samanow had identified. The Company came up with three basic masks. These masks are referred to as Fragment Masks representing 'fragments' of personality.

These masks were:

- Mr Fist: 'Don't mess with me!' – the mask of aggression and intimidation.

- Mr Cool: 'Everything is sorted. No problem.' – the image-conscious, 'streetwise' offender who knows it all.

- Stone Wall: 'I don't know…' – the bored, indifferent, uncommunicative and blank mask.

Later, Bergman and Geese (UK) went on to expand the spectrum of manipulative masks:

- Good Guy: 'All I'm doing is standing up for myself' – the 'John Wayne' who only does 'what a man has to do…'

- Bullshit: 'You see, it happened this way…' – the mask of sly, manipulative, deceitful avoidance that keeps responsibility and insight at bay.

- The Joker: 'It's just a laugh, that's all.' – the mask of cruel insensitive humour that is often sexist and racist and used to avoid the seriousness of one's behaviour.

- The Rescuer: 'You can't do that to him!' – and if I rescue you, then you must do the same for me, or else!

- The Victim Mask/Poor Me: 'You don't understand what it's like for me!' The 'offender as victim' for whom the 'cruelty' of the world and 'bad luck' relinquish him of any responsibility for the victims that he himself creates.

What is quickly apparent to the audience is that behind one mask is another and another and so on. It would be naive to think that there might simply be some God-given element of ourselves which we need only to communicate with in order for us to see the error of our ways.

The recognition of the sheer complexity of the concept of 'masks' inevitably motivated the need to identify the place beyond mask that seems to generate the offending behaviour in any given situation. It seemed clear that this 'place' was in some way beyond cognition, a place of impulse and reaction – a place that sparks the act of 'doing' rather than 'thinking'. Offenders talk about the urge to attack, the urge to steal or abuse. This urge may seem beyond their control, and sometimes extremely scary. This urge can take an offender to the very edge, to murder or rape.

The notion of a 'beast within' that drives an offender to commit crimes was translated into the character of Death Bird. This large mask, reminiscent of a skeletal vulture skull, became an integral part of the show *Lifting the Weight*[3] and, in later years, project work. However, the belief that this impulse or 'Death Bird' was somehow 'beyond control' was contested in both performances and workshops. If we can consciously recognise not only our masks but also our impulse to hurt, damage, bully, manipulate, cajole, steal or rob, and to gain power and pleasure from such abusive acts, then we are capable of confronting and 'pulling down' that 'impulse', controlling that 'Death Bird'.

Central to the Company's use of mask and Death Bird is the need to recognise choice and free will. Through this recognition, we can identify the masks that help to perpetuate the creation of victims, and drag the perpetrator back into prison. Without this recognition we are likely to remain a slave to our habitual behaviours.

The basic principle of using theatre and drama in group work with violent men is to explore offenders' violent and aggressive experiences and in so doing surface the thoughts and feelings which feed the behaviour:

Offender: If someone is coming at you with a knife, you have to use violence to protect yourself!

Project Worker: So why was he coming at you with a knife in the first place?

Offender: Well, we had an argument, and he was pissing me off!

Project Worker: How had he pissed you off?

As the offender goes into more and more detail around the offence one invariably finds more and more material that underlines the offender's role in instigating or contributing to the eruption of violence. By emphasising their responsibility for the violence they commit, the project worker can encourage the offender to identify the masks they may be using and anger management skills they lack, and through role play the offender can begin to explore and practice new skills that may reduce the likelihood of them continually re-offending.

---

3   *Lifting the Weight* was the second piece developed by Geese (US) and follows on from 'The Plague Game'. It explores life on the street post-release and the challenge of staying 'straight'.

From 'The Corrida' to 'The House of Four Rooms'

In designing a group work programme for violent offenders it is necessary to incorporate a number of basic ingredients: the exploration of the origins of violence; the recognition of responsibility for one's actions; a recognition of the impact of the offence on victims; basic skills that an offender would need in order to live a life free of violence; and an opportunity to test those skills prior to facing the real world. The final ingredient is perhaps the most difficult to construct. How, having tackled all these issues, do you test the effectiveness of what you have done? It would be very easy for someone to take on board the language and manner of change only to discard them on leaving the group room. It was in an attempt to address this dilemma effectively that the Company developed the concept of 'The Corrida'.

The idea of 'The Corrida' sprang from early discussions during the development of the Company's five-day prison residency 'The Violent Illusion'. The original performance, conceived as part one of a trilogy, was first developed by Bergman and Geese (US) in 1988. A full mask mime, it explores the origins of violence in the home. Bergman and Geese (UK) went on to develop the trilogy with 'Violent Illusion II', which looks at interventions in behaviour and 'Violent Illusion III' or 'The Corrida'. The image of a 'corrida' or bull ring was developed as some special place in which the offender would experience in 'real time' a process that would test his new skills and understanding. The set is a complete circle. At one end of the space sit the 'judges'; a Company member and three fellow participants. The audience is comprised of participants in the week's work, who watch through windows cut into the set. Another Company member takes the role of 'Corrida Host', a 'Master of Ceremonies' who facilitates the direction and conclusion of each 'Corrida.'

In 'The Corrida', violence is not an option. The participants must enter determined to deal with whatever the 'test' might be. They must first give a 'declaration of intent', in other words, their reason for being in the space and what it is they wish to leave behind in their lives. The test itself could be dealing with provocation or the temptation to get involved with violence. It could be more personal, such as speaking to or listening to the victims of his violence. The challenge is tailor-made for each person who enters, with Company members taking on whatever roles the 'Corrida' may require. No 'Corrida' has ever been repeated. Spontaneity by all participants is the key.

'The Violent Illusion' was designed specifically for use by the touring company in a prison setting and requires a minimum of seven company members. The demands of violent-offender group work in prisons and probation required the development and adaptation of the concept of 'The Corrida'. Unlike a prison residency, a maximum of two company members work on any given group work programme. This rules out the more complex performance-based approach of

'The Violent Illusion'. Yet it was clear that the essential ingredients of the residency were very powerful and had an identifiable impact on the participants. For some time the Company experimented with various exercises and approaches to the problem of integrating 'The Corrida' into ongoing group work. One such exercise, originated by the Portuguese psychodramatist Fernando Santos Vieira, when he was working with substance abusers, conceptualised the process of change as an exploration of 'four rooms'. Geese (UK) developed this idea, integrating it with Prochaska and DiClemente's 'Six Stages of Change' (1986a) (see Figure 5.1) into a powerful metaphor, 'The House of Four Rooms' (see Figure 5.2). This is a theatrical representation of the process which moves from

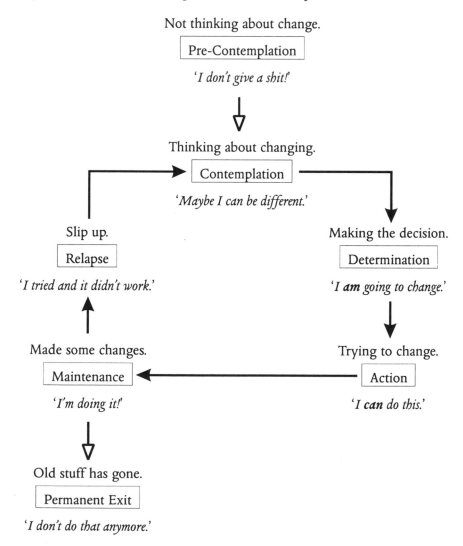

Figure 5.1: Adaptation of Prochaska and DiClemente's 'Six Stages of Change' (1986a)

'pre-contemplation' to 'permanent exit', incorporating masks, Death Bird, 'The Corrida', and other images designed to stimulate change.

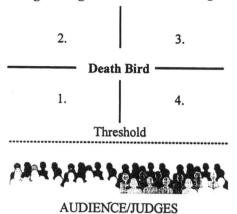

Figure 5.2: 'The House of Four Rooms'

The group work space is divided into four 'rooms' using chairs arranged in a cross, with a space at the axis to cross from room to room. The axis also represents Death Bird or 'lapse/relapse'. Whichever room one is in, Death Bird is ever present and thus so is the potential to ditch the process of change and return to old habits. Once the 'Four Rooms' are established, a 'threshold' is delineated at the entrance to room number one and the exit of room number four. The threshold establishes the line between 'the street' or old behaviours and the process of change as symbolised by the rooms. To cross the threshold and enter the first room a 'declaration of intent' must be made. The declaration must be a clear statement about the participant's reasons for wishing to leave their old life of violence and aggression behind. This 'old lifestyle' is referred to as 'the street'. They must leave 'the street' behind in order to step into the first room. This ritualisation is an important aspect of the drama, beginning to delineate the world of the possible from the criminal world of the known (Mitchell 1996; Rebillot 1993).

To begin with, the group as a whole enter the first room and are asked what it might represent to them in the process of change. The group may identify 'the past, bad memories, guilt, fear, anger, aggression, violence, family' and so on. The list will often cover two or more sheets of flip-chart paper which are then stuck to the wall. The group are then asked to name the room. One group decided to call it 'The Mirror Room'. This is repeated with each room. That same group ended up with the second room as 'The Room of Hope', and the third as 'The Sorting Room' or 'The Room of Struggle and Confusion'. The fourth room is left unnamed, as it is the final room in the process of change and therefore personal to anyone who reaches it. It is in the last room that the decision must be made to leave behind, once and for all, the destructive behaviours of a lifetime. In order therefore to cross this second threshold, they must make another declaration that reflects what they have learnt in the 'The House of Four Rooms', what skills they must now use and their commitment to permanent change. On completion, they step back onto 'the street', only this time they must choose to walk a different path.

Confronting the mask: preparation for 'The House of Four Rooms'

Day One

It's Monday morning on a sunny October day. Eight men walk into the group work room to begin a two-week violent-offender programme. Not yet a group, the men are about to be involved in an act of 'collective learning' (Boal 1994) and the Geese worker perhaps will be involved in some 'defusing of the bomb' (Jefferies 1991). Each man has been assessed by probation officers who will work with them and the Company through the course. There is a very mixed atmosphere. Some appear nervous but willing to see what will happen, others seem more hostile, only attending on sufferance.

The group work begins with a request: 'Give one reason why you don't want to be here, and one reason why you do want to be here.' There follows a series of replies, such as: 'I'd rather be in bed, but I agreed to be here so maybe I will learn something'; 'I could be doing something else, but I'm here because I want to stop getting into fights.' Once the group has had a chance to say how they feel about being there, and have what they say accepted (Heathcote 1978) the work begins. The content of the course is outlined, and the aims and objectives are emphasised. The week is about change, it requires commitment and hard work, and theatre will be the primary tool. As little time as possible is spent in sitting around talking. It is crucial to get everyone up on their feet and into the first exercise, a 'human knot'. Soon the atmosphere begins to settle. Many of the most resistant are forced to laugh at the hopelessness of the task. They are asked, 'what are the links between trying to unravel this "human knot" and the real world?' Gradually responses start to come: 'It's about trust', 'Working together?', 'Sorting out your problems!'

Every answer is acknowledged, and the group are encouraged to see how a simple exercise like this can have a connection with the real world. We go into further exercises which loosen any tension that might still linger from the beginning of the session. By the end of the morning, the men are creating 'frozen pictures', using images in the manner of Boal (1992), first of films they know, three of them showing a scene from *Jaws*, another group showing the last scene from *One Flew Over the Cookoo's Nest*. Having done this they move on to show scenes of an argument in a pub leading to a fight and the aftermath: arrest, prison, or simply the victim face down on the floor.

The energy is kept up through the afternoon, exploring more scenes of pub violence, arguments on the street and other similar situations. Always the same questions are asked: 'What does this character think?', 'How does he feel right now?', 'What does he do next?' As the questions continue, the group are encouraged to separate thoughts and feelings, and to understand how the two combine to form behaviour.

By now the purpose of the week and the rationale for using theatre and drama to surface issues and thus raise debate begin to make more sense. As the group workers process the work for the day, there is a sense of optimism; this could be a 'good' group, one prepared to work. However, in any group-work process it is not uncommon for there to be a rebellion at some point or another, as the seriousness of the process of making change and taking responsibility becomes increasingly clear.

Day Two

After a very positive start to the day, in which the 'fragment masks' are explored we move on to some more detailed scene work. The aim is to create a scene and characters, focusing on an imaginary offence, from which we can identify the concept of 'cycles' of offending, or repeated patterns. We ask the group to decide on an offence. 'A pub fight!' says John. 'A domestic...' suggests Ray. 'Nah! A football match!' offers another. They are given the choice of which one they want to explore. The majority choose the 'domestic'.

The scene is gradually created and the group are asked who is there and what is happening:

Well, there's the wife...and the bloke...and he's been on the piss!...Yeah, and he comes home and she's really pissed off!...Ha! And he's just pissed!

Ricky volunteers to play the man. John plays his partner. They start to improvise and it is very real. The scene is stopped periodically in order to ask more questions, and the characters' thoughts and feelings are written down. As the scene unfolds, the discussion gets more and more heated: 'Well, she is just asking for it!...', 'Yeah, it's always the man's fault!', 'If she talked to me like that I'd have slapped her!' As the group workers begin to (respectfully) challenge the group's attitudes to the imagined victim, the men retaliate: 'You're only interested in what he's thinking', 'Yeah, she's probably thinking "I'm just going to wind him up!"...She probably wants him to hit her, 'cause she really gets off on it!' Most of this comes from Ray, a domestic abuser with a long history of violence to his ex-partner. Interestingly enough the scene was actually suggested by Ron, who also had a history of domestic abuse.

The sense that he is the real victim, that only he really suffers and that she is the real abuser seems consistent amongst violent offenders who abuse in the home.

They see themselves emotionally torn apart by their partners who are always at fault. No woman is to be trusted. If she does not completely submit to her partner's will, then she must be punished.

It takes the rest of the session to pull the group back to the purpose of the programme and their own professed commitment to change. The group workers stand firm by their support of the victim. Throughout the sessions the group are asked to swap places or 'role reverse' with the victims of their offences. Whilst in the position of 'victim' they are asked to speak, act and think in that role, a technique championed by Moreno (1972). This is often a significant moment in the process as the offender, perhaps for the first time, is asked to experience being on the receiving end of his abusive behaviour. The victim's voice is the voice the men do not want to hear because for many of them the victim is always to blame. In challenging this thinking it is necessary to focus their attention on the distortions, irrational beliefs, prejudices, minimisation, denial and blame that they rely on to avoid responsibility.

Days Three, Four and Five

Over the next three days the group, one by one, re-create an offence that they have committed: a fight outside a club in which the victim loses an eye; a fight with the police; violence on the football terraces where a group member had videoed the violence as it was happening; an attack on a train guard; and three stories about domestic violence. As we explore these scenes the group members are asked to identify what their thoughts, feelings and behaviour are. They are also asked again to 'reverse roles' with the victim(s) and explore their experience.

From the mask to 'The House of Four Rooms'

Week Two: testing the change

The second week of the course focuses on the process of change. There are several basic questions which we need to ask: 'If you are going to change, how do you do it? What is the process you need to go through? What kind of life are you aiming for? What do you need to leave behind to get there? What skills do you need?' And finally, perhaps the too rarely asked question: 'What skills do you already have?'

Day Six: the group are introduced to the four rooms

The room is divided into 'The House of Four Rooms', and the group are briefed about the concept prior to entering the group work space. They go through the process of naming each room and identifying the issues that each room represents. In the afternoon they write their declarations.

Day Seven: group preparation

The group spend time preparing for their own 'four rooms'. They work on their individual declarations, cycles of offending, problem-solving skills and any other relevant material gathered from the previous sessions.

Days Eight and Nine

Before beginning work on the first participant's 'four rooms', we remind the group that anyone can choose to opt out if they feel that it is not the right time for them to go through this process.

Each participant does two circuits of the 'rooms'. The first time around, he gives his declaration, then steps in the room. He identifies what is there for him personally: what are the masks, people and experiences that he needs to deal with in order to move to the next room? This is repeated for each room, except the fourth room. He then goes back to the start and repeats his declaration. The rest of the group, who act as 'judges', then ask any questions they like to test the participant's sincerity. If they feel he has answered to their satisfaction, he is allowed to step into the first room and face whatever challenge may await him.

The challenge, as in the 'Corrida' in 'The Violent Illusion', is created spontaneously by the company member(s) running the exercise and can range from an improvised scene to individual tasks.

Ricky's 'rooms'

Declaration

> I've got to stop taking things personally.
>
> I've got to start dealing with problems instead of bottling them up.
>
> I've got to open up a lot more and talk to people.
>
> I've got to get on with my life and stop dwelling on things that happened in the past and partially got me here in the first place.

The first time through the rooms Ricky identified alcohol and his family as two major problems. He had been drinking heavily for some years, and after leaving the army had become the family problem-solver, frequently bailing out his brother and getting into many serious fights as a result. The masks he most used were: Stone Wall, Mr Fist and The Rescuer.

When he has completed his first run-through he returns to the start and the group ask him questions:

Mick:	How are you going to find a way of combating what is in the first room?
Ricky:	I've just got to face it, that's all. Stop the drink.
Mark:	It's not the alcohol, but violence, anger and aggression that you have to sort out.
Ricky:	I know, but the booze is a part of it.
Mick:	How sincere are you when you say you want to kick the drink?
Ricky:	I do like it – but I know it's going to screw things up.
John:	How do you propose to do that, gradually or in steps?
Ricky:	It would need to be completely…
Sean:	How are you going to stop dwelling on the past?
Ricky:	I've got to face the fear…

The questioning goes on for some time before the group feel he is ready to recross the threshold. Before he steps into the first room he is reminded that a challenge awaits him for which aggression and violence are not an option.

A company member quickly briefs John to play Ricky's brother. He then follows John into the first room.

The first room[4]

John:	Ricky, do us a favour, this guy is after me. If you don't help me I'll get hurt!
Ricky:	I can't keep doing this for you…stand up for yourself!

Mick is briefed to go in and put the pressure on Ricky.

Mick:	Is he coming then? Is it sorted?
Ricky (getting heated):	No! I've said I'm not doing this for you any more!
John:	Come on Ricky, I need you!
Mick:	You're some kind of joker you are! Are you going to wear a black tie when your brother's done in, are you? Are you going to walk away from your own brother then?
Ricky:	When's the last time you turned around and helped me? When were you ever there for me? When I get in trouble there is only one person to bail me out and that is me!

group suggested the title 'The Room of Mirrors' for this room.

John: And there's only one person to bail me out and that's you!

Ricky: Yeah…and this time you're going to have to do it yourself!

John: So, when you're looking down on top of him and he's going down with his little wooden suit on, everything is going to be all right for you, eh? You're laughing!

The scene goes on for some time with John and Mick pouring on the pressure. But Ricky stands firm. The whole thing feels very real and the group watch intently as Ricky pushes past John and Mick and steps into the next room.

John: You're just going to leave me then?

Ricky: Yeah! You get on with it!

The second room[5]

Ricky is asked what he needs to do in this room.

Ricky: I need to convince myself that what I'm doing will work – by knocking down the barriers.

He then selects 'Stone Wall' and 'The Victim' masks as the ones that stand between him and change. He tries to say what each of them does for him. 'Stone Wall' acts as a barrier that will not let him open up. He starts speaking to the mask, telling it that it is useful sometimes, but that it has to stop holding him back. Penny, a probation officer, comes over to stand next to him, puts her hand on his shoulder and speaks a thought she believes he might have: 'I'm afraid of something. I need to know that fear.' Ricky starts to talk about losing people who are important to him. Penny continues, 'I'm still frightened of losing something…' He asks for a 'time out'. This is an agreed break in the process of the 'The House of Four Rooms' in which the participant can take a breath and decide what to do. He must then return to the moment the action stopped and deal with the situation.

Sean, in talking about his own 'four rooms', offers this to Ricky: 'I had to push through it. If you don't confront it, well, you just keep walking away from it. You just got to do it.'

Ricky comes out of his 'time out'. He holds up 'The Victim' mask and says firmly, 'I need to lose all these fears that are building up! I've got to stop feeling sorry for myself all the time! I've got to put the past behind me and move on or else I'll always be stuck here!' He steps briefly into the third room.[6] He is asked where he thinks he is in the process of change. 'I'm between 'The Mirror Room' (the first

5   The group suggested the title 'The Room of Hope' for this room.
6   The group suggested the title 'The Sorting Room' for this room.

room) and 'The Room of Hope' (the second room).' The group feels that he has done enough work and his session is brought to an end. There follows a discussion in which the group feed back on how Ricky's work relates to them. Ricky also feeds back, saying how hard it was, but how he was really glad he had gone through with it.

Conclusion

The afternoon of the final day is an opportunity for the group to discuss and feed back on the two weeks' work. One by one the individual members discuss the impact of their experience in 'The Four Rooms'. All agree that it has been the hardest thing they have ever had to do. Ray's 'Corrida' had been to talk to his wife, and in 'role-reverse' to reply as her, expressing his partner's anger at years of abuse. Mick had to shut down the 'fragment masks' that prevented him from changing. John had to deal with the police and Mark had to speak to his four-year-old son. The final 'Corrida' was Ken's, in which he buried the destructive and violent memories of his life in the army, and talked to his family about his choice to change.

But change is a long and drawn-out process. It can take years. Consequently, after the two weeks of intensive work, the group meet for one day a month for six months. This provides the group with the opportunity to share their experiences in dealing with change and continue to work on their skills.

'The House of Four Rooms' has a clear impact on the group, but cannot be seen as a 'cure-all' for offending behaviour. In the follow-up sessions it is clear that there is so much more work that needs to be done. Many of the men are endeavouring to maintain the momentum of change but inevitably they face situation after situation that test their ability to control. We hit the 'yes but' factor:

Mick: I'm really trying to change! But I was in this situation where I was jumped by this bloke while I was trying to sort an argument between my mate and this other bloke and...

The process of change can often be accelerated by brief, and sometimes profound, experiences. Theatre and drama have proved to be instrumental in effecting change in offenders yet we cannot hope to undo the behaviours of a lifetime in two weeks. The dilemmas that each member of the group face in turning their professed desire to change into a reality can be almost too much to bear. At least with their habitual coping strategies they may have a sense of who they are and what their world is made up of. In stopping violence alone they face an enormous task. The temptation to retreat to the predictability and 'safety' of an aggressive

herefore a daily experience.

heatre provides is a framework to explore in three dimensions the past,
 future and in so doing assess the impact of destructive behaviour on

oneself and one's victims. It can stimulate the individual to start to ask questions of themselves which they have not asked before in quite the same way. In particular, theatre can underline the question of choice, because in whatever situation we may find ourselves in, there are always choices. Anyone who abuses makes the choice to do so, and no amount of self pity or blame can alter that fact.

Geese Theatre Company is moving into its tenth year, and still the work remains intensely challenging. Because there are no easy answers, because only a clear reflection of the offenders' world will engage them in the process, change means that one is forever searching for new ways of improving the work. This can only come from the offenders themselves, from their experiences, from their stories. We are familiar with our own world, where things are the way they are because we live within it and know its geography. My map of the world is not the same as yours, because my experiences are different. The Company moves on, therefore, by continually asking those we work with to share with us the landscape they inhabit so that we, through theatre and drama, can assist them in living their lives in a different world.

References

Berkowitz, L. (1978) 'Is criminal violence normative behaviour?' *Journal of Research in Crime and Delinquency,* July, 149–161.

Boal, A. (1992) *Games for Actors and Non-Actors.* London: Routledge.

Boal, A. (1995) *The Rainbow of Desire.* London: Methuen.

Braun, E. (ed) (1969) *Meyerhold on Theatre.* London: Eyre Methuen.

Cloward, R.A. and Ohlin, L.E. (1960) *Delinquency and Opportunity.* New York: Free Press.

Dart, R. (1967) *Adventures with the Missing Link.* Philadelphia: The Institutes Press

Dollard, J., Doob, L.W., Miller, N.E., Mowrer, O.H. and Sears, R.R. (1939) *Frustration and Aggression.* New Haven, Connecticut: Yale University Press.

Freud, S. (1923) 'The Ego and the Id.' In J. Strachey (ed) (1961) Standard Edition, 19, pp.1–16.

Gelles, R.J. (1983) 'An exchange/social control theory.' In D. Finkelhoe, R.J. Gelles, G.T. Hotaling, and M.A. Strauss (eds) *The Dark Side of Families: Current Family Violence Research.* Beverley Hills: Sage.

Gergen, K.J. (1972) 'The healthy, happy human being wears many masks.' In D. Krebs (ed) *Readings in Social Psychology* (Second edition). New York: Harper & Row.

Heathcote, D. (1978) 'Excellence in teaching.' In L. Johnson and C. O'Neil (1984) (eds) *Dorothy Heathcote: Collected Writings on Education and Drama.* London: Stanley Thorne.

Hirschi, T. (1969) *Causes of Delinquency.* Berkeley: University of California Press.

Hodge, J.E. (1992) 'Addiction to violence: a new model of psychopathy.' *Criminal Behaviour and Mental Health,* 2, 2, 'Psychopathic disorders' pp.212–222.

Jefferies, J. (1991) 'What we are doing here is defusing the bomb: psychodrama with hard core offenders.' In P. Holmes and M. Karp (eds) *Psychodrama: Inspiration and Technique.* London: Tavistock/Routledge.

Miedzian, M. (1992) *Boys Will Be Boys: Breaking the Link Between Masculinity and Violence*. London: Virago Press.

Mitchell, S. (1995) *The Theatre of Self Expression: Ritual Theatre Approaches for Drama Therapists*. Unpublished.

Moreno, J. (1972) *Psychodrama: Volume 1*. New York: Beacon House.

Prochaska, J. and DiClemente, C. (1986a) 'Six stages of change.' In W.R. Miller and S. Rollnick (1991) *Motivational Interviewing*. New York: Guilford Press.

Rebillot, P. (1993) *The Call to Adventure*. London: HarperCollins.

Sim, J. (1993) Paper to Conference on Masculinity and Crime, Brunel University. Quoted in J. Bensted, R. Wall and C. Forbes (1994) 'Cyberpunks, Ronnie Biggs and the culture of masculinity: getting men thinking.' *Probation Journal*, 41, 1, March 1994, pp.18–22.

Yochelson, S. and Samanow S.E. (1976) *The Criminal Personality Vol. 1: A Profile for Change*. Northvale and London: Jason Aronson Publishers.

Further Reading

Bergman, J. and Hewish, S. (1996) 'Violent illusion: dramatherapy and the dangerous voyage to the heart of change.' In M. Liebmann (ed) *Arts Approaches to Conflict*. London: Jessica Kingsley Publishers.

Best, D. (1992) *The Rationality of Feeling*. London: Falmer Press.

Johnstone, K. (1981) *Impro*. London: Methuen.

Prochaska, J. and DiClemente, C. (1986b) *Treating Addictive Behaviour. Process of Change*. New York: Plenum.

CHAPTER 6

Twisting Paradoxes
Chris Johnston

The characters and situation in this chapter are entirely imaginary and bear no relation to any real person or actual happening...

The staff common room in a prison taking category B and C prisoners, somewhere in the Midlands, England. A performance has just taken place in the prison, given by the Set Them All Free Theatre Company. John, the director of the theatre company, and Derek, a prison officer, are sitting down together.

Derek: Well done, John; it went really well. Smashing. Congratulations. First-class show.

John: You should say that to the cast.

Derek: They probably know it from the applause which our lads gave them. We don't get enough of this in the prison. Cheers! It's a shame we can't provide this kind of entertainment very often.

John: Is it entertainment only, do you think?

Derek: Obviously you've got a message, same as we have. We're all pulling on the same rope, John.

John: In that case, why did security try to ban part of the cast from coming in?

Derek: Hold on there. I sorted that for you. But I know their position and it's a fair one. Half of your cast are villains, that's why. Or ex-villains to give them their due. You never made that clear when you phoned. It's no good looking like Christ at a stoning, one of your guys has an armed robbery charge against him. And it's in the last five years, I believe. Is it any wonder security don't want him in?

John: Why, is the prison holding a lot of money?

Derek: Now you're being flippant. He's a security risk.

John: In what way?

Derek: He may have friends or accomplices in here.

John: So what's he going to do, smuggle guns? Do you not think joining
          a theatre company a strange way to go about gun-smuggling? Or
          perhaps I'm in on it as well?

Derek: I understand you feel strongly about it, John. But visitors passing
          contraband is a real issue for us. There have to be some guidelines.
          How are we going to tackle the drug problem unless we impose
          them? I'm not saying your lad is part of that, but why should secu-
          rity take a chance? Or do you think we make an exception because
          he's had a blinding realisation that he's an actor all of a sudden?

John: Why doesn't it make a difference if we vouch for his rehabilitation?

Derek: Don't. You might regret it.

John: Why?

Derek: Listen, I'm not saying the lad hasn't done well. But remember I do
          know these characters, and for me the old leopard/spots equation
          still holds true. After a bloke's been out for twenty years, then show
          me proof of real change – but after just two or three years, John,
          I'm not convinced. Yes, you get a kind of surface change, a friendly
          show of compliance but you'd be surprised what a friendly face can
          hide. Some of these blokes play the system better than Menuhin
          ever played violin. Change doesn't come with a packet of corn-
          flakes or even a few rounds of applause. I wager that any bloke
          with a record, put him in any kind of pressure situation, chances
          are you get a reversion to type. They just go back to the behaviour
          they know.

John: Which is?

Derek: Confrontation, possibly violence, certainly deceitfulness. I've seen
          most of the variations.

John: Some might say you were stereotyping people in revenge for hav-
          ing to do your job.

Derek: I trust you wouldn't be amongst them.

John: OK, sorry, that was a bit high-handed but what are you saying, that
          you don't think any kind of personal change is possible?

Derek: Well, this way you're not disappointed, are you? And it leaves open
          the possibility you might be pleasantly surprised.

John: So it's a case of 'Abandon Hope All Ye Who Enter Here'?

Derek: To be honest, John, my attitude's changed since my daughter's grown up. I have a family, a young daughter. Knowing what I know of these blokes, I'm frightened just to see her walk down that road to school. If there's a choice between giving some sex pest a second chance when we're not quite sure which way he'll go, and absolutely guaranteeing Judith's safety, I'll keep that bloke in for life if I have to. I don't care if it costs £30,000 per year, it's money well spent as far as I'm concerned. You take Danny who's just come back to us. He had three years on the out, spent it either pissed or walking out on job offers because they're not 'good enough' for him, then one day he's fed up so he gets a gun from somewhere and does four building societies in the same day. Admittedly he did the first one with a bottle of washing-up liquid under his coat but then he decided he needed the extra firepower. He didn't kill anyone, luckily, but he came that close. In fact the woman who was most distressed was the woman in the first place who screamed so much he decided he really ought to fire, so he did, but of course only green liquid came out. And that didn't make it through his coat. Back at the time when he got parole, some idiot will have argued that he was a reformed character. In someone like that, the despair, the anger that he's got inside is in so deep that no one understands it, least of all Danny himself. You can argue psychology till you're blue in the face but when it comes down to it you cannot predict how someone will react when life goes to pieces on them. So my answer is, if you want answers, the protection of the public is the first concern. Respect the human rights of the prisoner, of course, he has to have education and a chance to improve, but be very sure to keep him locked up, if necessary past his sell-by date. And I tell you something else, a lot of the wives would agree with that.

John: You don't think they'd rather have him at home, bringing in a steady income?

Derek: How many ex-prisoners do you know bringing in a steady income?

John: Not many.

Derek: I should wager very, very few. Now you may be making the mistake that I blame them entirely for their own situation: I don't. Fact is, society is not giving them a fair chance. We know there's this legislation and that legislation, but when it comes down to it, once you've bitten off a prison term, getting work is hard. We just don't trust a bloke with a record, and he ceases to expect any other kind of response. So it's a cycle all right, but society is helping turn the wheel. And blokes tell me when they leave, they say, Derek, when I'm out of here, I'm back on the same business – what hope is there for me doing anything else? And I have to agree: not much. So keep 'em locked up, I say. Another pint?

John: Thanks.

(Derek comes back from the bar.)

Derek: See, I admire people like yourself, John. We need people like you because you're optimistic and you've got ideals. It means people like me get challenged – otherwise…we…

John: What?

Derek: I don't know…tar everyone with the same brush, I suppose. Obviously there are a few good lads in here. Trouble is, they end up feeling like losers in this company.

John: That sounds distinctly like a criticism of the prison you work for and not unlike the 'university of crime' thesis.

Derek: I sometimes wonder that if we teach them anything, it's how to be an arsehole. Don't print that, by the way. It's depressing, working here. I think the most depressing thing of all is the lack of gratitude. When you make a real effort for someone, or a group of people, and they walk away without a word of thanks or any kind of recognition.

John: Maybe they're too caught up in their own troubles. Besides, they see you as part of the system and your actions as simply the machinery of that system. They hate the system and so they hate you.

Derek: I forgot you used to be a hippie. Is that your basic aesthetic: criminal as artist as victim of the state as misunderstood revolutionary? Perhaps you should come and work here to redress it.

John: No, it's not quite as romantic as that. But I do believe that the capacity for personal change in everybody. The trouble at the moment is, we've set up the circumstances which are designed to ensure that the opportunities for personal change are at a minimum. So it's no wonder you feel so pessimistic. Bringing these guys in here today may help to tip the balance just a fraction. Because it's useful for those who are still inside to see how others have made good for themselves after leaving prison. Because there you have a very clear example of how your view of offenders – can't change, won't change – just doesn't hold up. See, I don't believe it's in the genes. People aren't born criminal. Babies don't come out of the womb with criminal intent. Crime isn't genetic, it's the perceived solution to a set of problems, even though it does provoke behaviour which in many cases admittedly has become habitual. What's often happened in early life is a series of horrendous experiences usually involving parents or others in the place of parents – sorry to generalise but it's not completely unreasonable. Dad Fuckup usually features somewhere in this scenario and these people end up learning-disabled. They've essentially learned the wrong lessons about how to deal with problems of confrontation and deprivation. And if this is so, then surely we can unlearn some of that? Which is why the Education Department is the most important in any prison even though it's usually the first to be cut. I wager that if you take ten inmates from your prison, you won't find more than one or two who actually enjoyed a stable home life and a good education.

Derek: That may be true, but unfortunately if the roots of a tree haven't gone deep enough you can't put your hands in the earth and pull them downwards. You can only cut the bloody branches.

John: The analogy doesn't hold. There is the human capacity to extend our field of perception. We're not accustomed to learning about ourselves. Our traditional education is usually directed outwards but we can make our own behaviour the subject of study if we wish. And we can start to bring into consciousness aspects of the personal and collective psyche which we've allowed to remain unconscious. It's not that the self becomes like a glass box, because much of the unconscious will always remain unreachable and unapproachable except through its manifests, but when you have individuals who are consistently 'taken over' by strong impulses and emotions, it is possible to make them more conscious of how and why those impulses emerge. They've probably never attempted to learn those lessons. They've just shrugged their shoulders and said 'I dunno what come over me' or 'I was provoked' and that's the extent of their analysis. Surely you can't fail to acknowledge the success of Barlinnie and other institutions where they've placed learning about self and personal responsibility high on the agenda. And that's where the arts and drama come in, because they deal with human behaviour as their subject matter. Drama especially is an obvious tool. The language of drama is behaviour, and the currency is feeling. So we can set up a whole range of different kinds of situations, fictional, factual, metaphorical, analogical which all explore the range of behavioural responses to challenging situations.

Derek: Come off it, many of these blokes know exactly what they are doing. You make them sound like they're idiots. No way. A lot of guys have chosen to be burglars or con men. They reckon it's a great way to live.

John: You're missing the point. They can only legitimately maintain that position if they block out – consciously or unconsciously – the impact of their behaviour on other people. Drama is about bringing things into awareness, including those things we'd rather avoid.

Derek: Sounds like an argument for therapy to me.

John: A good number of these men would probably benefit from therapy. But the reality is, they won't choose to do that whereas they might get into the arts.

Derek: Why? I reckon football's a much better idea. Learn to be a team player.

John: But the thing is these guys are already accessing skills and experiences which bring them closer to the artistic realm.

Derek: Blimey. You don't talk like that to the blokes, do you?

John: I reckon crime generally involves talents which might otherwise be redirected into art.

Derek: Yeah? So what does that mean?

John: There's a natural affinity between crime and art.

Derek: Oh, we're back to this one? Criminal as misunderstood artist? Sort of 'smash-the-old lady-in-the-face-sorry-that-should-have-been-a portrait' kind of analysis? Interesting.

John: You haven't heard me yet.

Derek: You carry on, mate.

John: Certain kinds of criminal activity involve skills and experiences which parallel those of artists. In a way, criminals live in a kind of parallel universe, a fictional world of their own making. That's why criminal subculture is so intense, because it's fashioned. It's always had a natural affinity with showbiz. To live outside the law means you're engaged in a very questioning relationship with conventional morality. To invent your own codes you need imagination, wit, bravado and courage. And the experience of law-breaking itself is often a serious buzz, perhaps the only thing worth getting out of bed for. It's a heightened experience, there's a kind of ecstasy involved not unlike what the performer or musician experiences. You're engaged in this mighty struggle with the forces of law and order, and these forces, you, me, the police, we're just trolls, we're ignorant, stupid people who simply can't recognise our own banality. We don't have the intelligence to perceive that basically everyone is on the make and therefore the only ones who are really alive are those who accept that notion of an amoral universe. Everyone else is in a kind of fog which dulls the brain and the wits. So if you get caught, OK, so be it, there's probably a good many more times you haven't been caught. Getting caught is not the end, it just means the battle moves to a different territory. As Jean Genet says, there's only one thing more exciting than committing a crime, and that's getting caught. All I'm saying is that there are sharp comparisons between the profound experience of the artist or the performer, and the transformative excitement which some criminal behaviour involves. You can hardly argue that more than a small proportion of crime is about personal gain.

Derek: Now I shall look at Pam Ayres in a whole new light.

John: Genet fused these two identities of criminal and artist in his own life, and incidentally he was far happier as a criminal. You and I, we haven't tasted that heady kind of excitement, the real buzz that comes from invading and destroying someone else's property, that comes from sexual brutality, and until we understand that excitement, that emotional pleasure, then we're just bullshitting around like old-style Victorian teachers of morality, only with a kind of modern, politically correct censoriousness. And the language is so sterile! I mean 'offender' – what kind of language is that? We need something much more robust than that, something much closer to the actual argot of the street, and the language of the arts is about the closest we can get to these experiences.

Derek: I don't think I need to 'get close' to the experience of raping someone in order to deal with a rapist. Or to know it's wrong. I don't have to go to the North Pole to know that it's cold there. The feminists may tell me there's a rapist inside every man trying to get out, but I don't have to get intimate with him. What are you saying– that we should empathise with the rapist and ignore the victim? That's just barking! I reckon you're just hero-worshipping the criminal because he cocks a snook at society. Basically I reckon you're in love with crime same as many of them – only you do it from the luxury of an Arts Council grant.

John: We should try to empathise with both.

Derek: But why try to empathise with the rapist?

John   Because how are we going to manage any kind of rehabilitation process which involves bringing that individual back into a shared morality if we don't understand the attractions of his behaviour?

Derek: OK, but how can you legitimately do that without – I don't know – going out and burglaring and raping and so on? Is that what you're suggesting?

John: Well, my own way is to work within the aesthetic dimension as I tried to explain, through setting up a kind of parallel universe where experiences as profound as those of both the offender and the victim can be explored. So participants can begin to experience some kind of victim empathy because they see we also recognise the intensity and compulsion of the drives which make them want to offend. By linking these different kinds of experiences within the same aesthetic spectrum we can also start to reduce the sense which many offenders have which is that of operating alone, in a void where your actions make no difference in the social world. The idea of empowerment may seem a bit bizarre but actually nurturing a sense of potential powerfulness – the ability to influence events – coupled with an increased sensitivity towards the effects of how that power may be used – that seems a legitimate part of any rehabilitation process. Drama facilitates this through its ability to set up situations which are false in that they are not really happening, but true in the sense that they re-create all the essentials of real life. And of course the emotions they generate are as 'true' as any involved in a real situation. The emotional self makes no fundamental distinction between the real and the theatrical. So it may seem a bit odd to argue for empathy with the aggressor as well as the victim but I do believe we have to engage emotionally with all the players in the scenario. And if we fail to do this, if we just blanket-condemn a person, this only turns the offender in on himself and makes him secretive and inscrutable. He gets really stuck in then and mythologises himself so much that we can't reach him any more. Which is just one aspect of the outsider experience, which is really only an inside experience, which no longer connects with others' inside experiences – if you can follow that. But surely this is what happens and it leads inevitably to the situation where someone can burgle or rape and walk away unconcerned with anyone else's experience apart from their own. And if you challenge that person about it they just look blank. Or else they just talk about their *own* experience, casting themselves in a victim mould. I believe that crime will continue to increase as long as we continue to create outsiders. And to bang on a little longer, it could be said that this perverse self-mythologising may even become the norm if we fail to create enough binding rituals which genuinely succeed in bringing people together. Personally I don't count cod rituals like football which are completely lacking in any kind of spiritual dimension.

Derek: What?!!

John: Yes, they're just opportunities to indulge in a kind of mild sadism. And before you ask, I do believe there is a fundamental distinction between sport and the arts because the arts don't reduce everything to a banal, narcissistic competitiveness, albeit with a pseudo-intellectual gloss.

Derek: So, you don't support Arsenal? OK. But I have to ask, John, how can you realistically set up this kind of process?

John: Not easily.

Derek: It's Utopian.

John: Only looked at from inside the 'prison works' barbed wire fanaticism. It's really only a conjunction of drama and therapy. Sure, it requires money and investment to set up these kind of programmes but I suspect it would be money better spent than paying for a criminal justice system which is only punitive and never addresses the core problems.

Derek: I also wonder how many of our guys would honestly be interested, and it seems to me that your process does rather depend on blokes pitching in. What's in it for them? What would they have got out of it in the two hours we might have been able to give you today? Why should they be bothered?

John: I guess they might have got a sense that you can get a buzz out of drama, which for some, rivals the kind of buzz you get from breaking into a warehouse and lifting some computers.

Derek: So you'd hand over the running of the prison to the Royal Shakespeare Company?

John: That would be an interesting experiment, I'd like to see that. No, genuinely, I would. It wouldn't cost a great deal by comparison to what you might save. Where there have been high-profile drama projects in prison they always make a big impact on participants' lives. And the fact is, most of these guys are actors already, they've learned to maintain their masks out there. So it's less about getting them to become actors than getting them to realise the extent of the acting they're doing already. Then we can get them to realise that the best place to be acting is on the stage. Why are you laughing?

Derek: You've managed to reduce rehabilitation to a mechanical process! Come on, be honest, the truth of the matter is, you only get a few who are interested. We regularly get far more interested in soccer than drama. And you won't change that in a hurry. Drink up, I'll take you round the new wing. We've been expanding, you know. But still no drama studio, I'm afraid.

John: In a minute.

Derek: Where are your lads?

John: They should be here.

Derek: Know what? They saw you with me, so they took a walk. You picked the wrong company sitting down with me. I recognise one of them. Sorry about the workshop by the way. Again, not my decision. Sounds as if you ought to be doing workshops as a priority. I mean, what's the point of doing a play? It's very entertaining but it's hardly challenging in the same kind of way.

John: In a play we get the chance to take some fictional characters and look at the underlying paradoxes and dilemmas which are pushing them towards a life of crime. And because the cast themselves are mostly offenders, they're working analogically on their own situation. So doing a production is simply a different kind of approach to that taken in a workshop where you might be searching around a lot to find some key issues. The play is a more developed stage of the process. But both involve acting, playing, learning to control and express your energies. The actors can go deeper and further in a production process. There's also a whole other dimension in that they perform to an audience so the audience is witnessing a statement about their personal commitment to a process of change. Interestingly, offenders find it hard to perform in public if they're still offending. I don't understand that, but I have noticed it. Perhaps it's to do with the fact that you have to feel comfortable with a certain transparency. After all, any actor is opening himself up so his dilemmas can be looked at.

Derek: So there's a connection between the actor and the character he's playing?

John: Like the guy who says 'There's no way I'll try and do a blag again' then the following day agrees to drive the getaway car for some mates. He does that because he's in the company of people to whom he can't say 'no'. That's a problem for him. He claims the situation has changed, but it hasn't really changed except in as much as his girlfriend has been putting pressure on him for money, so the old ideas of going straight are now invalid. In fact what's happening is, she's always done this. So he's analysing his own situation wrongly. The situation isn't changing at all, he just doesn't know how vulnerable he is to peer pressure. That's what strikes me about guys like Desmond – he constructs a false reality for himself composed of insupportable tenets which allow him to function as a criminal. What this play hopes to do therefore is show how this kind of self-delusion works. The actor himself is in the process of trying to get on top of that. The chances are, those audiences which have some background in crime will recognise these kinds of dilemmas. The play is a kind of question if you like, which the actors are putting – about how you cope with this stuff.

Derek: And the answer...?

John: If we knew the answer, we wouldn't ask the question, because it wouldn't be a question which concerned us. No, we offer the question for others to answer – each spectator may come up with a different answer. Hopefully, our putting the question in this way extends their perception of the issues and helps to contextualise the dilemmas. For example, we always look at consequences. Plays are good at this. If I commit a robbery in life, I try to avoid looking at negative consequences. Usually, I can manage this, maybe by going out boozing for a few days or whatever. But in a play we can choose to show the consequences for all parties involved; thief, victim, family of thief, family of victim and so on. You as a spectator are confronted with that. You may be changed for life by watching our play.

Derek: I suppose what worries me about all this is it's all rather psychological in a clever-clever sort of way – especially coming from someone who's probably never done worse than ignore a rates demand, and I'm wondering – even if the lads do benefit from this – they still have to go out in the wide world and make a living. So shouldn't we just be spending the money on skill training, so when they get out they're actually as good as – or even better than – the next guy in the queue? I reckon that if they came out with an edge in the job market – now that would make a difference in the long run.

John: But I don't think it's either/or, is it?

Derek: What are you looking at?

John: I just thought I saw one of our guys go past the window. No, it's
             not one or the other, it should be both. The problem is at present,
             it's neither. Anyway, this work I'm talking about encompasses both
             social and communication skills which are a pretty important part
             of holding down a job.

Derek: So these guys of yours that you've been working with – they could
             get a job anywhere, could they?

John: Yeah, I reckon so.

Derek: So why haven't they?

John: Maybe they're just not interested in working for the capitalist state.

Derek: Now if I had the money, I'd set up a different kind of educational
             structure. See, the problem is, their patterns of thinking are fixed.
             So their answers don't change. It doesn't matter how you put the
             question. They have to learn to use their brains. Problem-solving.
             Doing drama is all very well but you're addressing a small propor-
             tion. What we need is high-quality education, linked to
             qualifications, a fast-track process so they walk out of here with
             pieces of paper that will counteract the terrible stigmatisation these
             lads are subject to. A good job is a far better disincentive to a life of
             crime than some...

John: ...poxy play... Yes, maybe. Certainly it's no good taking someone
             through a learning process then putting them on the streets with
             no decent home or decent job. These things go hand in hand. And
             I'd accept that cognitive approaches do work, but what I suspect is,
             guys just get very good at learning the jargon and feeding it back
             to the tutors. It's especially true with sex offenders.

Derek: Perhaps that's true and it's a limitation but ultimately you're going
             to have to find out what Fred or Dave wants to do as a career. And
             help him get into that, with qualifications or skills or whatever.
             Which means sitting him down and making him really think about
             that, creatively helping him to a decision and then helping to push
             through the implications of that decision.

John: Maybe.

Derek: Very probably. Because if he's drawn a map of his personal psyche
             but can't identify the spot marked 'career' then it seems to me he
             might as well throw that map away.

John: Yes, I agree, I'm only saying that identity is as much tied up with what we feel as what we think. Some way or other that guy has to get to a point where he can be passionate about his career choice. Which is a feeling issue, and if he's only emotionally caught up in negative feelings of rejection, revenge or whatever then he won't be able to access aspiration. Feeling emotionally disturbed or put-upon is a characteristic of many offenders. You can't pretend those disturbed feelings aren't there or hide them with lateral thinking puzzles. The correct thinking grafted on to the old insecurities and disturbed feelings will only cause a rejection of what the mind has come up with. Sadly, at present we're living in an era which is still dominated by the idea that 'prison works', really a euphemism for the previous slogan that 'nothing works'.

Derek: I think what you propose would be accepted if it came supported by the proper authority. But you do need proof.

John: Oh, we've got proof all right. We are the proof.

Derek: I suspect you need rather tighter evaluation procedures than that assertion.

John: But simply filling up the jails isn't the solution, is it? The government thinks very hard about how to put offenders inside but not very much about the fact that pretty much all of them are going to come out again. Why is it that we're prepared to put millions of pounds into a prison system that is proved not to work and not be prepared to put any money at all into an alternative practice which does offer some hope for the future?

(Another warder comes up and whispers to Derek. Then he goes. Derek gets up to leave.)

John: What's up?

Derek: Apparently one of your blokes has been caught smoking a joint in the toilets. I won't be long.

John: I'll talk to him.

Derek: If you're very good I will allow you to talk to him when I've finished with him. Possibly.

John (calling after him): It's hardly a major issue, is it?

Derek: That's for someone else to decide.

PART III

Working in the Institution

Preface

Victor Hassine

I entered prison theatre through the back door. I mean I wrote the first play in prison with no vision of it ever being performed. I was writing for a national prison writing competition conducted annually in New York, by Pen American, and I wanted to enter a manuscript in each category. One of the categories happened to be drama.

I had never written a play, but before being arrested I was a theatre enthusiast, and had gone to many Broadway productions in New York. So in preparation of writing a play I read a couple of plays and fanned through recollections of performances I had seen and enjoyed.

When I finally began writing the play, I never considered the power in a play's performance. In fact I wrote it as if it were a fiction made up of continuous dialogue. I believed the strength of my writing was all in my words being read, not in their performance. I had never given much thought to why so many people in prison will sit mesmerised in front of a day room television and for hours watch any show that it projected. I never even questioned why I watched movies more than once even though I knew everything about them.

After I finished writing my play, I entered it in the writing contest and it won an honourable mention. I was pretty proud of that, so I sent a copy of the play to the superintendent of my prison. The play I had written denounced the death penalty while the institution I was in was 'the place of execution' for the State, so I was not really sure how the superintendent would react. I was relieved when he wrote back to tell me he liked the play. But to me, the play was still only a piece of literary fiction.

One day, an inmate who had read my play, and in the past had performed in a prison theatre production, convinced me that the play needed to be performed. He knew the power of a performance. Almost reluctantly, I responded to his constant prodding by writing to the superintendent and asking for permission to stage my play. I was sceptical about any response I might receive, but the very next day the superintendent informed me in writing that if I could find a qualified director, he would be inclined to allow the play to be staged in the prison.

I was surprised and at a loss over the superintendent's answer. I immediately went to the inmate who had gotten me into this mess and asked him what I should do next. He gave me the address of the woman who had directed a play in the prison over a decade earlier, and suggested I ask for her help. I sent a copy of my play to the prospective director and asked if she would be interested in directing a prison performance. Amazingly, she agreed and this began my venture into the dynamic world of prison theatre.

CHAPTER 7

Creating Drama through Advanced Improvisation in Prison

Robert Clare

This chapter is a combined diary and commentary from a four-week, full-time drama residency, using improvisation to devise, develop, rehearse and perform an original play with an inmate group. The account is fictionalised, insofar as its detail is actually drawn from more than one such residency which I have directed in British prisons, most notably in HMP Manchester (Strangeways) and HMP Maghaberry (in Northern Ireland). Any names in the account have been changed, and no reference to any actual person is intended.

The week before

The Head of Education made his usual speech: 'it's a different world, don't give them an inch (they'll use you if they can), keep your distance, don't take anything on trust, keep an eye on your belongings.' I have heard this before, but the student observer who will join me for the project (Sam) was shocked. 'How can he talk like that?' she asked, as we waited to be taken back to the Main Gate. 'Does all good drama not depend upon trust?' But we do have to be more watchful here than for any theatre project on the outside. And on these projects nobody can merely 'observe'. Sam will have to participate, and may take some responsibility as the work progresses. The group will certainly look to her for approval, and support. This must be recognised from the outset, if an observer is to be an asset rather than a liability. If there is any doubt as to whether they can cope, they probably ought not to be invited in.

Sam has the requisite sense and discretion, as well as enthusiasm. She also has several books of theatre games and exercises, and was surprised when I told her we won't be using any of those for the first day or so. We will simply go to meet the men. Stress that: to meet the men – not just to put faces to their records. So I have asked (as always) that I be told only their names and numbers, rather than any information about their offences, or their release dates. They themselves will tell me as much as they want me to know, just as I will only tell them as much about myself as I see fit. I am not a social worker, or a therapist. I am a theatre practitioner, and over the next four weeks I aim to produce drama that is of a professional standard with these men, confident that the nature of improvised work will enable us to achieve first-class results. Others may then assess the therapeutic value of the process. But it depends not only upon trust, but upon respect. To recognise the men's right to reserve what privacy they can is simply to start as one means to go on. Roll on Monday.

Week One: Tuesday

Two days in. Eleven men in the group,[1] and the usual mixture of caution, enthusiasm, cynicism and indifference. Some are just curious, some more actively interested, others see it as a soft option, and some do not care what they do so long as they get out of the cell. A couple have been 'persuaded' to join us by the Head of Education, who is keen to have the numbers to justify his budget. As usual, there is some suspicion of me, and of my motives for coming into the prison. Why should a professional theatre director want to work with them? What am I getting out of it? None of them has any acting experience, and most have never been to a theatre, though they are of course familiar with TV drama. Fine. This allowed me to be mischievously dismissive of actors, and of mainstream theatre in general. I told the men that, in my experience, prison work can actually produce better results than a lot of work in the recognised theatre. And that is why I am here. And it is true. The prison work benefits mainly from the fact that the men do not think of themselves as actors. In fact I told them that the most important rule is: No Acting. This got a laugh, but of course I meant it.[2]

Our other main advantage is that there is no pressure to work towards set performances. We will only share the work with an audience if the men in the group wish to do so. As usual, I have told the prison authorities that I will do my best to get some kind of performance together (and so far I have always managed this) but I cannot guarantee it. There is pressure on me, then, but not on the men. This is important. To make our rehearsal room into the right kind of 'safe space', the men must be reassured from the start that they collectively have some control over the process, and that they exercise a degree of self-determination within it. None will be asked to stick his neck out any further than he wishes, whether in

---

1   As a general guide, I consider ten to be a minimum number for a project like this, and 15 or 16 a maximum. Twelve is just about perfect.

2   Cf. the director Lindsay Anderson's eloquent note to an actor at the Royal Court, 'Don't just act – stand there!' Or Marlon Brando's remark: 'Just because they say 'Action!' doesn't mean you have to do anything.'

our rehearsal-room games and exercises, or in any eventual performances. However, I did stick my own neck out. I told them that, if they go for it, by the end of four weeks they will be capable of work that will surprise them, and anyone who watches it. Not work that may be dismissed as amateurish, or patronised by the compliment that it is 'very good, considering...', but work that could hardly be bettered – if at all – by professionals. Having as yet nothing to go on they laughed at this, but they are nonetheless intrigued. And at this stage, that is all I need.

These first two days have been mainly talk, and almost as much about general topics (football, etc.) as about drama. I always allow plenty of 'social' time at the beginning of each session. Sam is keen to get working, and to get the men on their feet, but especially at this early stage it is important to let them relax and settle once they have arrived in the room. To give them some time just to sit and talk, or smoke,[3] and gradually to unwind, is to allow them to claim the space on their own terms. This is also why there are no officers with us as we work: not because one wants to exclude them, but because our space must be somewhere the men can feel more and more at ease. The social time also helps in getting to know them, and observing how they interact – spotting those who are already friends or allies, or who may be competitive, and any potential outcasts or loners who may need particular support. So there is no hurry to get things going to begin with. The moment to call them together in any given session is usually fairly clear.

This afternoon we got properly under way with some very basic exercises, to illustrate some of the fundamentals that will underpin our work. A chair was set out in the middle of the space, and I asked for a volunteer simply to sit in it, and do nothing. Not to freeze, but just to do nothing. No acting, no pretending, and no imagining himself anywhere in particular. Just to sit there, while the rest of us watched him. He could look at us or not, as he chose: it did not matter. After about five minutes, I thanked him, and told him to relax. Then, without asking him what he was actually thinking about, I asked the rest of the group to think of him as a character, and to speculate about what we had just been watching in those terms. What kind of situation might such a character have been in? Did he seem at ease, or on edge? Where was he looking? Did he seem to be waiting for something? Or someone? Or remembering something? Was the memory happy or sad? Did he laugh (possibly from self-consciousness)? And if so, what might he have been laughing at (besides us)? And so various theories were developed, as to what the story or situation of the man in the chair could have been.

This, of course, is an exercise in which it is impossible to 'fail'. Whatever the person in the chair does, or does not do, is of interest. And as we speculate about

---

3   Smoking is too important a relaxation inside prison for any vote as to whether or not it's
     allowed during rehearsals, as might happen in a normal theatre company.

their 'character' purely on that basis, their 'performance' is by definition flawless, and whether or not they seemed real or convincing does not even come into it (provided they really 'do nothing', and do not try to 'act' for our benefit). Other members of the group then took a turn, and we discussed their version of 'doing nothing', and always without the person in question telling us what they were actually thinking. Even the most reluctant or self-conscious can join in this exercise with confidence, and can then enjoy listening to the different ideas sparked off by what they did. I used the exercise to emphasise a couple of important points. First, that everybody is interesting, simply by virtue of taking the space. Each is utterly individual, with his own particular personal presence, that can be focused or dramatically deployed in different ways. And everyone is capable of an inner life, that can give even the most diffident authority on stage, particularly when that inner life is held in reserve. Second, all audiences are detectives, and are fantastically adept at spotting little signs, and at reading and interpreting them. Most actors tend to over-demonstrate, and to try too hard to impress their audience. One of the strengths of our work will be that we do not.

Once all who wished to do so had had a go in the chair, we started to have some fun. Four chairs were placed side by side, to represent a bench, and again one of the men sat on it, and did nothing. He could imagine himself wherever he liked, so long as he did not try to indicate anything to us. We watched him in silence for a few minutes, to give us time to speculate about him and his situation. Then any other member of the group could decide, in their own time, to go and sit on the bench as well. We then watched the two of them. Very quickly, such twosomes became comic. Would they look at one another? Would either acknowledge the other? How did the body language of the first person change when the second arrived? Was there tension, or interest, or indifference there? Might they speak? What might happen between them? And of course what we were watching now was a play, albeit a very simple one. We then tried three on the bench, and then four. By now the situation was bristling with possibilities, and shifting interactions and relationships. Those watching picked out whatever aspects they particularly enjoyed, and any moments that they thought were especially telling. And suddenly the group found they had taken part in a series of dramas, without consciously doing any 'acting' at all. And we are off.

Week One: Wednesday

I came in early this morning, to drop in on Security, and introduce myself. This was to help to allay any apprehensions they might have as to who I am, or what the group is up to. Drama projects are sometimes dismissed as frivolous, or a waste of precious resources, so they may cause suspicion or even hostility in some quarters. Ours may well involve extra headaches for Security, particularly if we do any performances. The sheer vulnerability of a project such as this to the whims of those who administer the prison's regime makes good relations essential for political and pragmatic reasons, as well as being desirable for their own sake.

We took the bench exercise a stage further today. I suggested simple locations (such as a waiting room, a bus stop, or a launderette), and the men built up short improvisations simply by entering the space – again one by one, and in their own time. This began to get them talking and (just as importantly) listening to one another, picking up on whatever their colleagues say or do, and trying to avoid all talking at once. Again, the point was simply to be there and to occupy the space, rather than to try to be in any way dramatic or entertaining. At this stage, silent participation is fine. The improvisations went well. Sam led the group in a 'warm-up' at the beginning of each session, using some of the games and exercises in her books. My only strictures were these: nothing that might embarrass anybody, or make them look ridiculous; and nothing yet that involves any significant physical contact. Inmates cannot be expected simply to throw down any defences they may have erected around themselves. Personal space is important.

That said, I did judge that we could end the day with one of my favourite improvisations, which involved the group getting very close together. Four chairs were placed in a small square, to represent a lift. The group then stood inside (the space was not so small that this was uncomfortable), and the improvisation began as the lift 'stopped', for no apparent reason, between floors. This exercise would have had to be interrupted if anyone in the group had become – or acted – at all hysterical or claustrophobic. But it went very well. Laconic irony and understatement was the general tone, which led to some very funny moments and remarks, as they discussed their predicament. When eventually they all started shouting 'Help!' together, an officer put his head in to see what was going on. The exercise collapsed into laughter, and we ended the day's work there.

Week One: Thursday

A day of starkly contrasted halves. At this stage, I try to use exercises that develop the group's basic skills and levels of awareness while also being enjoyable. A good example is the mime version of 'Chinese whispers', which was the highlight of today's morning session. The men divide into two groups, and each then works out of sight of the other (today Sam took one lot into another classroom). Each group devises a mime, which realistically shows a commonly recognisable task – such as making breakfast, or changing the bedclothes. A simple mood is also decided upon – such as boredom, or preoccupation. Once the mime has been worked out, it is then refined and fixed by being exactly repeated a number of times by one of that group to the satisfaction of the rest. A member of the other group is then brought into the room, and is shown the mime without being told what it is. He then repeats it, as best he can, to a second member of his own group who is brought in to watch, but who of course has not had the benefit of the first demonstration. The challenge is to reproduce as exactly as possible the actions observed and (equally importantly) the mood of the person enacting them. One by one all of the other group come in, each to observe and then to perform the mime himself to whoever comes in next. Meanwhile, the group who originally devised it sit watching it change and/or deteriorate (and it almost always does deteriorate) as it is relayed from person to person, with (usually) diminishing certainty as to what it was originally intended to represent. Once the relay is complete, the original demonstration is repeated to show how far from it we have drifted.

Today, as usual, the results were hilarious. The first group's mime was changing the wheel on a car. By the time the second group had finished with it, the 'wheel' had grown to about eight feet square, and the motion of fastening and unfastening the nuts had become a determined hammering. The last actor to attempt it guessed afterwards that he was meant to be nailing up plasterboard. The second group's mime was somebody trying to make a phone-call, realising that the payphone he is using does not work, and going into an adjacent box to make the call from there. As the first group relayed this to one another, they did retain the phone box and the failed call, but the initially relaxed attitude of the caller was hilariously transformed – first, gradually, until he was tipsy; then into drunkenness; then reeling and incapable drunkenness, such that the last couple of interpreters could not finally make the call at all.

I used the exercise to make a couple of important points about basic storytelling. First, responsibility for the story is collective – it is, and must be, a team effort. Second, the narrative may deteriorate if the actors get so hung up on certain details that other important elements disappear. If they over-emphasize anything to the point where it acquires disproportionate significance, it is progressively magnified until it distorts what was originally intended. When we come to use improvisation to perform a play, rather than relying upon an existing script, an enhanced awareness of these dangers will be very important. Now these points have been made, of course, this exercise will lose part of its effectiveness. As the men get better at it, it will become less funny, and therefore much less fun. But it is a good one to use at this stage of the work, partly because any element of 'failure' is collective rather than individual, and can be celebrated for its comedy, rather than causing self-consciousness or inhibition.

The afternoon session was very different. The men were not unlocked at the appointed time, and one wing was held back longer still while certain security checks were made. By the time they were assembled, the anger and tension in the room was such that I judged it best to spend what time remained on a long relaxation exercise. I had the men lie flat on their backs with eyes closed, and talked the tension out of them as best I could. I encouraged them to feel the tension draining away, first from their toes, through the bones of their feet, their ankles, down to the bone of the heel, and into the floor and away…from their knees, their thighs, and so on. This process can take anything from ten to twenty minutes. If the instructions are sufficiently rhythmic and modulated, there can be an element of hypnosis in it. Where appropriate – as today – it can then be sustained for much longer, and made the basis of a kind of meditation. One advantage is that, while their muscles are at rest, the minds of the men can be kept focused.

Once they were fully relaxed, I asked them to think through their bodies again, to feel all the latent power in their fingers, their arms, their shoulders, the whole of the fantastic machine at their disposal as they lay there in utter repose, to feel the blood circling as the breath circles inside and out. Each of them individual and special. Complete. I reminded them that these are the raw materials of our work. Each needs to be able to feel good about who he is, or who he can be, in order to make the best contribution to the work that he can. We spent nearly an hour in this kind of contemplation, and afterwards most said they felt better for it. One went to sleep, which got a laugh when we all realised. A less extended version of the exercise is something we will use again and again. Sometimes it is better to begin a session thus, rather than with a more conventional 'warm-up'. Adrenaline and energy can be valuable, of course, but they are more so when married to an inner equilibrium, and a focused sense of strength.

Week One: Friday

I ended the first week's work, as always, with one long improvisation. Again, the situation had to be one that the men could enter and leave freely, with the emphasis upon simply being there, rather than any pressure to perform. So we set up chairs and tables as though for pub furniture, with a couple of the tables arranged as a bar. Mugs of water were glasses of drink. One of the group became a barman, to start us off. The others watched him, and then (again in their own time) gradually entered the scene. As always in these early improvisations, I encouraged them to use their own first names for ease and familiarity, as though they were all in their local. I had saved this improvisation until the end of the week, because I have found that it can be sustained for an unusually long time. Today it lasted for just over one and a half hours, only finishing when the officer knocked on the door to indicate the end of the session. The men were amazed at how much time had passed. As I pointed out, it was the equivalent of three episodes of *Coronation Street*, while no play that we might eventually put together would be longer than an hour. As the exercise went on, the men glanced out at me less and less to see what I was thinking. That showed that they are already beginning to grow in confidence, and in the ease with which they inhabit the space. Afterwards, they were very enthusiastic. Some claimed (as they always do) that they could even

taste the beer. They went off keen to resume on Monday. To give them something
to think about over the weekend, I asked them to write down the five best film
titles (real or imagined) they could think of.

Week Two: Monday

One of the men (Paul) has left the group. Apparently, he simply is not interested
any more. I was surprised. I had noted that he was a bit of a loner, but when I spoke
with him at the end of Friday's session he had seemed to be looking forward to
resuming today. None of the group seemed able to shed any light on his decision.
As a director, it is easy to take such things personally, as a rejection or an implicit
criticism of oneself or of the work (either or both of which may of course be true).
But in the prison context especially one must simply get on, as the men may be
trying to deal with all kinds of problems away from their class that one has no idea
about. That is why we must also be careful when starting to identify possible
storylines, to make sure nobody is compromised by the group's choices, or by
whatever issues we may eventually touch on. In this, of course, ours differs from
some prison drama work, which specifically requires inmates to confront aspects
of themselves and their past experience which are negative or problematic. Such a
process could damage our project. Starting as we do with only the proverbial
'empty space'[4] and a group who have chosen to work in it, ours is a necessarily
collaborative exercise, where success depends upon team work, but also, crucially,
upon the confidence of those involved. This is to some extent true of all drama,
but in the prison context it is more so than usual, if one aims for excellence. The
emphasis must therefore be upon empowerment and encouragement, identifying
the actors' potential and building upon it as supportively as possible. This means
focusing upon characteristics which may be positively harnessed, rather than
upon those which might otherwise need to be dealt with or overcome. What each
has to offer may thus be incorporated into the group's work as a strength. At the
same time one encourages mutual trust, and one helps them all to recognise and
celebrate their interdependence in developing and shaping that work.

We used the film titles which (most of) the men had noted down over the
weekend as a basis for improvisations. The two voted the best or most intriguing
titles on the list were *Midnight Express* (which almost always comes up) and *One
Flew Over the Cuckoo's Nest*. I divided the group again. Each half took a title and
discussed what it might have been about, if not about a drug smuggler in a Turkish

---

4   Cf. most notably, Peter Brook, and his book of the same name, *The Empty Space* (1968),
       which begins:

         I can take any empty space and call it a bare stage. A man walks across this empty space
         whilst somebody else is watching him, and this is all that is needed for an act of theatre
         to be engaged. (*op. cit.*, p.11)

prison, or a maverick inmate of a secure psychiatric ward. One group suggested that *Midnight Express* might be about a nightclub of that name, where the bouncers are involved in some kind of racket. The other group decided that 'the Cuckoo' was a good nickname for a criminal mastermind, and that the title could refer to one of his men outwitting him, and cleaning him out. It is often the case that a group's initial suggestions will revolve around crime like this, and usually in a way that involves money and/or power, and the characters getting away with something big. Clearly, there may be elements of fantasy or of wish-fulfillment here that might be deemed unhealthy or at best undesirable, and I myself would argue that such sensational scenarios should not become the basis of anything that might be taken further than just an exercise, or shaped for any kind of performance.

But the time for that discussion with the group is not yet. The primary concern now is with developing skills, and it is important for the men to feel that their ideas are welcomed. So we went with the storylines as suggested, setting up very simple scenes around each, involving only two or three characters at a time. Again, the task was, risking dullness if necessary, to inhabit the situation (so far as possible) in an absolutely realistic way, rather than trying too hard to make it dramatic, or underlining anything in a way that might seem false to those watching. The rest of the group commented and made suggestions. The vocabulary of criticism becomes more and more important from now on, so I encouraged the group to express their ideas as supportively as possible (saying 'you *could* have done such-and-such', rather than 'you *should* have done', etc.), and to pick out and remark on whatever was done well, rather than whatever they thought might have been improved. I then encouraged those making suggestions to take a role in the scene in their turn, so that they themselves worked in their own ideas. Even in relatively crude exercises like these, no one role should become associated with any one member of the group. It is important to celebrate the differences between what various actors bring to a role as alternative possibilities, which could help to take the work in different directions, rather than getting into potentially damaging comparisons as to who might be 'better' or 'worse'.

Week Two: Tuesday

I had an argument today with the Head of Education, who wanted to give the place in the group vacated by Paul to a man newly arrived in the prison. Although we are only just into our second week, and have not yet begun to shape anything for performance, it is my experience that it can be risky to introduce new members to a group after the very first couple of days – especially somebody whom nobody knows. So I resisted, arguing that trust, and a sense of confidence in one another's developing skills, had already begun to be established, and that it would be foolish to risk damaging this by introducing an unknown factor. The Head of

Education thought I was being a bit precious, until I told him how an extra group member had once been imposed upon me in exactly that way in another prison.

The man in question (Cesar) seemed bright and intelligent, but he was also very tense. The rest of the group had been together for two weeks, and they were already doing exercises for which he was not prepared. It was frustrating for them when things were explained to him that they felt they had already grasped. This may have helped to increase his own tension, and about a week later he snapped. During what was (I thought) a fairly innocuous relaxation exercise he had a sort of fit, and began speaking in tongues, while threatening us all from the centre of the room with elaborate martial arts gestures. Some very hard men were pressed up against the walls. The fit passed as suddenly as it had begun, and I quietened the session down (into a discussion of possible storylines), and then spoke to him alone at the end of it. That too was a mistake. Although he denied it, Cesar clearly had a drug problem, which perhaps partly explains how he came to believe he was possessed. He sat pouring out his delusions to me, while challenging me to disbelieve him. I found myself murmuring sympathetically and simultaneously calculating the distance to the door, wondering whether I could make it out of there. Finally, a couple of officers came in and escorted him on his way. Whatever his problems were, the drama group was not the place for him to seek help. He was removed from it, of course – but the sense of the 'safe space' had been damaged, and it took time to get the others back on an even keel. Of course, his was an extreme example, and the danger of that scale of disruption is remote. But I made a rule for myself after that, not to risk upsetting the balance of an already productive group if I could possibly help it, even if it might mean nothing worse than the other men having to mark time while the new person came up to speed.

In the class, we continued to work with the scenarios suggested by the film titles. These improvisations are generally fairly crude, being primarily designed to encourage the men to keep stepping in and out of the space, and to spark ideas as to how scenes and stories may develop. One of the men, Tony, had a problem. He was not unwilling to step into a scene, but when he did he tended to crack up laughing. To begin with, this was quite funny, but some of the others began to be irritated by it. I encouraged them to use his laughter, and to incorporate it into what they were doing. However, this was easier said than done, as their efforts made him laugh all the more. He was not being deliberately disruptive, and he kept apologising. Because he is a bit cocky, he is not always popular with the officers and with some of the other inmates, so this problem needs to be dealt with before it becomes more significant.

Week Two: Wednesday

This afternoon I personally did an improvisation with Tony. I do not like doing this, and I would not if we had already been shaping a piece for performance, as the work must come from the men. But there seemed no other way to tackle his problem. He and one of the others were supposed to be a pair of detectives in a car, watching some premises. Tony cracked up again, and the other actor threw his hands up, and simply stepped out of the scene. Tony apologised, still laughing, and I took the other actor's place. He laughed all the more, so I stayed in character and asked him what he was laughing about. This went on for some time, before eventually he calmed down a bit. The scene thus shifted until it was actually about the laughter, rather than what had originally been intended. Once the laughter was thus integrated, it was of course legitimised, rather than being something he felt he must suppress. It stopped being self-perpetuating, and Tony himself began trying to steer the scene back towards its original intention. I resisted that, and kept going on about his laughter until the subject began to be galling even for him. The scene ended up being a tense depiction of two partners who fall out, because one bursts out laughing for no apparent reason and then cannot explain why to his friend.

Once we had finished, this sparked several suggestions from the group as to what the reasons might have been, in terms of possible storylines. As I pointed out to the group, this shows that whatever happens in an improvisation is viable so long as it is used. The audience will accept almost anything, as long as it is acknowledged and incorporated by the actors within the developing action. It is only if they try to pretend that something is not happening, or if they appear to ignore it, that they can seem awkward and self-conscious in a way that will undermine whatever they are doing.

Week Two: Thursday

Alongside the simple scenes we have been improvising, we have been continuing to use various basic games and exercises to develop the company's skills, their ease in the space, and their confidence in themselves and in one another. We are now at a point where we can begin to use more sophisticated versions of some of those basic exercises, aimed more specifically at refining the special skills and disciplines which improvisation demands. For example, we have been playing a basic 'status' game, where half of the group are each given a piece of paper, with a number on it between one and ten. High number means high status, and so forth. The men are then given a situation to improvise, while also playing the status indicated by their number (which is only known to them). The other half of the group watch, and then have to arrange the improvisers in a line in order of status, on the basis of what they have seen. This is usually fairly simple, as 'high status' individuals tend to throw their weight about, while 'low status' shrink to the sidelines. The exercise is fine so far as it goes, but it does tend to encourage the participants to focus on their own performances, by 'acting' or overtly demonstrating whatever their status is.

The more sophisticated version which I introduced to the group today is one in which the numbers (which are not consecutive) are stuck to their foreheads, so that each can see everybody else's number but not his own. After improvising a scenario, each then has to place *himself* in what he guesses to be his correct position in the line, which he can only discover by paying close attention to how his colleagues respond to him. This forces the actors (and those towards the middle of the status scale especially) to watch and listen to one another closely, making the exercise one of more advanced team work. It is not a competition, and the exercise is only a success if everyone in the team ends with a clear idea of where they stand, and if all have acted realistically within the given scenario.

Another exercise that we have been using is the 'sentence' game. The group is again divided into two halves. Each half thinks of a phrase or sentence that would not readily come up in normal conversation (but is not so odd as to be ridiculous), and selects two of their number to try to work that phrase into an improvisation which I then give to them. Two representatives of the other half of the group are also in the improvisation, also with their own sentence to work in. Each pair tries to work their sentence in without it being spotted by the other side, who of course do not know what it is. The group had begun to be quite expert at this. In the more sophisticated version, however, which we began to play today, the two halves of the group choose two sentences as before, but this time the intention is to try to get the representatives of the other side to speak the sentence which one's own side has chosen, even though they again have no idea what it is, and again, within the general objective of keeping the framing improvisation as natural and convincing as possible.

In their first couple of attempts, the men came nowhere near getting the sentences worked in, and protested that it was impossible. But once I had again stressed to them that the exercise is not a competition, and that is only a success if both teams' sentences (or something close to them) are seamlessly worked into the conversation, they began to make real progress. What is important is to watch and listen closely to what one's fellow actors are doing, and thus to be able to help them to achieve their objectives, while trusting that they will reciprocate. Whatever games and exercises we use, it becomes more and more important as we go on that they are designed thus to promote the collaborative disciplines that are essential to improvisation. The actors must encourage and work for one another, rather than simply focus on themselves.

We moved on from the film title scenarios today. I brought in photographs which I had cut out from newspapers, without their captions, none of which involved any person or place that the men might recognise. These anonymous faces in differing situations then became the focus for speculation as to what their stories might be, and so for more improvised scenes. This got us away from the gangster-dominated storylines of earlier in the week. As in the games we have been using, I encouraged the men to concentrate in these improvisations upon helping each other to make as telling a contribution as possible. If anybody becomes marginalised during any exercise, it is up to the others to involve him. They are beginning to understand that, in improvisation, asking questions of one another is more important and more fruitful than simply stating what they themselves might think or feel. It also helps to keep the scene going without the conversation flagging and the energy being dissipated with it. In even the most trivial exercise from here on, the emphasis will be upon working together thus, to achieve whatever is the shared objective. Even if the characters are in conflict – and of course all good drama depends upon an element of conflict – the actors must be working in harmony. Improvisation implies a kind of freedom, and this is especially so in the early stages of a project when new ideas are still being thrown in. But (as I tell the group) it is a mistake to imagine that it is ultimately a free-for-all, where anything goes. In order for the work to be effective, and especially for controlled performances to be given, it comes to require a much higher than normal level of collective discipline and co-operation. In theatrical terms, it is the ultimate team effort.

Week Two: Friday

The concept of team-building took a bit of a knock today, when the Head of Education told me he had learned why Paul dropped out. Apparently, it was a case of intimidation, somebody having 'persuaded' him that he did not want to be involved any more. He will not say who it was, but it is possible that it was somebody else in the group. This happened once before on one of my projects, when a young sex offender was frozen out by the rest. I did what I could to prevent it happening, but that aspect of the prison culture was simply too strong in the institution in question, and the man himself refused point-blank to continue coming to the class. Paul's offence was nothing like that – I am told he was a serial burglar. I asked the group about him again, but they insisted that it was nothing to do with any of them, and all I could get out of them was that he 'owes' certain people in the prison. I passed this on to the Head of Education, and it is probably all we will ever know.

We are now halfway through the project, and next week we must start in earnest to examine possible scenarios to build into a viable drama if we are to stand a chance of getting a performance together. Three major factors will inform the process. First, we have no money to spend on costumes, or props, so we will have to beg or borrow whatever we need. Second, so far as we know, our only available performance space is the room in which we are already working. Third, and most obviously, our actors must be drawn from the group (Sam and I will not take part). Given my determination that any work we perform must aspire to professional standards, the challenge is to make these limitations into strengths, by tailoring a piece of work so precisely to our circumstances that we would still choose to spend nothing on it, and to perform it in our space with our actors, even if a large budget and innumerable alternative spaces and actors were available.

So I asked the men to spend some time over the weekend thinking of possible settings that our relatively spartan and institutional room might feasibly become, and also to think of stories and situations that need only involve actors such as those in the group. A prison play was immediately suggested; but the one constraint that I now imposed, was that the setting must not be a prison or a police station, and that the characters must not include prison officers or the like. Quite rightly, the men want to work on something which is hard-hitting, and not merely entertaining – but it would be irresponsible to do this by being so blatantly controversial or confrontational in the eyes of the prison authorities that we might jeopardise future projects. Everyone agreed that this made sense. I also asked each of them to think of a character over the weekend. It must be somebody they could feasibly play – somebody of about their own age, physique, background, and so on. It could be someone they know, or an amalgam of more than one person, or someone entirely fictional. But I asked them to begin to think through the detail of the character's life, so they can share it with the rest of us on Monday.

Week Three: Monday

We have lost another member of the group. He sent a message saying he was sorry to drop out, but he has been offered work in the kitchens, which of course means more and better food. He felt he had to grab the chance while he could. So the group is now down to nine. Eight is about the minimum number that is effective, so I hope we do not lose any more.

We spent part of the morning talking through various scenarios that were thought up over the weekend. There were some interesting suggestions. Paratroopers waiting for a jump was one that got a good response – as did the idea of a five-a-side football team getting ready for a match in a changing room. Monks in a monastery was laughed out of court, and a Social Security waiting room was reckoned to be too boring. The man who just dropped out sent a message suggesting a gang of decorators going on a job. Homeless men in a shelter was another suggestion. We will start working on some of these tomorrow.

In the afternoon, we turned our attention to the characters the men had prepared. I took them through the long relaxation exercise where they lie on their backs with eyes closed (see Week One: Thursday, above). Once relaxed, I asked them to focus their minds on the chosen characters, and asked a long series of questions about them. Where were they born, and into what circumstances? Where did they go to school? To work? Were they married? Were they happy? What were their dreams? Their expectations? What made them laugh? And so on, for about 20 minutes. Then I asked them to keep the characters firmly in mind, and to sit up. We placed a chair in the middle of the room. Each in turn sat in it, and answered questions from the rest of the group about his character as though he were the character answering. This is a common enough exercise, of course. Some call it a 'hot seat', though that is a term I dislike, as it sounds confrontational. I prefer simply to call it 'character chairs', and ask that the style of question and response be as if the character is questioning himself, rather than being challenged externally. That is not to say that the questions cannot be difficult, or even challenging; but they must be phrased quietly – gently, even – as though they come from inside the character's own head.

One of the best today was Tony, who seems to be over his laughing problem. Maybe he simply needed the subtle screen that adopting another character can provide. Not that any of the men is going very far from himself here – there are no major transformations, and it would not be fitting if there were. Tony, like the others, is simply adjusting and channelling aspects of his own manner and personality, as appropriate to the character in question. There is no need for us to know where the line is drawn between what is invented and what is drawn from personal experience. And so it would be in performance. As we in the audience have no preconceptions, we will simply accept whatever version of a character steps on stage before us. Variations on these emergent characters will be incorporated into whatever scenario we eventually develop as a play.

Week Three: Tuesday

I am beginning to accelerate the work gently now, though still allowing social time at the start of each session, and still using games and exercises to keep things varied and interesting, so the men feel no increase in pressure. We had a look today at the scenarios that were suggested yesterday, and the group quickly discarded two of them. Improvisations around the group of homeless men drifted alarmingly quickly towards violence, perhaps partly because alcohol figured so prominently in them. This was the first time I have had to remind the actors of the absolute rule that I impose on all improvisations with regard to potential violence. If at any point in any improvisation any actor feels inclined to hit or to lay hands on another, he must stop at once, step out of character, and tell us. We then discuss whether or not we want to incorporate anything physical into the scene. If not, then the group make suggestions as to how we might avert it. If so, then the action is choreographed according to the recognised principles of staged fighting, as practised by the Society of British Fight Directors,[5] which provide for absolute control and safety. Otherwise, I would avoid fights, as nothing would be more

---

5   The Society of British Fight Directors, 56 Goldhurst Terrace, London NW6 3HT (tel. 0171 624 1837).

likely to wreck trust within a group than one actor being hurt by another, or fearing that that might happen. In the case of the homelessness improvisations, the violence was not a problem in itself, but it did not seem to be leading us anywhere. Also, the scenario seemed to encourage over-acting, rather than the kind of controlled realism that we have been trying to encourage. So that option was discarded – as was the suggestion of the group of paratroopers. The latter idea had seemed dramatic, but nobody could come up with the beginnings of a storyline. As we had no chance of getting hold of military gear, we would have had to dress the characters in 'civvies'. We ended up with the vague suggestion of a group of soldiers off duty somewhere. Initial improvisations subsided fairly quickly into silence and/or banality, and the group abandoned the idea altogether.

In contrast, the two scenarios that seemed more promising are the five-a-side football team preparing for a match, and the gang of decorators. Each proved to be a situation in which conversation can be sustained for some time, with energy and humour. We do not have a full storyline for either of them yet, but they do provide a context in which different characters can readily engage with one another. Importantly, each involves some physical action – getting ready to play, or getting ready to paint – so that the actors have something to do besides just sitting or standing and talking. In order to turn either of them into a viable performance piece, we will need a basic story to be developed – around the match, or the painting job in prospect. We will then look for a secondary story or stories to emerge from the relationships of the characters, so that the drama is a function of the tension between these different developing narratives. This is a simple but effective dramatic model, which enables the play to cover more ground than its context might at first suggest. Within this, we will need what is sometimes called a dramatic 'hook' – something to keep the audience guessing, or wanting to know what will happen. Above all, there must be conflict between the characters, whether this manifests itself in comedy or in more serious confrontations. Over the next couple of days, we will improvise around both scenarios, introducing into each of them different versions of the characters which the group has been preparing, to see what we come up with. I will also check with the prison gym and the paint shop (and of course with Security) to see if we could borrow costumes and/or props from them. If so, then we can probably get what we need to make a performance look convincing at no cost. If not, we may have to think again.

The Head of Education came in to see some of the work today, was impressed, and is now very keen to know whether or not we can perform next week. He of course needs to make the necessary arrangements, if other inmates and/or selected prison staff are to be able to come and see the work. We have not yet made a group decision as to whether or not we will attempt to perform anything before an audience, but I hope the group are becoming sufficiently confident that I might be able to put it to them before the end of this week, if by then we have a strong enough story developing to make the prospect appealing. Much earlier on in the work, I asked the men to try to keep the second half of next week as clear of visits and other commitments as possible. They have done this, so we could perform if we wished to. I told the Head of Education that it does look as though we are headed that way, so that he can make whatever provisional arrangements are appropriate this far ahead.

Week Three: Thursday

The gym have offered to lend us not only football kit and a ball, but also some furniture – lockers, and a couple of benches. The paint shop were unsure, until the Chief Security Officer rang them and told them that we had his OK to go ahead. They also have plenty they can lend us, and we could even paint a wall of the room that we are in, so long as we return it to its original colour afterwards. We managed to get some bits and pieces from both sources to rehearse with, and for the last two days we have been improvising around both scenarios to develop basic stories for each. We spend less time on games and exercises now, but it is important not to abandon them completely. Although I am very aware of the time ticking away, I must keep the men as relaxed as possible. Most professional actors would be terrified at the thought of putting a play together in the week or so that remains, and Sam is beginning to be worried. But so long as I keep working calmly the men will do so too. They themselves have begun to ask whether or not I think they could or should perform to an audience. I tell them I have no doubt that they could do so if they wished, but that we do not yet need to decide.

So far, we have the basis of a story for each scenario, but not the secondary plots and how they are to be resolved. The initial structure for each mirrors our early improvisation exercises, and indeed the way we have worked over the past two days, as the characters enter gradually by ones and twos. The painters scenario involves six characters: four old friends, who are working while also signing on, their boss (who is also a friend), and the boss' 'gofer'. The room which they are to paint is our rehearsal room, of course. Two arrive, only to find that the others are not there as arranged. They argue. One would rather leave, but he is worried about his family, and various payments he has to keep up. He blames his friend for getting them both sacked from a previous, legitimate job. The friend denies responsibility for this, and tries to persuade him to stay. The gofer arrives. He does not know where the boss is, but gets the paint out and starts getting the room ready anyway. Another of the friends comes in. This one is a bit of a clown, and tries to defuse the tension between the first two, by telling jokes (laughter is always useful, especially if we want to hit the audience harder later on). At last the boss comes in, having been held up in traffic, and eventually so does the other worker – but he refuses to speak to anyone, or even to explain why he is late. And that is as far as we have got. The open questions are, why was he late? And what might be the matter? And how can whatever it is bring things to a head between all of the characters, and perhaps especially the first two, on-stage? We have no answers to all of this as yet.

The five-a-side option involves seven characters, which is perilously close to our limit, as there are only nine actors in the group. Even though none has any commitments that he knows of which might clash with possible performance times next week, there is always the chance that one or more may be prevented from coming to any given session. This is one reason that I will continue to keep switching the men in and out of different roles. Each will ultimately be able to play more than one character, and no one role will depend for its performance upon a particular actor being there. Besides thus providing ourselves with a built-in understudy capacity, there are other important considerations behind this way of working. First, as no one role is the special preserve of any one member of the company, all feel they can continue freely to contribute ideas as to how any character may interact with the others. Second, and by extension, all the actors are thus helped in remaining focused on the broader story, rather than becoming fixated by any one character, and thus becoming blinkered and self-regarding on stage. This helps to ensure that whatever they do serves the needs of the play as a whole. Third, and perhaps most importantly, this approach emphasises that the characters are themselves flexible, and can change – sometimes subtly, and sometimes more radically – according to which actor is performing them.

This is of course one of the major advantages of presenting new work through improvisation. As noted above, the audience have no preconceptions, and will simply accept whatever version of any one character we choose to present to them. The actors do not have to 'live up to' their characters in any sense, except in so far as they must take responsibility for how they contribute to the collective telling of the story. Similarly, they are of course speaking their own words, rather than trying to make what somebody else has written sound natural and spontaneous. The story itself, and the way it unfolds, will be very tightly structured; but although the actors will know what they must talk about at any given point, they will not need to worry about 'getting their lines right'. So long as they collectively keep things going, mark the important moments, and focus the narrative in what they have come to know is a mutually supportive and disciplined way, none needs fear that there is any danger of him 'failing' in performance. This all makes for confidence and naturalness, and helps prevent the kind of artificiality or self-consciousness that can spoil so much theatre work, whether amateur or professional. If the play is also well-structured and compelling then the work can achieve a standard of excellence that is rare in the theatre, and that is all the more powerful in the case of a prison group because it is so far beyond what anyone expects. All of which brings me back to the storyline...

The story of the five-a-side football team so far has certain elements in common with that of the painters, though unlike the other it is divided into two scenes. The team are a group of friends, playing in a local league. One of them is up to something which the others do not know about. He is the first to arrive in the changing room, and then the other players and the manager come in one by one. Again, there is a mixture of argument and comic banter during the early stages. The match in prospect is important – a cup-tie. Preparations for it are interrupted by the arrival of a stranger, who wants to talk to the one who came in first. To the bewilderment of the rest of the team, and despite the manager's protests, the player goes out to talk to the stranger without saying what is going on. On his return he seems shaken, but still refuses to say what is wrong. After some further team-talk, they go to play the match. The second scene starts as they return to the changing-room, having lost heavily. The one who talked with the stranger seems to have cost them the game, as his mind was clearly not on it. Eventually the rest confront him, demanding to know what is going on.

Again, this is as far as we have got. As in the painters scenario, the basis of some good conflicts and relationships is there. Each allows for lively conversation, with some humour, that may be kept going fairly easily, and for the gradual emergence of something more dramatic. In each case, what we lack is the kind of revelation that makes sense of the plot so far, and then allows us to take it to a resolution. If we can avoid moralising, then ideally this would involve touching upon an issue of some kind – so that the play is not only a good story in its own right but also has something to say, or at least gets the audience thinking.

Each option has enthusiastic advocates within the group, so we will have to keep both open for now. I would like to have decided between them before the weekend, so we could be a bit further ahead going into the final week. Then I might also have been able to ask the men whether they feel they could perform to an audience. But all that might have to wait until Monday now.

Week Three: Friday

I had a long conversation with the Head of Education and the Chief Security Officer with regard to possible performances next week. Impressed by what he saw on Tuesday, the Head of Education wants us to perform in the prison chapel, so that as many inmates and prison staff as possible can watch. Security reckon this would be feasible, though some of the workshops would have to be temporarily closed in order to cover the performance. I argued against it, for a number of reasons. First, the men have not yet agreed to performances at all, let alone one on that kind of scale, which would be intimidating in itself. Performing in the chapel would also make technical demands on their voices and 'projection' skills that we do not have time to address. They are comfortable in our current working space, which is home territory to them. To cope with a relatively small audience invited into there would be one thing; to venture out into what might prove to be (for these purposes) the alien environment of the chapel would be quite another. It would also be hard to make the chapel into a convincing set for either of the stories we are working on.

Furthermore, we will need to give more than one performance, if nobody is merely to be consigned to understudy duty. By performing only within our own space we would contain the work, so minimising disruption to prison routines – disruption which could cause resentment, when the quality and thus the potential value of the work are perhaps not generally appreciated. This is of course partly why the Head of Education wants as many as possible to see it, so that if its quality does become generally acknowledged he can then more effectively argue the case for the funding of further projects. I argued that we should therefore do all we can to make this first project successful, by containing it, and thus protecting the actors, upon whose confidence everything will ultimately depend. A second project, at a later date, might then make performances on a larger scale more desirable, and more appropriate.

Once I had joined the group, things moved fast today. Sam had already done a couple of exercises, so we went straight on to considering our two scenarios. Two of the men had had strong ideas as to how each could be taken forward. Tony suggested that the manager of the five-a-side team could be a probation officer, and that the players could all be his clients. If one of them is mixed up in something illicit, then for him (and perhaps for the whole team) there could be much more at stake than just a football match. Another suggested that the player in question could be carrying something which the stranger is after – such as a package of money, or drugs, or a weapon. We could even see what was in the package, as he hid it before the others came in. When they eventually find out what's going on, that could mark the end not only of their cup-run, but also of the team itself.

For the painters scenario, it was suggested that the character who is late could have discovered that he is HIV positive, and that the circumstances in which he must have been infected were such that some (or all) of the others might unknowingly have been infected as well. If they had all gone away somewhere together – for a football match, or on an extended stag night – they might have shared a prostitute, or otherwise indulged in some kind of group sex without taking sensible precautions. Whatever else they were arguing about would then be intensified, or would pale into insignificance, when viewed in the light of this new development, as they argued first about who was to blame, and then what to do.

We worked on both scenarios, and each could clearly be shaped into an effective piece of drama. Everyone agreed that the five-a-side option was perfectly viable. In contrast, some of the men were dubious about working on a play involving HIV/AIDS, although a couple of others argued strongly that the very things worrying them are precisely the reasons that we should go for it. The subject is clearly worthy of attention, and arguably particularly so in the prison context. But that also makes it sensitive and potentially dangerous ground. I simply do not know how serious a problem shared needles are in this prison, nor what is the incidence (or just the threat) of homosexual rape. Nor can I know whether anyone in the group – or any potential audience member – is actually HIV positive. They would hardly volunteer the information. Two of the group have also said that if we do work on the HIV option, they refuse to perform it to an inmate audience in case it opens them to ridicule or abuse. I do not want that to be the deciding factor, so I asked everyone to think about the options over the weekend, so that we can decide on Monday.

Afterwards, I told the Head of Education that whatever arrangements he makes for performances can still only be provisional. He now agrees that if we perform at all it should be in our current workspace to small audiences, rather than trying to open up the work to the prison's population in general. One performance could be to whomever is working in the Education Department on Friday. Few outside tutors come in that day, and there are no examinations imminent, so we would not compromise anybody's studies. That would leave us needing one more performance and audience. In other prisons, it has sometimes been possible to arrange a performance for the men's families, in the Visitors block. This also enabled representatives of outside agencies (such as local theatres, and funding authorities, to whom one might look for help or support for any future projects) to attend and to assess the work. However, that will not be possible here – at least, not this time around. One of the other teachers in the Education Department overheard our conversation. There is a small Young Offenders wing in the prison, and she suggested that, so long as the play was suitable, we might perhaps perform it to some of the lads from there. I guaranteed that any play which we produced would of course be suitably responsible. The general rule is that the Young Offenders never mix with the adult inmates, but the Head of Education will ask if we can make an exception in this case.

Week Four: Monday

We have decided to go with the story of the five-a-side team, as the group are all happy with that, while they cannot agree on the HIV issue. Given more time, we might have stayed with the latter option for longer, to test their reservations more fully. Whether or not to perform to an audience played no part in making the decision. Had the group decided to go with the HIV play, and then not to perform it to an audience, then I would have had to accept that, and to justify the decision both to the Head of Education and to the Governor for Inmate Activities. After all, if the work is adjudged to be worth doing, then it must be worth doing for its own sake   for what it is and for what it means to the men involved – rather than for whatever entertainment or instructional value it may also have for members of an audience (and in this sense our project is markedly different from any professional theatre production). Once the men had chosen between the two options, they also decided they were confident enough to go for a couple of performances, on the understanding that these would be to relatively small audiences in our own space. The Head of Education has obtained permission for some of the Young Offenders to be brought over on Thursday, so we now have three days to prepare ourselves.

We spent most of the rest of the day confirming the main points of the story as it stands so far. Once the afternoon session had finished, I typed out a synopsis (it came to half a page of A4) and duplicated copies for each member of the group. These were taken to them in their cells by the Head of Education, so they can make sure they know the essential structure of the story overnight.

Week Four: Tuesday

Today we kept running our play, or sections of it, while continuing to swap different actors in and out of the roles. The group then identified the strengths of whatever they had just watched, thus confirming their collective grip on the story so far while also discussing whether any new details may usefully be incorporated. What the characters say and do is thus very precisely ordered, within an ever more detailed structure. The actual dialogue is improvised, for naturalness and spontaneity, but the detail of the structure is not. The group are coming to know precisely what is required of them to tell the story and to enhance its impact, at any given moment.

Today's work resulted in some significant developments and adjustments. First, we concluded that it would increase suspense if the audience did not see what was in the package at the start. Then it was suggested that it might be better still if the package disappeared during the action, so that the audience never knew what was in it at all, but were left to speculate. If the other members of the team also did not know what was in it, but only that it was something seriously illegal that the stranger was after, then that could be almost worse for them than actually finding out. So we tried the stranger returning during the second scene, and taking the package away. But this meant that the crisis was effectively over once the stranger had gone. So then it was suggested that somebody else should remove the package, so the stranger never got it. It would also be more powerful if the player who brought the package in had been pressurised into carrying it against his better judgment, so that consequently he was out of his depth, and did not fully know what was going on himself. If he had been told simply to leave the package in a locker, and it was then picked up while he was playing the match, he himself might not even know that it had been taken, or by whom, when the stranger came back to get it. Finding it gone would further harden the stranger's attitude against him, making the situation more desperate for everybody involved.

So we invented another character: a caretaker. He first provided a comic element, coming in to complain about the mess the team made, and being jeered at and mocked off the stage. Then he returned once the team had gone out, and unbeknown to any of them, to remove the package from the locker. In order to keep the number of characters to seven (so we still have two in reserve) this meant losing one of the players from the team, and turning the manager into a player-manager. As we have still not finally allocated roles, this kind of adjustment can still be made without adversely affecting anyone in the group. Only after tomorrow will that no longer be possible.

Again, at the end of the day, I typed up the story in all its developing detail (it now comes to almost a page of A4) and copied it, so that the men can continue familiarising themselves with its precise narrative sequence overnight. They must also now think about which of the main characters (if any) they are keen – or would feel comfortable – to play.

Week Four: Wednesday

It is a good job we kept the number of characters to seven, because Tony was told last night that tomorrow he will be moved to another prison. He was bitterly disappointed, and will not be coming to the class again. The reason given was overcrowding, but some of the group suspect that somebody somewhere has made sure he will miss the performances for more calculated, personal reasons, Tony having made no secret of the fact that he was hugely enjoying the work. I have no idea if this is true, but it perhaps emphasises the need for some discretion and caution in the way the men carry themselves within the prison while engaged in this kind of project: one never knows who may be alienated. So now we will have only one actor in reserve, for any given performance.

We settled the casting this morning. The two oldest will take a turn at the player-manager, to give him added weight and authority alongside the other (younger) characters in the team. The stranger will be played by the two quietest men in the group. One of these in particular has always found it difficult to speak much during our improvisations, being somewhat introverted, and more a watcher than anything else. His casting is particularly pleasing. The stranger is the most obviously imposing character in the play, the suggestion being that he is a hard man, whose very presence threatens the others. The actor in question is actually rather gentle, and not tough at all so far as one can tell. But his performance has menace not because he 'acts' tough, but because of the focus and ultimately the respect that the other characters accord him. The stranger actually needs do little more than just enter and stand there, almost without speaking. By the way they respond to him, the others create his 'performance' for him. And this is true to some degree of all. It is the company who in this way collectively define who each of the characters is, and how he fits into the story, thus carrying through the emphasis in so much of our work upon the need for closely watching, listening to, and supporting one another. This one actor's case also provides a perfect illustration of how personal characteristics may be positively exploited. The very quietness and withdrawn personality of the actor has been made into the character's strength, rather than becoming a weakness or a liability.

Once the casting was settled, we ran the play several more times, with the actors now taking the role(s) that they will actually play. As their grasp of the play's detail becomes more confident, so its length is gradually increasing. Earlier in the week it took 20 minutes, whereas now it is closer to 40. In performance, I would expect it to take anything between 35 and 45 minutes, depending upon audience laughter, and performers' nerves (if they are tense, they will get through it more quickly). Again, at the end of the day, I retyped and recopied the story structure sheet, so that each has his revised page of A4 overnight, to continue to remind himself of what is required. Nearly there.

Week Four: Thursday lunchtime

Last minute tension. One of the men told us this morning that his nerve had gone. He said he would understudy, but he didn't want to perform after all. I was delighted that it was the rest of the group, not me, who persuaded him to rethink and take part, reassuring him as to how strong he is in his allocated roles, and that they will all be there, supporting him. This is an excellent sign. They no longer need me or Sam to give them belief in themselves, and they are truly taking responsibility for one another. They know that the work can be impressive, and that they could have a notable success on their hands. Whatever happens this afternoon, they have put together something of quality. For some of them, this may be the first time for a long time that they have had anything to be unreservedly proud of. They own this play. It is theirs. They are clearly very nervous, but they are dealing with that in the right way, and it is making them even closer as a company. Their determination was very evident this morning, during the final couple of run-throughs. And they are confident. Not in an arrogant way – they are much too nervous for that – but confident because they know what they are doing, and they know that they are ready, and equipped. If they can keep their discipline, and keep working for one another in the way they were this morning, they will knock the audience's socks off. Roll on this afternoon...

Postscript: a couple of months later

The Head of Education has been in touch, and tells me that he has learnt that one of the men in the group is HIV positive, and must have been so at the time of our work together. He was not one of those who argued against the HIV scenario, but it is entirely possible that his condition was known to one or more of the others who did.

References

Brook, P. (1968) *The Empty Space.* Harmondsworth: Penguin.

CHAPTER 8

'Silent Voices'

Working with Black Male Inmates – A Perspective

Martin Glynn

My experiences in the UK…so far

Ever since I started working in prisons, I have pondered over the reasons why I put myself through an experience which at times is fraught with contradiction, pain, and conflict. I could state the obvious by using a whole range of sociological reasons. This would be justifiable, but rhetorical at the same time.

Working in prisons is a deeply personal and important part of my own development as a Black man, where there is the need to connect with those forgotten and invisible voices who, despite their crimes, come from the same cultural, political, and social bond as myself. I am neither a liberal nor someone who condones behaviours where people get hurt. I also do not see myself as an archetypal Black community leader who needs to get even with the system. It is quite basic…there is something within me which sees potential in the most disaffected individuals, and I feel I can offer a few outlets for self-examination and creative expression, leading to possible ways of finding solutions to becoming people who contribute to the overall well-being of society.

This is not an ideal, this is a fact. Jimmy Boyle and John McVicar are living proof of this. The artist in any society has many keys to unlock many different changes; be they social, political, personal, or cultural. In saying that, I am also a realist and know the limits of what is achievable, but my experience alongside countless others like myself *has* brought favourable results. So where does all this start? It is my intention to present my experiences, pertinent issues, emotional feelings, and some basic analysis of working inside prisons, which will enable you as the reader to question your own relationship and responsibility to a section of the prison population, which is over-represented, marginalised, and who despite so-called 'Equal Opportunities' continue to be casualties of right-wing, racist policies, namely…BLACK INMATES.

What kind of person should I be?

To me this is the most fundamental question of all. There is no definitive answer, but when I am bringing new people into a setting like a prison, I usually have a long discussion, which is both personal and professional.

Working with Black inmates is not a joyride, and should not be seen as either a personal crusade or a liberal statement of reform. At times it can be painful, unrewarding, and scary. So much rests on your temperament, attitudes, and beliefs. Being a good actor or writer will count for very little, if you have no understanding of the core of the inmates' social reality. Merely having Black skin counts for very little. It is the type of Black person you are.

We are not all the same, we speak, think, feel, and act differently. You need to look at yourself and identify your strengths and weaknesses, emotionally, spiritually, and psychologically, as they are all key points needed to give you at least a start. Morally you will need to be honest with yourself, see where you stand on issues such as rape, murder, and a whole range of criminal activities, and whether or not the issue of race figures in how you approach these issues. You will need to be able to know how to handle difficult people, not just inmates, but racist guards, and those who will not share your views and ideals.

Prison creates a strange irony, on the one hand it is exhilarating, but at the same time it is a fearful place to be. I seldom work supervised, which sounds crazy, but that is my choice. I need intimacy, which in my case can only be achieved through contact which is conducted in a safe and confidential space. For many Black inmates, I can be the first outsider with whom they will have had contact who is interested in them, and not what they have done.

This is a difficult experience for many Black inmates, who at times will tell me they feel like a social experiment. In essence, they feel scrutinised by probation officers, the structure itself, community workers, and so on, where reports with no action, research for dissertations, and a whole series of tactics can be used to diffuse and confuse the real issue – namely creating an equitable system, which allows *all* inmates a chance to participate in activities which will lead towards the growth of individual potential and an increase in life chances, when sent back into the wider community.

When things are tense, you can come out feeling totally drained of all emotions. My advice is simply: *Know what you want from yourself, the men, and the institution itself.* Also, locate other people who have worked with Black inmates and learn from their experiences. You also need to be clear about your own level of ability. Black inmates need to know that you not only understand your subject, but that you are skilled to pass the knowledge and skills on, to enable them to move forward. You are there for them, not for furthering your career.

A final point on this issue. Once you have gained their confidence, Black inmates *will* become very attached to you. This is in itself not enough to get you through. You need to have a sharp awareness of the dynamics within any group. Never try to find out the crime that an inmate has committed, unless they volunteer that information, and even if they do, you should not take a position on the issue. All inmates have a story to tell, but you must never let your personal feelings lead you into potentially dangerous situations. Despite any rapport struck, you should never place yourself in a position which will compromise you and your work. It is easy to work with Black inmates, sympathise, empathise, and want to collude with their way of wanting to take on the system, but the danger will emerge when other factions within the prison hear about it, and may act to prevent you from going any further. Prison is made up of many constituent communities, Black inmates being just one. My advice is to do your homework and know the territory you are treading. A guy serving three life sentences has nothing to lose by taking your life if you pose a threat to his own survival within the prison. Act with common sense, but as a friend of mine always tells me…sense is never common.

Can I work alone or do I have to be part of a company?

I have always worked alone, mainly by choice. This is more cost-effective from the prison's point of view. In saying that, working alone can be isolating, and at times stressful, so if you are going to work alone, ensure you have a good emotional support structure. This will act as an important release. Prison is not an easy place to work, and will affect the way you think and feel, which is normal, but it can be harmful if you do not deal with the feelings you have. There are many drama companies who work in prison, to whom you may want to attach yourself. It is personal choice, but be clear about what you aim to get from working with them.

What kind of work should I do?

For me the key issue here is the need for inmates to find their own voice. Your job is to help them find it. I have tried several models which have been quite successful. Once again these are not definitive, there are many tried and tested methods, which you should look at before selecting the one which suits you. Working with Black inmates takes many forms and approaches of which mine is just one. Whatever the approach, it should be professional, dynamic, and positive for all concerned. Respect should be given to the diversity amongst Black inmates' experiences. To the political, cultural, and religious, to the spiritual and linguistic.

Language is such a major issue amongst Black inmates. Not only do we have the different layers of articulation shaped by urban experiences, but we have other language communities, such a Caribbean English, African-Americanisms, the expression of Black politics, and so on. Without a respect and understanding of this, it is unfair to inflict yourself on Black inmates. If I were to teach Shakespeare, I would be expected to understand and respect the language of Shakespeare, despite putting new meanings and interpretations on his work. The same right should be afforded to Black inmates' stories.

Eurocentric, monocultural, and White Liberal notions of what is best for Black inmates do nothing to promote the search for the voice of the Black experience within prison. It is not that White attitudes, beliefs, and values are not valid, but they must be presented in a true historical, cultural and political context, free from notions of White superiority and Black inferiority. This would mean the inclusion of Black-led thought and ideology within the policies and practices of any institution, whether there was a visible Black community of inmates or not. This would demonstrate the institution's commitment to realistic equity, informed by the need to represent a fair system, and not by a crisis management response to visible numbers of minorities. Unfortunately, recognition and status is seldom given to Black-led thought and ideology. This can give rise to biased perspectives around Black issues. There needs to be a sharing and a pooling of different options available, in collaboration with knowledgeable artists and scholars from a broad range of Black opinion.

The role of Black artists can be fraught with problems, as institutions themselves by definition have foundations based on a White power structure. Unless the power structure you are appealing to is sensitive enough and understands the context of your requests, the path is long and arduous, and usually culminates in you being worn down with your original demands diffused. Because of this any programme of activity for Black inmates must be linked to the overall ethos and development of the prison itself.

Case studies

The previous paragraphs are really food for thought. I think it is also valuable to share experiences, which will enable you to question, debate, and discuss relevant and pertinent issues. I would like to use two very different examples, as a way of contrasting the difficulties of not only working with Black inmates, but the problems associated with being a Black practitioner.

Long Lartin Maximum Security Prison
(One day per week from August 1993 to December 1993)

The Education Department in Long Lartin had been aware for some time that the existing provision was not meeting the needs of a particular group of Black inmates. They had voiced their frustration at not having a programme which was conducive to things they wanted to learn. The prison responded by contacting a community organisation which provided link services to the prison. Ranging from Black history to computers, Black professionals from this organisation gave inmates an input, as well as being people whom the inmates could 'share a vibe' with.

I was contacted, as I was seen as someone who could handle such a challenge. My brief essentially was to work with a 'difficult group of Black lifers' using creative writing as the vehicle. Basically, I saw it as more of a ploy to calm a situation which could have been tense if not remedied. In essence, Long Lartin needed to 'keep Black inmates quiet' by employing a measure which, despite its genuine orientation, was merely a short-term solution to the long-term problem of the lack of Black-led ideas across the range of the Education Department's provision. To be remedied this would of course involve resources, time, and commitment (a familiar get-out clause often used to justify why something cannot happen!). The fear of a raised Black awareness, be it cultural or political, poses a threat to institutions such as prisons. This also covertly tends to support the reluctance to do something more long-term.

The issue was initially who the inmates wanted to work with and therefore I decided it would be best to meet them first. This was preferable to me simply landing on their doorstep. After my security clearance came through, an initial meeting was arranged. Entering the prison, I could feel a tension, which was to stay with me to this day. The stares and aggressive body language from White guards resentful at yet another Black face sent to work with a section of inmates most would like to see have nothing was quite chilling, but it also prepared me for the many challenges that lay ahead.

Sitting nervously in the Catholic chapel with a couple of colleagues, one Black, one White, the men burst, and I mean burst, in. The entire meeting was a form of interrogation, where my motives, politics, consciousness, and fear were all tested. Inmates threw many questions at me, as well as trying to assert an overt physical presence to see if I would squirm, or break down. I made my position clear. The only difference between myself and the inmates was they had been caught and sentenced, whereas I had yet to be convicted. I went further and told them that I was also a victim of the same system, had chosen different routes, and made different choices with my life, some of which I was prepared to share and pass on. This seemed to bring a wave of approval as I had shown that intimidation, bravado, and machismo did not impress me. I explained that I had worked with Vietnam veterans in America, as well as other Black inmates in maximum security prisons in the US and Jamaica. Quite simply I had worked with so-called 'Bad Men'. I realised that the key to gaining access to their lives was through my own life experiences, which were also fraught with danger and fear, although in my case not because of a criminal lifestyle. Another factor, and a major reason why so many people do not get access, was my implicit knowledge of the world from which they came. Would you send a plumber to do an electrician's job? I passed the test... I was in. I agreed to undertake the job.

Every day I arrived the inmate constituency changed, but there was a hard core of between 15 and 20. The closeness grew to a point where any delay in getting to the sessions would result in a near rebellion and desire to deal with the guard responsible for hindering my movement into the prison. Each day the agenda was shaped by burning passions, which many of the inmates had never felt comfortable discussing before. I felt very powerful being able to harness such a strong group of inmates, who had previously been written off. However it was not always easy and despite being the facilitator, I became very aware of others within the group, who saw me as their own route to leadership. Consideration of this was important when maintaining a sense of direction. You should never let the inmates dictate that role – share it, but never give it up.

Black inmates like any other group in prison are living in a confined space, stripped bare of status and identity. However they have the added pressure of being contained inside an infrastructure which is steeped in racism. This will always lead to individuals, who were previously known in the community, being demoted to a nobody in prison. This can and does lead to those inmates possibly seeking to exploit outsiders by assuming some level of control within the work you do. It can come through the loudest voice in the group or sheer physical and psychological intimidation. You need to negotiate the basis on which that happens. My way of tackling the problem was to place the responsibility on to the group. Basically if anyone other than me took charge of something, the group would take full responsibility if anything went wrong, which would usually mean a loss of some privilege imposed by the prison. Doing it this way usually resulted in a process of natural selection, where the group would not want to place responsibility in the hands of irresponsible inmates, who could not be trusted. Your powers of persuasion, reason, and negotiation have to be honest and truthful, as well as you having integrity to back them up. If you say you are going to do something, carry it through. Failure to do this and you will lose respect from the group, and that is a disaster.

So why should I have felt so stressed at times?

First, working alone made me feel vulnerable, as there were several different factions operating in my group (anti-White, Black Muslims, different drug/gun posses, etc.). When tempers flared, I had to call on all my skills to calm it down. Second, each day, each guard, each experience was different, and would affect my mood prior to entering to the prison. I met hostility, intimidation, racism, as well as the occasional well-meaning individual (who, despite being welcome, never made me complacent about how I was perceived by them). Seldom did I respond outwardly. Instead I used a complaint mechanism and was quite successful. It got to a point where I made an official complaint to the Governor, based on an incident which I cited as conduct unbecoming an officer representing an institution like Long Lartin. I had to be clear in making my complaint that it was not rooted in race, as I could not directly prove it. Goading and overt aggressive posturing from some guards happen all the time to many artists, and is orientated to the artist's difference. In my case it was not only being Black, but also it was based on their resentment of the level of access and rapport I had with Black inmates. There was a strong underlying feeling of being despised or feared. White institutions can easily diffuse Black assertion by trundling out excuses based on 'your word against theirs' and this weakens your chance of proving a point. I knew from that day I would be seen as some Black radical, here to make Black inmates rebel, and that is what happened. This bred fear amongst those who were not locking *me* up at the end of the night.

Next, the continuing flux of inmates transferring to and from other prisons meant that I had to be really flexible in my input. I frequently had to change my methods of working and this upset my planning. Luckily it worked out, but by the same token if I was too rigid a facilitator I would have had problems. Even regular attenders could be quite fickle and reject something they had agreed to accept the previous week.

Finally the thirst and hunger for knowledge took my role way beyond that of a writer. I became politician, writer, activist, cultural critic, brother and friend. At times I wanted to take the whole system on, as each week inmates would bring to my attention a catalogue of issues which had restricted their civil and human rights. It was at those times I felt under the most pressure, as inmates relied on me to take things further. I cannot separate my politics from my art and therefore this produced for me great internal conflict.

As I walked up and down those corridors, hearing the keys, looking at inmates living in a racially divided institution, I always knew I was going home to my own comfortable existence. There were times when I was challenged by inmates who were angry that I was out and they were in. I recognised that the line between us was so thin, and based on society's misunderstanding of Black people. I knew that I could be the next person coming through those gates. However I also knew that it was important for my own sanity to detach myself from the work once I had gone home.

Imagine being an individual who has grown up in a system which has encouraged you to rebel, react, and justify the criminal justice system by making you a prime candidate to scare society, and meeting someone armed with ideas which could help you challenge things, to enable you to survive. You would be angry, feel that you have been deceived, and made powerless to do anything about controlling your own life. The net result I would equate to a form of post traumatic stress. Many inmates cannot handle or do not have the internal capacity to deal effectively with having a raised political and cultural consciousness. This is something the prison knows only too well (as the amount of punishments meted out to Black inmates demonstrates). A way to help these inmates is to allow them the option to participate on the level which helps them cope best. Some inmates will want to go the full way because they see the benefits of such personal growth. Other inmates, who have different survival strategies, may only want what is required to get by. Therefore flexibility is the key. Ramming it down inmates' throats is not what it is about. It is about alternative coping strategies. To assume that what you are doing is essential and not an option is not only arrogant but foolish, as it suggests that all inmates' needs are the same.

There was a weird paradox of seeing young Black brothers acting out their badness on the streets, thinking they would be able to get away with it, and then meeting them the following week in Long Lartin. It hits you when you realise that you cannot separate yourself from the community and be totally objective about what you do. You know at any time you could end up in the same place. This is a perspective which helps me focus, and provides me with an important grounding.

Despite the hardships, pain, and frustration, the residency resulted in a concert performed by the inmates and other artists from the community. It was truly a collaborative and memorable affair. The success of the whole residency hinged around a fairly progressive and open Education Department which collaborated with me, and did not restrict the way I wanted to work. This in my own experience is rare, but not to be negated.

Overall, I managed to deliver my programme, which could have failed had I not been focused, with clear aims and objectives. I won through, despite the usual lack of resources, and limited space. These are just things you learn to deal with. Technological provision will always be a priority in a prison. Resources which will empower inmates to look for new ways of seeing their lives are rarer. There are prison libraries, but the selection of materials, and who makes that selection is questionable. (There are of course Black consultants, librarians, writers, and artists, who are every bit as important in the area of resource provision, who should figure in this equation.)

Brinsford Young Offenders Institution
(A two-week residency – 1995)

Having previously done a couple of one-off sessions in Brinsford, I was asked to undertake a two-week residency with a group of mixed, majority Black young offenders. As Brinsford was a remand centre I knew that the group would not be stable, so I prepared a very flexible programme similar in orientation to Long Lartin, where inmates would explore issues of self, through writing, performance, and in this case video.

I was told that I was working with a particularly volatile group whom the guards resented and did not want to have anything remotely recreational. Each day an orchestrated pattern of vindictive events, designed to thwart my work, emerged. This was confirmed when disgruntled and angry inmates eventually made it to the sessions and needed time to express their disgust at their treatment which included such things as:

1. Inmates being detained, making them late for the sessions.

2. Inmates having their own work seized and confiscated by guards.

3. Some guards voiced open resentment at not being able to keep a full eye on the inmates.

4. Inmates being provoked, leading to being denied a chance to participate fully in my sessions.

All this culminated one day when I was in the library having a very important and cathartic discussion with the inmates, when the Head of Inmate Activities burst in, and started shouting, making accusations about me being a security risk. He continued that I had breached the prison rules by working unsupervised in the library. This was quite strange. I asked how I could be a security risk in a prison, when I had only gained access with the prior knowledge of the prison itself.

His intervention was potentially dangerous, as the inmates prepared themselves for conflict. I took the officer outside, and proceeded to calm the situation down. We were moved to another room, and I continued my session. That was the end of that, so I thought. At lunch in front of the whole staff, the Head of Inmate Activities came back into the office, bawling and shouting at me, as he was obviously upset by the way in which I dealt with the situation. He felt undermined in front of the inmates. His tone was threatening, loud, aggressive, and not the behaviour you would expect from a senior officer within the prison. I responded by challenging him openly in front of everyone, pointing out that I was not there to be verbally abused or attacked in such a disrespectful way. The ensuing argument brought no support whatsoever from the rest of the people in the office, which was more hurtful than surprising.

After being humiliated, I met with the person in charge of the Education Department and made a formal protest. He disclosed that the officer's actions were prompted by a conspiracy of other officers who resented what I was doing. This officer had then proceeded to create a situation where I was seen to be unsupervised, as a conscious act of sabotage on their behalf.

Feeling angry and upset I proceeded to go for a meal in the prison canteen which is in a separate building away from the prison, and is not a secure space. On making my way over I was prevented from entering by two large and aggressive White prison guards from the neighbouring men's prison Featherstone. They gave me the third degree, and insisted I give them some ID. This was in a building where many people entered, who did not need ID. Eventually after some fierce negotiation I was allowed into the building. At the table my hosts were happily enjoying their lunch until I relayed my dissatisfaction at what had just taken place. Most people heard me as I was angry and raised my voice. Like a scene from *High Noon* everyone stared at me, making me feel very self-conscious. Once again there was a look of 'we don't know what to do' on people's faces, which added to my anger. To compound things I was overheard by one of the guards with whom I had had the altercation. He turned around, came over and threatened me in full view of everyone. For a couple of seconds we stood nose to nose. His breathing was quick and I could see his fist curled. When he became conscious that he had aroused attention from his other colleagues he backed off issuing threats under his breath. At that moment I felt humiliated, vulnerable and extremely distraught because of my lack of support in my ordeal.

Why such a long speech about a small incident? In Long Lartin I was dealing with bureaucracy, racism, and fear of change. In Brinsford I encountered something which was in some respects more sinister. Professionals who were allowed to abuse their position inside and outside of the prison, with little or no accountability. Why is it so dangerous? Quite simply, I have no control or mechanism to prove their behaviour as wrong, other than my word against theirs, which raises another question: what safeguards do I have in preventing myself from being set up or accused of something on the strength of a prison officer's word? If it can happen to me in a place like an open canteen, what does that say about what is going on inside the institution?

It is this type of behaviour which makes me question the morality of who polices our prisons. Should we allow a system which cannot detect racist individuals (who are given a legal right to act out their own biased ideologies on Black people) to go unchallenged? It would appear that the criteria for selection is fraught with problems or can only accommodate a certain type of person who is prepared to do such a job. There are a vast amount of hard-working, conscientious, and able people working in prisons, but unless the bad ones are rooted out, there will be major difficulties in prisons dealing with legitimate complaints that inmates have in areas such as racial abuse, intimidation and provocation. The day I received such bad treatment I made an official complaint, and received an apology from the prison.

Needless to say it has strained the relationship I have with the prison itself. Over my many visits to prisons I have tried to rationalise why I get so many problems, when I am the one who is invited in. I have come up with the following list:

1. Fear of Black assertion.

2. Inability to manage change coming from artists.

3. Inappropriate and poorly trained staff whose perception of outsiders is shaped by their own past.

4. A lack of coherent policies when dealing with artists whose methods of working conflict with the strict regimes within prison.

5. A reaction to the difficult encounters the prison has with Black inmates who are not prepared to accept second-class status within White institutions whose ethos accommodates many racist attitudes, practices, and policies.

6. The contempt and fear of Black practitioners who can make Black inmates politically aware, giving rise to what they would see as possible *Blacklashes*.

As I stated earlier, there is a tendency to avoid Black insurrection by creating diversions. It could be sending in a Black person whose job it is to stifle Black development, a tool of the establishment in Black skin, designed to thwart moves towards Black self-determination. Or simply the institution can use economics as a reason why things cannot happen. The history of slavery, colonialism, the dismantling of apartheid, indeed the story of Black survival, is a testimony to the fact that no institution can stem the tide of opposition against inhumane and brutal treatment. The predictable outcome usually results in a range of temporary, ill-thought-out, reactionary measures, replacing the previous ones.

Conclusion

No one is born a criminal. Capitalism needs to feed off something to justify its existence. It just so happens that Black people historically have always been packaged to allow that machine to be fed. The problem with much sociological analysis around Black people is context and orientation. I remember being told by a university sociology lecturer that there was no such thing as a Black Social Theory. I asked him about his knowledge of Pan-Africanism, Black Nationalism, the economic and political systems within Africa and the Diaspora, Marcus Garvey, Walter Rodney, and so on, hoping that he would at least have knowledge for a debate. He apologised for his ignorance, and asked me why I was so angry. My response was to pose a question: 'Why do people such as yourself get jobs with such a limited and biased view of their subject?' He walked away, stunned that I knew something he did not.

As a Black person, I am sick to death of being defined, examined, miseducated, and generally dissected by those racist structures and institutions, which strive to maintain a position of superiority. I am sick of decisions taken on my behalf without consultation or a sharing of ideas. I am not a student of Black history, I am someone who shares a world history and recognise that my experiences make up part of that overall picture. Should I not expect that those in charge respect that experience, be it personal or communal, as an integral and important part of what is a truer reflection of the ways things are now and have been in the past? This does not mean there will be no disagreement and that we have to see the same thing the same way. It merely means choice and difference adds to the democracy of change. My role as an artist is to let society see itself through the eyes of those I work with. Black inmates, like any other constituent community in prison who become victims of an oppressive regime, will rebel and kick back until that force is driven back or re-evaluates itself. If the casualty in my work happens to be a system which discriminates on every level, then so be it.

Despite its efforts, prisons will not be able to stop inmates from writing poetry, plays, watching films, developing journalistic skills, painting, and using many other forms of artistic expression. The power of Rap, an ever-evolving Black film culture, and desire for Black self-determination will give rise to many new voices contained within the prison system, who will articulate their dissatisfaction at their present state, as well as providing a documented history of Black life in prison.

Statistics regarding Black incarceration are not relevant when it comes to human rights issues. It is not about how many Black inmates receive bad treatment. It is more about the institution's ability to deal with itself in areas such as Cultural Diversity and Race Relations. Like most people I am concerned at the level of Black involvement in crime, and want to do something about it, but I will not be palmed off by dealing with Black inmates without making Racism and White superiority accountable as a contributory factor to the problem.

What is not so easy is to determine the number of Black inmates who have been victims of racism and discrimination in prison, how many have been victims of racial attacks, how many have been denied a cultural and political voice, how many have been pushed to the point of committing suicide, and so on. I will never condone breaking laws if they are justifiable and equitable, but I will also not condemn those who strive for Black self-determination, when it is a necessary part of survival. I will not condemn struggle…

I started by posing the question about my reasons for working in prison. I realise that as a Black man who has had many friends pass through the system, I have a responsibility and a role to play, in ensuring that those silent voices are seen, heard, and, most importantly, understood.

CHAPTER 9

The Prisoner's Voice

Joe White

Introduction

I do not think that in the course of arguing the case for theatre in prisons over the
last 12 years, I have once thought it appropriate, or indeed necessary, to focus on
the profound personal benefits it has held for me. I believe the reason for this has
been due to the nature and context of such deliberations. The simple fact of the
matter is that the vast majority of these arguments, and certainly the most
hard-fought, have been angled directly at the prison authorities. Be they petitions
to prison governors to sanction the performance of a given production, or appeals
to security officers for a more flexible and supportive attitude, I have always
approached such discourses from the standpoint of a group representative and I
believe this is how it should be. Theatre is, primarily, a collective undertaking and
prison authorities are no more impressed by proposals driven by an individual's
personal goals and ambitions than theatrical agencies should be outside of the
prison system.

As I approach the latter stage of my sentence, and begin to make my first
tentative steps back into the free world, I feel compelled to express my gratitude
for the existence of theatre in prisons. Re-emerging into the world, after more
than a decade of institutional life, I am more conscious than ever of the scale of my
indebtedness. Rather than face a daunting transition steeped in uncertainty and an
overwhelming sense of dislocation, I feel able to walk forward with a certain
degree of confidence and genuine optimism. There is no doubt that without the
bridges that theatre has provided – both in terms of opportunity and, perhaps
more importantly, with regard to maintaining and consolidating a more personal
sense of worth and purpose – my reintroduction into society would be
considerably less hopeful.

What has finally convinced me that some sort of personal testimony should be
made is the steady erosion, throughout the prison system, of opportunities for
prisoners to become actively involved in the making of theatre. Admittedly, there
does now appear to be a more open-door policy extended towards professional

theatre companies aiming to bring thought-provoking and challenging productions into prisons. From my own experience, as a member of the audience on such occasions, these, usually offence-related dramas, invariably result in extremely positive response and debate. I should make the point that when speaking of theatre in prisons I shall be referring to theatre in prisons by prisoners, rather than that of touring professional companies. Recent trends in prison policy, however, now make the possibility of prison-based theatre groups even more remote, with activities such as theatre being labelled 'a soft option'.

With calls for more punitive and austere prison environments, with education departments under threat of closure throughout the system, one has to question whether punishment is not being sought at the cost of meaningful attempts at rehabilitation. Within the type of prison system currently being advocated the opportunities I have taken advantage of simply would not exist. I never thought I would look back on my prison sentence and be able to say that I have been fortunate but, in the light of such policies, I am acutely aware that my experience could, quite easily, have been very different, with an equally different outcome.

The prisoner's voice: questions of identity and change

Despite my many years of incarceration and institutional life I have managed to retain some sense of personal identity. By this I do not simply mean a stubborn adhesion to the person I believed myself to be on entering the prison system, but a living identity: a sense of self that remains keen and able to adapt. Although furnished with the inevitable routines and crushing uniformity of the penal regime, my own passage through the prison system has also included a space in which to evolve: a domain that enables questions of identity, character and self-expression, to be explored as part of an on going process. To give voice to emotions and attempt meaningful expression to psychological states denied expression elsewhere. I have been permitted to probe and delve, not only into my own personal character and make-up, but also into other lives, other situations and viewpoints that lie beyond immediate experience. This space we call theatre.

This, of course, is not a new phenomenon. The creation of theatre is as old as history itself. All civilisations have, in some form – either as something we might recognise as 'theatre' or as a more ritualised activity – employed the enactment and portrayal of what they perceive the human condition to be, or what it could be, through the dramatic medium. Theatre defies any one definition; however, I would suggest that its requirement as a platform becomes that much more apparent within societies and communities where any alternative means of expression are limited or even restricted altogether. Theatre may offer one of the only legitimate voices for communities where the human condition is suppressed.

I am not suggesting for one moment that a direct comparison should, or could, be drawn between the restrictions required by the prison regime and those imposed by political bodies on their citizens, or that theatre in prisons should necessarily be driven by a desire to subvert the prison authorities: rather, that given the undeniable existence of a severely repressive environment, theatre can provide an invaluable platform and a much needed outlet for quite natural responses. Theatre is not produced within a vacuum and as such any meaningful attempt at analysis must take into account the particular circumstances and background to its creation.

There can be few subjects that are guaranteed to provoke such immediate and emotive responses as those arising from the mention of prisons and imprisonment. As crime and punishment increasingly take centre stage in the political arena it is inevitable that opinions and viewpoints have become equally vehement. What I would seek to relate here, though, is a sense of context to the production of theatre in prisons by prisoners: what it means to be in prison and where the need for theatre stems from.

It is perhaps something about the very nature of legitimised punishment that, almost by necessity, it requires no credence to be given to its effects upon the

For King and Country 1991
HMP Wayland Drama Group
Reproduced by kind permission of Eastern Daily Press

individual other than to further instil feelings of condemnation. The mere mention of prisoners experiencing any degree of emotional or psychological discomfort invariably provokes loud, indignant protestations about how 'they should have thought about that before they committed the crime', or 'isn't that what prisons are meant to do?', etc. There are those that even question whether prisons are particularly distressing places at all, painting an almost attractive picture of three meals a day, no bills to pay and access to all manner of recreational facilities. In such a climate, to focus on the emotional or psychological pain of prisoners not only amounts to a sympathy that is seen to be grossly misjudged, but it also offends the moral contract that allows the punishment to be sanctioned.

This latter assertion is just as unpopular within the prison system as it is within the wider community. So strong is the feeling of censure that I cannot help but feel a qualifying apology is required in making what, to my mind, is a quite obvious statement: that prison is a painful experience. I mention it simply as a fact, and one that I believe to be fundamental in understanding the function and, ultimately, the enormous benefits that theatre in prisons has to offer.

Unlike the prison regime, which necessarily places emotional control toward the top of its list of priorities, the theatrical space actively encourages self-expression. Many of the prison system's associated problems – violence toward prison staff, prisoner assaults and bullying, drug abuse, suicide – I believe to be as much a direct consequence of an inability to articulate emotional responses to imprisonment, as simply something that is seen as intrinsic to the 'criminal mentality'. As pain and frustration manifest themselves in the form of angry and violent outbursts, these can only be seen as disruptive by the prison regime and are subsequently dealt with in a purely negative way, namely further punishment, and so the cycle continues. In a great many cases the use of both prescribed and illicit drugs only serves as a further means of suppression and escapism.

But it is not only the limitations of the prison regime that create an environment of emotional intolerance. The subculture of prison life itself forms a tight-knit community with its own pecking orders. In this highly discriminatory and fickle community natural responses to imprisonment such as grief, fear and insecurity in general are deemed as weaknesses and will not be tolerated by the more dominant members of the population. Deviation from the 'hard man' image is generally met with taunts and bullying and it can easily escalate to actual physical assault. The combined effect of this dual repression by both the prison regime, and the prisoner population's own intolerance, results in individuals being effectively trapped in a community that both denies and censors. Prison theatre provides something of a refuge from this inherently intolerant community. Similarly it is one of the only available outlets for the more sensitive but equally forbidden emotions such as pity, love and friendship. Individuals can exercise a subtlety of expression within the theatrical arena without fear of derision.

There is, of course, a problem in attempting to refer to prisons in terms of 'communities' at all: by definition, prisons involve the segregation of those incarcerated from the rest of the country's population and, with expulsion, any claim to the term should be relinquished. Ironically though, one could argue that it is precisely through this act of exclusion and group chastisement that conditions are set in place for the intense form of communal life experienced by prison populations. Certainly one can think of few situations where individuals are thrown together involuntarily for such prolonged periods – irrespective of race or background – and subjected to an existence of enforced 'equality' and uniformed regularity. But although there would appear to be, on the surface at least, aspects of prison life that might suggest a potentially strong collective identity, in reality any such parity is endemically shallow in its nature and in no way constitutes either a healthy or a harmonious environment.

I believe the need for emotional expression arising from an intolerant prison environment to be only part of a much deeper and fundamental necessity: the need to establish, or to re-establish, a sense of identity. Reception into the prison environment immediately entails the systematic stripping of an individual's reference points in terms of personal identity. All that is offered by way of replacement is a prison number. All the various constituents that previously contributed to an individual's definition of themselves – personal relationships, home environment, occupation, familiar surroundings – are effectively removed. The most basic of expressions such as personal interests, styles and the myriad of daily choices that contribute to our self-image are no longer available. This is the reality of what it means to have one's freedom taken away. In the free world I believe self definition to be a recurrent question, rather than any fixed notion, that we unwittingly 'answer' each day of our lives through interaction and choice. When these reference points to our sense of identity are removed the question 'Who am I?' becomes an increasingly literal one.

Of course, the premise is that the lifestyles and behavioural choices made by criminals prior to their conviction were the wrong ones, leading to their receiving custodial sentences in the first place and, therefore, the curtailment of such freedoms is not only deserved, but should be welcomed in initiating change. Problems arise when one considers what the available alternatives might be, in terms of possible redefinitions of identity once within the penal environment and, perhaps more importantly, what such an environment might contribute in actually reaffirming certain criminal attitudes and beliefs.

First there are those immediate definitions proffered by the courts and, to a greater extent, perpetuated by the prison regime: 'You are a criminal', 'You are a social failure', etc. Such statements, although inevitable, are not particularly helpful in promoting positive development. The most prevalent characteristics of prisoners entering the penal system, and I include myself in this, are a deep lacking in self-confidence, low self-esteem and self-worth. This is not just a reaction to having been brought to call in the eyes of the courts – such perceptions are often well entrenched prior to arrest – and, although not an excuse, such attitudes can be seen as at least 'symptoms of crime'. In a great many cases these existing self-images and perceptions in offenders are simply confirmed and consolidated through society's rejection.

Then there are the day-to-day cultures offered by the prison environment. Broadly speaking, I would say that there are two readily accessible avenues open to the individual, both are potentially as degenerative in their impact and lead, ultimately, toward their own forms of institutionalisation. One is the perpetuation of a criminal identity through association with and adherence to the criminal subculture, the other takes the form of a passive acceptance and absorption of institutional life. The latter, although earning the rather ambiguous term of 'model prisoner', involves an identity which necessarily negates any exercise of free will or personal responsibility. The former gives credence to the belief of prisons as 'schools of crime'. Neither in themselves succeed in making any significant inroads towards facilitating change, or in addressing the 'symptoms' mentioned above. In fact, I would argue that quite the opposite is true. For the greater part, imprisonment 'succeeds' in the erosion of confidence and the ability to emotionally communicate, resulting in the release of extremely disturbed individuals whose chances of positive reintegration into society are considerably less than when they entered the penal system. Certainly the rate of reoffending would seem to bear this out with 51 per cent of all prisoners discharged from custody in 1992 reconvicted after two years (this rises to 89 per cent of all 14 to 16-year-olds).[1]

Expression through the arts, but especially through theatre because it takes the human condition and human interaction as its starting point, offers one of the few positive opportunities to challenge these depressing forecasts. No matter how many times one is told to change, or whatever coercion can be brought to bear, lasting or genuine change cannot be made until an individual has reached a point of personal discovery that holds real significance in his or her own emotional and psychological life. Theatre in prison provides a realistic arena for such growth and development.

Other worlds

I distinctly remember my first exposure to theatre in prisons. Having spent several months on remand awaiting trial – an experience which had left me floundering in a world of failure, isolation, fear and apathy – it would never have occurred to me that such a thing were possible. As a result of a casual invitation from a fellow prisoner (that I have to admit I had attributed to an unfortunate state of delusion

1   Prison Statistics England and Wales 1994, HMSO Cm 3087.

on his part) I suddenly found myself in the wings of a small stage in the recreation hall of HMP Wormwood Scrubs. Hardly able to believe my eyes, I observed the familiar sight of a company in the throes of a technical rehearsal and a director grappling to maintain composure. I could have been in any community theatre in the country. Here was a part of the world I had left behind that not only appeared to be intact, but which was positively thriving.

My experience of theatre prior to coming to prison had been limited to amateur college and community theatre groups. Although serious in their intention, these companies did not function with anything like the sense of urgency and dedication with which prison-based companies operate. Having since worked on 13 full-scale prison productions, it never ceases to amaze me the ease with which so many prisoners, with even less experience of theatre prior to coming to prison than my own, can inhabit a character and enter, with such enthusiasm, worlds alien to their own.

What the initial attraction might be in joining a prison theatre group varies a great deal. For my part, the discovery of theatre in prison was nothing less than a lifeline: a gateway not only into other worlds where it was possible to breathe life into otherwise benumbed or disabled faculties, but also into a community whose positive ideals and values had somehow survived the transition inside the prison walls. For others it may simply be curiosity that draws them towards a drama group, or the sheer relief of discovering a space that offers a respite from the apathy and stagnation of prison life and which gives licence to full and free expression.

Once established, the group's immediate aspiration invariably points to the production of a play, with very little interest in activities that are not tuned toward a distinct end result. Although this desire to get started on a production could be true of any theatre company, for a prison group there is an added incentive in working towards a fixed objective: unlike so much of prison life, which amounts to a never-ending sequence of routines, a production schedule offers a series of pre-set targets that lie within a foreseeable time-scale. In effect a sense of 'real time' is created within an otherwise boundless experience where weeks and months represent nothing more than loathsome obstacles to be wished away or blotted out completely. Suddenly there is a sense of purpose, but, of course, along with this comes the necessity for sustained commitment and responsibility, qualities that are not generally encouraged by the prison regime.

For the theatrical process to function at all there are certain prerequisites that a company must seek to achieve before any real progression can be made. One of the most basic is the establishment of trust. As in the production of all theatre there can be little hope of creating believable drama without first establishing its solid foundation. Before the imagination can be exercised there must be a strong sense of confidence. Within the prison environment though, trust is a rare commodity indeed and its creation is one of the biggest challenges facing a prison theatre company. Mistrust is part of the bedrock of the prison ethos, with every movement and action being underpinned with a relentless suspicion.

It is the nurturing of confidence within the individual that facilitates the growth of belief within the group. Conversely, it is the support and acceptance of the group that enables the individual to trust. In order to encourage the function of these dynamics there are certain prerequisites that should be promoted from the onset of rehearsals. First, an acceptance of equality within and toward all company members, including any prejudices toward type of crime or racial or cultural differences, and, more generally, the equality and worth of individual comment and opinion. This approach, along with being desirable for the creative process, also establishes an alternative to the daily intolerance of the wider prison environment. Second, the promotion of the company and its aims as the 'property' of its collective members; this is undoubtedly the most important factor in the binding of the group and equally is invariably seen by the prison authorities as the most threatening aspect of prisoner theatre groups. Basically it is simply a matter of control. There is a common and strongly held belief amongst many prisoners that any pursuit sanctioned and facilitated by the prison is not for the benefit of those individuals involved, but is primarily used by the authorities as part of either an exercise in PR, or an opportunity to observe and make psychological assessments (to 'get into our heads' as it is commonly referred to). To secure any modicum of genuine enthusiasm and commitment it is necessary to dispel the assumption that their efforts are 'for the system' and believe that they are, first and foremost, for ourselves. This is easier said than done. There is the similarly ardent belief, amongst a certain contingent of the uniformed staff, that to permit any sense of autonomy amongst prisoners ultimately results in a loss of control. Even in placating such fears – allowing rehearsals to continue with relative immunity and without strategically placed officers about the rehearsal space! – there are always the expectations of prison governors and various heads of department to contend with. There is nothing more certain to shatter the confidence and spirit of a company than the impromptu appearance or proclamation from a prison governor, joyfully stating what their hopes for the group might be, invariably beginning with the choice of play.

Of all decisions, the choice of play is the most fundamental in terms of the group's identity. The process of reaching agreement on a particular script effectively defines the group's voice: what it is they want to say. It is imperative that the choice reflects a true consensus of the company, and that it inspires and excites. In this way the play will lie at the heart of the company's purpose: a constant centre of gravity that both holds the group together and continually reminds its members of their goal. Any outside body attempting to impose a script upon a group invariably results in an immediate loss of interest and the eventual disbanding of the company.

The desire of the establishment, in terms of theatre, is usually something along the lines of, 'What we need is a good comedy. Something to make us laugh'. This wish to limit the range of expression employed by prison theatre groups towards the light and ineffectual is a clear manifestation of the prison authorities' reluctance to recognise, or give any credence to, the emotional reality of imprisonment. Certainly it is not my experience that, given the choice, prisoners will opt for pure comic relief. On the contrary, the relief that theatre offers us is the discovery of other worlds which portray characters and events that both hold a significance and offer interpretation to our own lives. It is not pure escapism that is craved, but the need to give and find meaning, albeit to an imagined life. Active use of the imagination is not the same as delusion. Whereas the former, I believe, seeks to expand comprehension, the latter is merely a retreat and a denial of self. Whether these worlds be located in eighteenth-century Australia, as in Wertenbaker's *Our Country's Good*, in World War I – Wilson's *King and Country* and Barker's *The Love of a Good Man* – in nineteenth-century Russia – Dostoyvesky's *Crime and Punishment* – or set in Chile in the aftermath of a dictatorship, as in Dorfman's *Death and the Maiden*, these plays were chosen because they embody something about the nature of humanity. More specifically, with what it is to be human and where the shift to the inhuman exists. Exposure to such complex questions of morality and ethics would perhaps appear beyond the reach of a prisoner company and, in the purely intellectual sense, this may be true. However, in terms of personal experience and the ability to imagine, I would suggest that we have more than sufficient means at our disposal to comprehend such matters.

The rehearsal process

I distinctly remember the shocked silence that befell a newly formed group after the first reading of Steven Berkoff's *East*. Here was a play of unrestrained passion, a torrent of uncensored emotion from the first syllable to the last. The silence was a mixture of longing, coupled with an uneasiness at having tasted the forbidden fruit: we had not only given voice to the words themselves, but, more importantly, to the associated emotions that they licensed. The script contained a passage to freedom, a vehicle for life that was denied elsewhere.

Typically, rehearsals would begin with an open forum where current 'events' and personal responses could be aired. Our own life experiences within the prison environment were brought to the rehearsal process. This procedure developed naturally and served not only to bind the group and establish a trust between us but often these renditions provided fertile ground in which to root the drama. All good theatre depends on a strong element of conflict. For a prison-based company there is no lack of examples to draw upon! Perhaps one of the most potent examples of this came during the course of rehearsals for Wilson's *King and Country*. The actor playing the character of Private Hamp – a young shell-shocked soldier who is sentenced to death for desertion – was told, quite suddenly, of the death of his father. One of the greatest fears for any prisoner is the loss of a loved one whilst in prison. This actor demonstrated tremendous courage in channelling his loss, and very personal grief, into his character and the support he received from all the cast was a tribute to the humanising power of theatre.

This is not an isolated case. In portraying dramatic scenes where there is conflict of an emotional and occasionally violent nature, where actors inhabit the roles of both persecutor and victim, there would be many contributions and renditions from company members that help to illustrate and illuminate. The same is true of conflicts arising from the differing status or authority of characters. This is not surprising in itself given the background and present standing of the company members. What is surprising is the degree of perception and discernment demonstrated when dealing with these issues in the context of the rehearsal process. Grappling with the sense of a given dramatic situation – the question of motive in particular – immediately raises and encourages a sense of personal awareness within members of the group. The questions, 'What would I do in this situation? What alternative action could the character take?' and 'What are the consequences of such actions?' are all questions that, as prisoners, hold enormous significance and import to our lives. For many this line of discussion would in other circumstances provoke a strong resistance but in the creative arena there exists an astonishing degree of willingness. Partly this can be attributed to the fact that by placing the emphasis on a fictional character and not directly upon any individual there are no accompanying feelings of judgment. I believe the main reason lies in the fact that by this stage it is the play's production that has taken priority and, therefore, such inputs are seen as genuine and legitimate efforts toward this end.

In retrospect, it is evident that there were tremendous therapeutic qualities at work here. I have since heard the term 'psychodrama' used in connection with theatre in prison but, at the time, it seemed a purely instinctive and spontaneous experience. I do not think, however, that this quite profound and cathartic experience would have occurred if the primary motive had been something other than a striving for artistic achievement.

I have long been of the opinion that the imagination is one of the most powerful tools available for human growth and survival, that it is only by first imagining the possibilities that one can seriously begin to comprehend and conceive of alternative choices and begin to formulate their expression in reality through 'new' courses of action.

Exposure to the rich and subtle language of plays not only serves as a sound educational exercise but also acts in extending emotional vocabulary. Outside the rehearsal room the communication of the play soon begins to creep into any available space. We would take great pleasure in quoting lines from the script to each other at any given opportunity (much to the confusion of those around!). Whether walking on the exercise yard, in passing in corridors, these exchanges, though perhaps a novel technique in line learning, were much more than that. They gave us the chance to demonstrate and delight in our secret world and in turn provide something of an insulation against the monosyllabic dirge of prison rhetoric.

Performance

Ideally prison theatre productions fulfil their true potential when they are performed to both prisoner audiences and those comprised of members of the general public. Due to problems of security these two groups are never permitted to mix, so separate performances have to be arranged. Surprisingly, it has only ever been a problem gaining authorisation for prisoner audiences; even in maximum security establishments invited audiences have been sanctioned.

Whilst at Wormwood Scrubs prison, productions of Berkoff's *East* and Barker's *The Love of a Good Man* were deemed by the prison authorities to be too unwholesome and possibly too disturbing for the prisoners to attend. Aspersions about the use of obscene language in the play and the depiction of violence seemed nothing short of absurd: the vast majority of the day-to-day interaction in prison is scurrilous and violence, if not an active ingredient in the lives of many prisoners prior to entering the prison system, is certainly in great evidence once within the prison environment. The notion that prisoners should be shielded from the meaningful theatrical portrayal of these facts seemed naive to the point of foolishness. Moreover, this 'cultural guardianship' failed to extend to the content of gratuitously violent videos showing each week, or to pornographic magazines which were also readily available.

Such was the determination of the drama group in Wormwood Scrubs to show something of our *East* production that an impromptu performance was staged. It was a wet Sunday afternoon, and subsequently, the standard hourly exercise period was being conducted inside the prison block. We had marked our stage area at the far end of the third landing – this being the only level, apart from the ground floor, to have space other than the narrow gangways which ran the length and width of the wing. The effect was such of creating a balcony above us on the fourth landing, where one or two curious prisoners were already leaning over. We were well into the first scene before it became apparent that something other than mere 'exercise' was taking place. By the end of the second scene, we had gained the attention of a large percentage of the block's 230 prisoners who had congregated toward the spectacle and encircled our rendition with much amusement and lively banter. Each scene was received with energetic applause and, thankfully, the nonplussed guards allowed the play to run its course. As the doors slammed and I found myself once more in isolation it dawned on me just how big a risk we had taken, but as I listened to the charged effusions emanating from above, below, and all around, I knew that our belief was right and that we had reached the audience; for a few hours we were not separate, but had been joined through the experience of theatre. We were permitted to show subsequent productions to the prisoner population and in performing to them, they have proved to be the most receptive and appreciative of audiences.

Often individuals would express their gratitude in having been given the chance to witness our theatre, some having gained tremendous personal insight as a result. I remember a life sentence prisoner, convicted of the rape of two women, stating after a performance of Ariel Dorfman's *Death and the Maiden*, that while watching the play he had begun to realise, for the first time, something of the terror he had caused his victims. At that time he had already been in the prison system for 14 years and had never been challenged about either his attitude toward women or his offence.

In terms of what the act of performance holds for those prisoners on stage, the effects can be equally a revelation. As the end result of many weeks of effort, performance offers a sense of achievement and pride that qualifies as one of the, if not the, most positive and uplifting accomplishments of our lives. To receive appraisal and applause, against the usual prison backdrop of relentless contempt, amounts to nothing less than a light of supreme hope. I can think of no better illustration than to quote the Governor's speech in Wertenbaker's *Our Country's Good*:

> Some of these men will have finished their sentence in a few years... Should we not encourage them now to think in a free and responsible manner? And we, this colony of a few hundred will be watching this together, for a few hours we will no longer be despised prisoners and hated gaolers. We will laugh, we may be moved, we may even think a little. (Wertenbaker 1996, p.206)

The way ahead

To say that prison 'works', solely because prisoners are prevented from committing further crimes whilst in custody, is a wholly negative statement and one which effectively abandons any credence towards the notion of change. It amounts to a sweeping admission that prisoners are as, if not more, likely to continue a criminal lifestyle when they re-enter society and that prisons do nothing in offering alternatives to this sad consequence or in facilitating change within the individuals in their charge. If this is true, prisons are not only failing in their responsibility to offenders but ultimately towards the rest of society as well.

In order to put this into some sort of context I should like to draw an analogy that may appear somewhat inappropriate at first glance, but it is one that I believe to be valid in exposing the critical state of the prison service.

Let us imagine that one is afflicted with a medical condition that is considered serious enough to warrant admission to a hospital for treatment. All the various resources and expertise of staff are immediately brought to bear. There exist clear objectives in the policy of that institution: first, diagnosing the problem and second, treating the patient in the most efficient and professional manner. If necessary, advice and counselling are offered on discharge to aid the recovery process and to take all possible steps to avoid any recurrence of the condition. It does not take a great deal of imagination to predict what the reaction would be if these primary goals were to be ignored or deviated from. What if, for example, a patient admitted to a hospital for treatment were to be discharged without having received the required treatment? What if the hospital environment were such that a condition was to be exacerbated, with an additional risk of contracting further ailments whilst in the hospital's charge? Of course this would be quite unacceptable. This analogy is not meant in any way as an attempt to liken crime to disease, but to demonstrate the deficiency of a public service that appears to promote the very problem it seeks to eradicate.

metaphor of hospital

Clearly rehabilitation poses a far greater challenge to the prison system than simple containment, the boundaries of 'success' being more easily defined when dealing purely with matters of prison security than the facilitation and assessment of an individual's potential rehabilitation. Without meaningful attempts at rehabilitation though, no amount of security will succeed in protecting society in the long term.

I have seen many actor-prisoners come and go. Most have returned to society with at least one positive experience to show for their time 'inside'. Some have continued their involvement with theatre, in some capacity, on release. One or two have succeeded in making professional careers in the theatre. These achievements stand out in stark contrast against the counterproductive waste that constitutes the bulk of the prison experience in this country.

If there are still major obstacles and a growing cynicism towards the benefits of theatre in prisons there is, thankfully, increasing evidence of an acceleration in the achievements of post-prison theatre. A recently formed theatre company for ex-prisoners, Escape Artists, now stands alongside the well-established women's company, Clean Break. This is extremely encouraging, but it would seem that most of the potential groundwork that could be taking place whilst we are actually serving sentences is still under threat. As I write this, the Education Department here at HMP Lincoln has been threatened with a drastic cutback in the number of hours of education as part of a national reduction in prison spending. I can only hope that my own experience and those of my companions will not be rendered inimitable in the wake of current and proposed penal policy.

References

Wertenbaker, T. (ed) (1996) *Timberlake Wertenbaker: Plays 1*. London: Faber and Faber Limited.

CHAPTER 10

Drama and the Institution

Anne Peaker

In this chapter I propose to look at work developed in Manchester Prison by the Theatre in Prison and Probation Centre (the TIPP Centre) in conjunction with Manchester University Drama Department. Changes in the approach adopted by the Centre over the past few years and the development of its relationships within the prison are interesting in themselves and also because they reflect much that has been taking place more generally within the world of arts education and within institutions in the criminal justice system.

The interviews, during which much of the information and views expressed in this chapter were obtained, took place in September and October 1996 in HMP Manchester and with members of the TIPP Centre.

Background

The TIPP Centre's relationship with the prison goes back nearly ten years, to a time when Paul Heritage, then a lecturer in drama at Manchester University, joined Rob Clare, a theatre director, and Caroline Munroe, an actress with the Royal Exchange Theatre Company, to run a six-week drama workshop with some of the prisoners in the Education Department. These sessions built on work already carried out by Rob Clare which had led to writing workshops being undertaken over a period of 16 weeks. This had resulted in the play *Strangeways* being performed by the National Theatre Company and a documentary being made about it by Granada Television. In both cases the play created in the prison was performed outside by professional actors.

Paul Heritage also worked with Geese Theatre Company (then in the early stages of its development in this country) when it ran a week-long residency with remand prisoners. This time the agenda was set more clearly by the prison. It was to enable the young offenders on remand to explore their concerns through group improvisation, with the hope that they would be prepared to share the outcomes with other prisoners in a performance at the end of the week. It was hoped that the residency would: demonstrate the need for young prisoners on remand to be given more opportunities of this kind in the future; highlight the need for more appropriate space for performance work; and offer in-service training to two members of the education staff. This approach to the use of drama, was more clearly directed at addressing prisoners' offending behaviour than at creating a drama about prison life and imprisonment. The issues explored included: drunkenness, child abuse, truanting, pickpocketing, drugs, family relationships and adoption.

Soon after this James Thompson, Director of Apt Theatre and Visiting Lecturer with the Drama Department, sought permission from Paul Dennerly, the Education Officer, to bring in two ex-students from the Department to work with him towards another production. This was given, and during a period of two weeks in 1993 they worked with a total of 16 prisoners. The population changed from day to day as a result of the campaign to empty police container cells in the area and only one prisoner was present throughout the residency. This disrupted plans to hold a performance inside the prison at the end of the two weeks.

However, 'At Her Majesty's Pleasure: A Royal Remand Performance' was performed in the Green Room in Manchester, with professional actors taking the parts. The performance provoked a mixed reaction from its audience. Teachers from the Prison Education Department 'were very positive, stating that the prisoners' work had been presented professionally and truthfully', whilst others criticised it on the grounds that it said too little directly about prisons and prisoners. According to an internal company report on the project by James Thompson, the focus was not intended to 'challenge offending behaviour or to intervene in prison life but to run a creative theatre project with prisoners, leading to a legitimisation of prisoners' work and a sense of achievement'. The performance raised a number of significant issues concerning the role of the theatre practitioner in the prison context, and in conveying material and information from the inside to the outside. It was noted that the 'reckless driving' offence and scenario in the piece was very much victim-centred. It was also pointed out that processes of crime and punishment do not easily divide into victims and perpetrators. He suggests that while theatre practitioners working in this context need to 'seek clarity in terms of setting the boundaries and objectives of their projects', they 'do not need to simplify the issues involved.'

After this project it was agreed that each year four or five final-year students would work in the prison for one to two weeks towards the production of a performance or a video. Whilst the end product was felt to be important, according to Paul Dennerly, in an interview with the author, the emphasis was always intended to be on the process rather than the product, 'the final product was much less important than the journey towards it'.

The creation of the Theatre in Prison and Probation Centre

Although a substantial number of drama projects of different kinds had been undertaken in prisons during the 1980s, little was done within Britain to raise the profile of this work until the early 1990s, when there was a renewed sense of optimism within the prison service that group work might have a greater effect on the rehabilitation of offenders than researchers looking at rates of recidivism in the 1970s had previously accepted. It was part of the attitudinal shift amongst criminologists from 'nothing works' to 'what works?' (McGuire 1995).

A number of events served to create a much greater level of interest in the use of the arts. The first of these was a one-day conference on 'The Arts and Crime' run by the newly formed Geese Theatre Company of Great Britain in 1989. Then in 1991 the Centre for Research in Social Policy (CRSP) at Loughborough University reported on the findings of its research into the arts in prisons, a study which had been commissioned jointly by the Arts Council of Great Britain and the Home Office with some additional funding from The J. Paul Getty Junior Charitable Trust (Peaker and Vincent 1991). These indicated that the arts were seen to have an important part to play, not only in the education and rehabilitation of offenders, but also in the life of the prisons in which they took place. These findings and those resulting from a study of the visual arts in prison carried out by Colin Riches at the Royal College of Art (Riches 1992) were widely disseminated at a series of conferences and seminars on different aspects of the work.

In each case participants expressed a wish for further opportunities to develop professional networks, for a means by which they might access advice and information, and for the availability of training both for arts practitioners and for criminal justice staff who wished to develop arts programmes. Two professional organisations were developed in response to this demand.

In 1992 the Unit for the Arts and Offenders was established within CRSP and, in the same year the Drama Department at Manchester University, APT Theatre and the Greater Manchester Probation Service jointly ran 'Acting for Change?', a participatory conference on drama work with offenders. Following this the TIPP Centre was set up under the direction of Paul Heritage and James Thompson. The final year of the Drama Department's Community Theatre Course was then narrowed down to focus solely on work in criminal justice settings.

This structure continues today, with the TIPP Centre existing as a professional organisation which delivers staff development and a wide range of practical programmes. It is also contracted by the Drama Department to run the second and third year Project Course 'Prison Theatre' and the MA in Applied Theatre (Prison and Probation). It is a very symbiotic relationship which is sometimes difficult for outsiders to fully comprehend. In practical terms the division is often between professional work and supervised student course work. The establishments which host student placements do not pay for their work; however, the TIPP Centre does charge for the programmes which are run by its own staff.

The change meant that other institutions were also needed for student placements and that a more formal structure had to be adopted to support this whole area of work. All involved considered it to be essential that the students should be well prepared for their work 'inside', and Paul Dennerly was asked to come and talk to them before the placement to give them some sense of the people that they would be working with and of what they could and could not do within the context of prison. He also talked about the need to maintain security, confidentiality and about the difficulties involved in the development of relationships with prisoners.

However, these placements were not without their difficulties, largely, according to Paul Dennerly, resulting from 'immature students working with mature and highly manipulative people', and he felt that they needed either him or a member of his staff to be with them all the time. James Thompson usually set up and supervised the placements and there was daily feedback to the other members of the course so that the students working in other prisons could learn from each other's experience.

The prison's slender education budget was substantially augmented by the provision of drama work funded by outside sources and it greatly welcomed the introduction of new ideas and fresh faces. The benefits were felt not only by the prisoners directly involved, but also by those who watched the productions and by the prison management who enjoyed the positive publicity and interest which they attracted. Indeed in 1992 plans were afoot for a space in the prison to be converted into a drama studio, which would avoid drama work having to share the much used chapel.

Placements in the Education Department have now come to an end. According to Paul Dennerly this is due to a number of factors including the increasing pressure which is being felt by Prison Education Co-ordinators, who all have teaching duties now in addition to those of administration, and the particularly tight security demands in prisons where Category A prisoners are held. Whilst the student placements do not cost the prison anything, nor do students necessarily require individual security clearance, they do inevitably make demands on staff time. Although the TIPP Centre has not found that this has affected its work in other prison education departments, each establishment operates very differently. It may also be because Strangeways Education Department's energies have recently been concentrated on the development of some innovative and high-profile work with music.

Work with the Probation Service

During this time the TIPP Centre had also been undertaking work in Probation Service Day Centres. In 1993 it was commissioned by Greater Manchester Probation Service (GMPS) to develop a 'Challenging Violence' programme, and by Lancashire Probation Service to produce a 'Crime/Employment' package.

One programme called 'Blagg!', proved to be extremely popular in Probation Day Centres. It involves probation clients in the exploration of offending behaviour through a fictional group-created character called Jo. It is a very physical, visual and participatory workshop relating directly to the group of offenders' own experience, and can be included in ongoing group work run by probation officers. The programme was designed and piloted with GMPS and initially sessions were run by James Thompson in conjunction with a member of their staff. However, it soon became clear that, with sufficient training from the TIPP Centre, probation staff could facilitate the sessions on their own. This had the twofold advantage of giving probation staff a greater sense of ownership of the programme and of freeing up TIPP staff time for more developmental work.

The Blagg! Workshop, devised by the TIPP Centre, 1992
Designed by Jocelyn Meall
Picture by Bridget Eadie

In September 1993, when Shirley Johnson came to Manchester Prison, as Senior Probation Officer, she had to restructure the work of the department following the closure of the prison for refurbishment after the riots. She expanded her team from four to ten and divided their time evenly between routine welfare work on the wings and group work. She was aware from her previous experience that the prisoners did not generally respond well to the kind of group work which involved them in 'just sitting and talking about things', so, having heard about the work developed by the TIPP Centre in conjunction with GMPS, she made contact with the Centre through the Probation Service Practice Development Unit.

In 1994 she managed to obtain sufficient funding to cover the cost of the props and to pay for the TIPP Centre to run a training course for her staff. According to Shirley Johnson, the approach was 'very lively' and with the prisoners responding enthusiastically 'the work took off'. Two members of the probation team were particularly keen and they transmitted their enthusiasm to the others, although some of the less outgoing members still found it quite hard to take on the role of facilitator. Indeed, Paul Donnelly, one of the two enthusiasts (now doing the Applied Theatre MA at Manchester University) says that he had personally always hated drama and role play, but that his experience in the training sessions showed him that it could be 'an effective way of working'. TIPP Centre staff still remained available for consultation, although after the initial training they have had no further direct input to the sessions.

Shirley Johnson says that the scheme is 'ideal' because she finds that prisoners respond well to work which keeps them active and their energy level high. It makes it easier then to move on to address their thinking. One aspect of the project's design that she particularly likes is its use of large and colourful props: 'They are cumbersome and not really portable which was problematic until we got a group work room to put them in, but they need to be like that in order to create an impact.' When they come into the room the prisoners 'have got to think "wow! this looks interesting" – if they sit with their anorak hoods up and feet on the table, it is a dickens of a job to get them active and engaged.'

The 'Blagg!' programme has been run on average twice a month since that initial staff training session, with four probation staff willing to take the lead but always working with another member of the probation team. Different people bring a different style to the work, says Paul Donnelly, but the variation lies in how you get the message across whilst working towards the same end. The programme is so carefully structured that it provides a very safe vehicle for exploration through drama.

In 1995 the Prison also introduced the TIPP Centre's Anger Management Programme 'Pump!'. Once again it had been designed in conjunction with GMPS and was already in use in a variety of settings outside the prison. In Probation

Centres it was being run as an eight-session course over a period of eight weeks. Clearly such an extended programme was not appropriate for a local prison with a high turnover like Manchester, and so the programme was reworked into an intensive four-day course run over a period of two weeks.

In the event, the pilot for the course only ran for three of the four days because the Vulnerable Prisoner (VP) Wing, in which it was to be held, was 'closed down' on the first day. Seven VPs took part, with offences ranging from rape and sexual assaults (some involving children) to burglary and violent assaults. Prior to the course, Pat Milnes, one of the probation officers, had carefully interviewed the participants to ensure that they would be suitable and that, if they wanted to take part, they would be prepared to forgo all visits and other disruptions during the four days.

As with 'Blagg!', each day was divided into two sections. On the first day the morning session was used to create a fictitious character and a scenario in which he is wound up by a situation and becomes angry. The afternoon was used to explore the psychological factors, alternative responses and strategies that he might have used in that situation. The second and third days returned to and built on the original scenario in a variety of ways, looking at triggers and interventions, at some of the situations which occur outside of the prison, at the perspective of the victim, at assertiveness skills and other strategies for coping. Once again the mixture of different approaches (such as drama games, forum theatre, improvisation and brightly coloured props), held the interest of the group and helped them to develop a new language with which to discuss difficult situations.

The initial course proved quite difficult to run. Not only did the work have to be substantially condensed but also the terms of reference of the Programme had to be changed in order to make it appropriate for people in prison. By the end, however, Michael Balfour from the TIPP Centre and the two probation officers involved were well pleased with the outcome. The following are some of the comments received from the participants during the programme follow-up:

I've spent three years being angry with someone else, now I realise I was actually angry with myself.

I've been to groups for violent men in the past but this group has had an impact, I've addressed my own attitudes and where I went wrong.

I always thought that I just snapped, now I realise there is a build-up so I may be able to do something about it.

I have become angry over the last week since I attended the group but unlike before I have not resorted to violence and afterwards I have sat down and thought a lot about things and how I could have handled them better; I would never have done that before the group.

The course has only been run about five or six times so far because all group work had to be suspended during the summer of 1996 whilst programmes were reassessed in light of the reduction of funding available to prison governors (by 13.3 per cent over three years in addition to the need to implement expensive security measures, following the Learmont Report). The Probation Department in the prison has had to lose two of its ten members of staff. However it is planned that the course will in the future be run once each month, for three days with remand prisoners. 'It is not ideal,' says Shirley Johnson, 'it would be better run over a longer period, but prisoners move on so rapidly. It won't improve the course but we hope it doesn't take too much away from it.'

Another change is that all sessions will be run by a probation officer in conjunction with a member of the custodial staff. Initially there was some concern that the prison officers would consider the work to be 'silly and just messing about'. 'Presentationally with this drama work we have to keep them with us and not introduce something that appears too wacky,' says Shirley Johnson. However, she feels that once they get involved they see that it works and there are now several officers who are keen to take part, in fact one is so keen on the work that he is now prepared and able to run the sessions himself.

Whilst this is seen in most respects as being a positive move, enabling prison officers to become much better informed about what is being done with prisoners on their wings and ensuring their help with referrals, there is also some anxiety on the part of the probation staff that this might be the thin end of the wedge. They believe, that for the sake of economy, the management would like to see the work taken over completely by prison officers. Their concern lies not only in the potential loss of jobs but also in that, traditionally, custodial staff have had a very different approach to running group work. As Shirley Johnson puts it, most are much more inclined to 'tell rather than sell', and the nature of the work could be totally changed.

Other links with the TIPP Centre

One of the reasons why the probation staffs' group work has been so successful can probably be attributed to the continuing enthusiasm of the initially reluctant participant, Paul Donnelly. His involvement in the MA course at the Drama Department has meant that he has been able to recharge his own batteries and to experiment with other programmes as part of his study. For example, he contributed as a member of the prison staff to a project on drugs, run by Lisa Sissons and Rowan Davies, two other MA students. During the project they used drama to discuss what drugs are used, what is 'safe', and also to examine opinions on drug use. Paul considered that the project was very successful, and in no small measure because of the two leaders' own energy and enthusiasm.

For his own MA practical project, Paul ran a three-day 'Relationships Group' in the prison. Whilst framing it carefully so that individuals were happy to participate, the intention was to explore prisoners' attitudes to sexuality. The sessions were structured so that discussion progressed, through drama exercises, from an introduction to the other members of the group, into thinking about friendships. This was extended, through role play, to an exploration of what happens to a fictitious character within a relationship. Participants were gently led into considering the issues of homosexuality, rape and the nature of masculinity and femininity. Still sculpted images in which participants used their own and each others' bodies proved particularly effective. The images were so strong that it helped participants to realise that the type of relationship was not important because often the problems were the same. Initially there was some thought that the problems in a heterosexual relationship would be different from those in a homosexual one, 'however,' Paul said, 'this myth was soon dispelled'.

Paul commented: 'Drama freed them up to be able to talk, and they are still talking about it on the wing five months later. Because they all came from the same wing they seem to have been able to give each other support, in a way that had not previously been the case.' One prisoner specifically said that 'he now found himself challenging his own attitudes.' Another reported 'before the workshop I kept myself to myself because I did not trust anybody on the wing. Now I realise that some of them are okay and I can trust them to some degree at least.'

Conclusions

Over the past ten to fifteen years Manchester Prison has been one of the establishments where some of the most innovative work in all the different art forms has taken place. This has come about through a hard-won relationship of trust which has developed between the Management, Education and Probation Departments and the custodial staff. In looking specifically at the work of one organisation, the TIPP Centre, one must remember that what the Centre has achieved has been done in part as a result of the goodwill created by other visiting artists and by prison staff. By the same token other work in the prison has benefited from the achievements of the TIPP Centre. The sense that effective work in any community setting, but in particular in prison, can only be carried out where there is a respect for all the interest groups, for what has gone before and for what will come after, is still a relatively new concept, and by no means all artists pay more than lip service to it.

The drama work that the TIPP Centre has developed in Manchester Prison has ranged from:

1. activities which through a creative drama process have allowed
    prisoners to articulate their own feelings, ideas and experience through
    the construction of plays performed for a prison or an outside audience;

to:

2. programmes, carefully devised to address offending behaviour, which
    can be integrated into the prison system and run by members of staff
    without the continuing assistance of drama practitioners.

To some extent any organisation will have the nature of its work dictated by the
funding which it can attract, and as the Prison and Probation Services have
become increasingly conscious of the need to be accountable for their spending
and to demonstrate that the work they commission is of direct relevance to their
client group, so theatre companies working in this field have had to rethink their
activities. This has been exacerbated by a reluctance on the part of the Arts
Council and Regional Arts Boards to recognise work as part of their remit which,
whilst not therapy, is of a therapeutic nature. This reluctance is not echoed by the
arts training bodies, and there are now a number of Arts in the Community/Arts
in a Social Context degree courses which include an option to work in criminal
justice settings.

The TIPP Centre's current relationship with the Probation Department would
appear to be a very healthy one, in as much as it is able to support the development
of drama-based programmes without having a permanent presence within the
prison; however, the extent to which the continuing success of the work depends
on the participation of at least one member of the probation staff on the MA
course remains to be seen.

Another question which cannot yet be answered is to what extent such short
courses are able to make a real impact on individual prisoners. There are plans
afoot for the prison psychologist to undertake pre- and post-course interviews on
a sample of the participants; however, whilst those involved may show an
immediate shift in attitude, it is likely that they will also need some continuing
support if any lasting change is to take place. Where the ethos on the wing is
encouraging the response so far would seem to be good, but much will depend on
the attitude and commitment of the prison officers not only in Manchester Prison
but also in the other establishments to which the men will transfer. It is therefore
clearly a good thing that officers are to be involved in the groups, but having to
take on such a very different way of working in order to lead the sessions
effectively will be challenging to most.

This is a matter which has been drawn to my attention within a number of
establishments where prison officers are now being encouraged to run
offence-focused courses. For the successful leadership of such work, staff have to
have done much more than 'read the manual'. Unless they have a substantial

understanding not only of the issues but also of the techniques used in group work, prisoners very quickly become bored and the exercise can be counter-productive. This is particularly the case with drama which requires a considerable degree of self-confidence and expertise on the part of the leader.

The involvement of participants is another matter to which probation staff have been giving much thought. With group work of this kind it is essential that everyone is prepared to take part. Some initial reluctance can be handled, but on one occasion a whole group refused to turn up for the afternoon session of 'Blagg!'. It was thought they had not all contributed sufficiently to the creation of the character, Jo, and therefore did not feel any sense of ownership and were not able to move on to the more difficult, analytical aspects of the course.

Another problem encountered was that in one group there were several people with learning difficulties, who were unable to take part in the sessions at the same level and speed as the others. In a very condensed programme this clearly presents a difficulty for the other members of the group. Perhaps there is a case to be made for sessions to be run specifically for people with learning difficulties. Careful selection is, however, not easy in a prison where prisoners are constantly moving on and to some extent, according to Shirley Johnson, it has to be a case of 'accepting the first ten who will still be in the prison when the course is run'.

Manchester Prison and TIPP have clearly developed a fruitful partnership, let us hope that the work already established will carry on, despite the current threats to budgets, and that together they will continue to break new ground.

Postscript

It is perhaps appropriate to end this chapter by mentioning two encouraging events which have taken place during the past 18 months, and to express a note of caution. First, in 1995 the Prison Service established a Standing Committee on the Arts in Prisons, on which theatre practitioners are represented, and second, in conjunction with the Geese Theatre Company and the Unit for the Arts and Offenders, the TIPP Centre ran 'Creative Time', the second European Conference on Theatre and Prison, in April 1996. This event marked an important stage in the development of the whole area of work. It was attended by theatre practitioners, prison and probation staff, management, academics, funders, and prisoners and ex-prisoners, from 11 different countries. Following the conference an International Network was set up to support further development of the work.

The conference programme allowed participants to experience and discuss the wide range of approaches currently adopted by organisations, and they were encouraged to consider ways in which effective policies could be put in place to ensure that theatre can be used to best effect. The event received support from the Prison Service and the following is a quotation from the keynote speech given by its Director General, Richard Tilt:

I am delighted that your organising committee has invited me to deliver a short presentation to this important and timely conference. It is important because theatre and the wider arts make a huge contribution to the regimes in our young-offender and adult establishments. It is timely because the Prison Service, like other public services, is having to implement budget cuts (in our case 13.3 per cent). One of the effects is the need to reconsider and prioritise all aspects of our management, staffing and the activities which we provide for inmates. (Tilt 1996)

Since April 1996 the number of people being sentenced to prison has continued to rise at a dramatic rate, placing even greater pressure on budgets, with the result that the creative work which has been developed in so many prisons is now seriously threatened and it will only survive if prison governors can be successfully convinced that it is not only 'good value for money' but also crucial to the well-being of prisons and of those in their care. Sadly, hard times are ahead, despite a now widespread recognition of the value of theatre in prison.

References

McGuire, J. (ed) (1995) *What Works: Reducing Reoffending.* Chichester: Wiley Publishers.

Peaker, A. and Vincent, J. (1991) *Arts in Prisons: Towards a Sense of Achievement.* London: Home Office Publishers.

Riches, C. (1992) *There is Still Life: A Study of Art in a Prison.* MA Thesis, Royal College of Art. Unpublished.

Tilt, R. (1996) 'Creative time: Second European Conference on Theatre and Prism conference report.' Manchester: HMP Service Publisher, Manchester University.

CHAPTER 11

Shakespeare and Broadmoor

Timelessness Updated

Murray Cox

The paradox implicit in the title of this piece has caught an essential attribute of *Shakespeare Comes to Broadmoor* (Cox 1992). Timelessness is a theme which applies both to Shakespeare and Broadmoor, within aesthetic and clinico-legal frames of reference respectively. It is one characteristic of Shakespeare's language whose relevance can be asserted without fear of contradiction. It is also true that the majority of patients in Broadmoor are legally detained 'without limit of time'. How then can the *collage* of concepts which *Shakespeare Comes to Broadmoor* conveyed be brought up to date? Two options present themselves.

First, I could describe in detail the various activities within the Hospital which followed in the wake of 'Hamlet Day' – 6 August 1989. This was the day when, with Mark Rylance in the name part, the Royal Shakespeare Company (RSC) performed *Hamlet* before an audience consisting largely of Broadmoor patients. To be more precise, the book itself described the more immediate events which followed the performance of Hamlet so that this present 'post-script' could simply extend the time frame. Nevertheless, though this approach may be of domestic interest to those involved in the life of the hospital, it is in itself parochial and unlikely to hold the attention of a wider readership.

Second, a wider survey could be attempted which looked at drama, therapy, dramatherapy – and (it is impossible not to hear Polonius prompting with a whisper) therapeutico-drama! In other words, a more distanced editorial commentary could reverse and adapt the lines from the last editorial page in the book: 'How these things came about'. We could explore the impact on the hospital of 'What came about after these things'.

I have taken the second option.

There is undoubtedly widespread interest among many informed and enquiring people from associated professional disciplines and a wider public. There is still great curiosity as to how this extraordinary initiative ever took place at all. I am glad of this further chance to acknowledge my debt to Sue Jennings, who convened the original Dramatherapy Workshop in Stratford-upon-Avon where I met Mark Rylance. But, more specifically, it was Mark's intuitive flash, sensing inherent possibility, when he said 'It would be good if we could bring *Hamlet* to Broadmoor,' which set the wheels turning. This was the fulcrum upon which everything balanced.

I am usually asked two supplementary questions. 'What was the effect?' – although, for obvious reasons, this question is only asked by people who have not read *Shakespeare Comes to Broadmoor.* 'Is the RSC still coming?' is the second question. I do not want to enter into detail here of which plays, actors, directors have visited Broadmoor. Suffice it to say that there is usually 'the next play' on the horizon and this depends on many factors on both sides of the wall. There is considerable enthusiasm among those outside who might come to take part in a performance within the hospital. And this is reflected in the eager anticipation shown by patients, staff of all disciplines and management as to what the next play will be and 'do we have any idea of a date yet?'.

Within the hospital itself, two distinct developmental lines can be detected. The first is the establishment of dramatherapy as a professional enterprise within the broad range of psychotherapeutic initiatives. Two Broadmoor nurses have trained in the discipline and are now qualified dramatherapists, being supervised by Jessica Williams-Saunders, Consultant Dramatherapist, who writes (December 1996):

> Currently two dramatherapy groups have been established for male patients, with one for female patients aiming to start at the beginning of January 1997. Patients are also seen for individual dramatherapy sessions. In addition to this the dramatherapists attend clinical team meetings and are liaising with wards about further referrals to the dramatherapy service.

> The hospital is currently seeking to employ a Senior 1 Dramatherapist to work for two days per week and is in the process of advertising this position.

A more focused Broadmoor dramatherapy project was organised by Sue Jennings and is vividly described in a chapter entitled 'Masking and Unmasking: Dramatherapy with Offender Patients' (Jennings, McGinley and Orr 1997). This is well illustrated and is an excellent account of the project in detail, as well as conveying much of the ambience and background of the teeming life in a Broadmoor ward. Furthermore, it demonstrates the value of psychological assessments of patients both 'before' and 'after' dramatherapy.

The second unfolding sequel to *Shakespeare Comes to Broadmoor* has been a series of dramatic performances by visiting theatre companies. An established format has gradually crystallised. The performance tends to start in the early afternoon and after a short break the actors return to join the patient-audience for a discussion which I, informally, 'chair'. Although this is scarcely necessary. Questions are as direct as they are numerous. They speak volumes. After a performance of *Macbeth* the first question was to the actor playing the 'physician': 'You retreated when Lady Macbeth approached you. Did you feel you would be contaminated if you touched her?'. This production of *Macbeth* was in fact the fourth play which Mark Rylance has bought to the hospital and his continued interest is a source of great encouragement to us all.

On another occasion, after a performance of Ibsen's *The Master Builder* (with Brian Cox as Solness) we heard that those who had 'endured the rigours of schizophrenia' would be 'steering well clear of Ibsen in the future'. This was because to Solness' wife Aline, dolls were of more value than people. An intolerable state of affairs. And it is a cause for reflection that the audience which could tolerate the 'out vile jelly' scene in *King Lear* found Aline's line 'I didn't just keep them. They lived with me' as something appalling and beyond comprehension.

We have almost established a 'convention' that, if possible, the actors will return to run a 'workshop' with patients who attended the original performance. It is a creative opportunity of great therapeutic potential.

A third initiative which needs 'updating' was the return of the Geese Theatre Company in 1993 to visit one ward to undertake a workshop entitled 'The Violent Illusion'. This was a programme of performances and group work which was held on the Young Persons Unit for a week in December 1993. Marie Quayle, Jenny France, and Eric Wilkinson (1996) – representing psychology, speech and language therapy, and nursing disciplines respectively, within the clinical team – write as follows:

> The purpose of the programme was to examine some of the reasons why individuals become violent and in particular encourage participants to explore their own behaviour and underlying cognitive processes. The aim is to demonstrate destructive cycles of behaviour and to provide new skills, such as anger management and problem solving, to help the individual deal with situations differently in the future. The programme consists of performances and workshops and ends with a final challenge, named the 'Corrida', because of its association with bull fighting. The challenge, open to five participants only, was specially chosen for each individual by Geese Theatre actors and staff members. The patient was challenged to use his new insight and skills in a task relevant to his past history designed to be very demanding but at the same time possible. Patients who are not chosen to take part in the Corrida were asked to be judges alongside Geese Theatre actors and staff members.

> The Corrida was videoed and available for follow up work with individual patients who took part. A small group was organized consisting of two patients who had taken part in the Corrida and one patient who had acted as judge for the

other two. They were able to continue the work begun during the Geese Week as well as reflect upon the overall impact, particularly the emotional tension and release feelings such as tears when witnessing their own or another patient's Corrida. It was interesting to note that one patient admitted that he had deliberately blocked feelings about his offence both during the Corrida and in the follow up group session, whereas the patient who had been his judge, noting similarities to his own offence in the video recording of the Corrida, was visibly moved both during and after the group session.

Patients and staff involved in the Geese Week continue to talk about the experience three years later on, both in therapy and in other situations. They have clear memories of the immense impact of that shared experience, which have influenced and been incorporated into the ongoing group work on the wards.

This overview would be incomplete without reference to the 'Broadhumourists', the patients' own dramatic group, which had certainly started before I joined the staff in 1970 and is currently 'alive and well'. The teams involved in the production, the stage management, the casting, the rehearsal and, of course, the actors, are all staffed by patients in the hospital. There is a traditional slow crescendo during the rehearsal period, which tends to take place between the late autumn and early spring, leading to the performances in March and April. These are open to the public. It is always encouraging to see coach-loads of visitors arriving to bring the outside world of the audience into contact with the dramatic creativity in the Central Hall. Last year there was a production of *The Wizard of Oz* and this year it is to be *Cinderella*. In some ways the wheel has come full circle, as it is good to be able to report that Mark Rylance officially 'opened' the refurbished Central Hall with its purpose-built staging area. This augmented the living link between the professional RSC performance of *Hamlet* which had taken place in the same dramatic space which most recently echoed to 'Somewhere over the rainbow.'

Summary

I remember sitting in a hotel room in Stratford in May 1991 wondering how 'to present something of the kaleidoscopic impact of Hamlet Day itself, and of its liberating effect on the creative life of the hospital. For the insurgence of the *Hamlet* Company and its non-judgmental energies opened doors of possibility which have not closed.' These words actually come from the first paragraph of the second page of *Shakespeare Comes to Broadmoor*. Fortunately, in spite of increasing financial constraints, it is good to be able to say that these 'opened doors of possibility' still remain open. Indeed, under the new Broadmoor Hospital Authority, I am repeatedly asked by Alan Franey, the Chief Executive, 'When is the next play coming?' and one could not possibly ask for more encouragement than that!

References

Cox, M. (ed) (1992) *Shakespeare Comes to Broadmoor: 'The Actors are Come Hither': The Performance of Tragedy in a Secure Psychiatric Hospital.* London: Jessica Kingsley Publishers.

Jennings, S., McGinley, J.D. and Orr, M. (1997) 'Masking and unmasking: dramatherapy with offender patients.' In S. Jennings (ed) *Dramatherapy: Theory and Practice 3.* London: Routledge.

PART IV

Evaluation and History

CHAPTER 12

Evaluating Theatre in Prisons and Probation

Michael Balfour and Lindsey Poole

The material for this chapter is drawn from the working experience between the Theatre in Prisons and Probation (TIPP) Centre and the Practice Development Unit of Greater Manchester Probation Service. The working relationship goes back four years and covers a number of innovative drama-based projects, such as the 'Blagg!' offending-behaviour workshop, the 'Pump!' challenging-violence programme, the 'Living Together' project for bail hostel residents and the 'CLEVER' project looking at issues of education, training and employment for young offenders.

Introduction

Evaluation can be regarded as a bit of a boring formality, something which is conducted long after the fire of creativity has died down. In this chapter we would like to argue for the benefits of evaluation, and the increasing necessity for arts practitioners working in the criminal justice system to build evaluation methodologies into their work. The chapter will set out our definition of evaluation before looking at the advantages and difficulties that are involved in applying theories to practice. Along the way we will share some of our practical experiences before offering some guidelines which may help practitioners develop evaluation skills.

During the 1980s the concept of evaluation in probation work gained wider acceptance in Europe and America in a political climate of accountability, efficiency and value for money. In the US, some arts organisations sell their projects to the public by advertising how many tax dollars are saved by successful arts intervention programmes (Gutierrez-McDermid 1990). In the UK, evaluation can also be a specific requirement for funding projects and is an essential part of a theatre company's approach to ensuring the continuation of their work in the criminal justice field.

As evaluation itself is a new and developing discipline, it is hardly surprising that the term can give rise to confusion and misunderstandings amongst arts practitioners and probation staff. There is not one agreed definition of the process, although the increasing body of literature around the subject provides practitioners with an overview of the different approaches (Everitt and Hardiker 1996). It is far beyond the scope of this chapter to offer an absolute definition, but what is required is a general framework of what evaluation may entail.

The process is one by which a piece of work is monitored, examined, researched and ultimately assessed within a political, economic and social framework in order to establish its value against a set of predetermined criteria. The very word 'evaluation' implies defining value, although who decides what value means and how it can be measured needs to be taken into account.

A common misconception is that evaluation measures those who do the work rather than what they are doing. Some of this confusion is caused by certain approaches adopting the jargonistic language of management (performance indicators, performance targets etc.). The greatest difficulty with this misunderstanding is that it ignores the fact that programmes of work are processes rather than entities in their own right and that the political, social and economic contexts in which organisations and programmes exist are directly relevant to their achievements. At the end of the day, evaluation is there as a tool to help answer those thorny questions of 'have we done what we thought we were doing?' and 'if we have, was it any good?'.

The broader perspective

To some extent evaluation has already proved itself to be an important ally in the continuing political debate over the relative importance of punishment and rehabilitation in criminal policy. A major influence on criminal justice policies in the 1970s was the landmark academic paper by Lipton, Martinson and Wilks (1975) of 231 treatment outcome studies of offenders. The researchers found that programmes were ineffective in reducing offending and drew from this the conclusion that 'nothing works'.

Since the 1975 paper was published researchers and organisations have fought hard against its findings: developing programmes, using better evaluation techniques and hosting events that widen the debate on what constitutes effective work with offenders. The research findings that have been produced enhance the development of existing work, maintaining standards and promoting evaluated practices to sentencers and policy makers. The use of meta-analysis (a statistical tool for comparing the results of a large number of separate programmes) has played an important part in recent criminology studies. The studies reported by

Andrews *et al.* (1990) and Lipsey (1992) have made a significant contribution to identifying factors in programmes that show a high effect in terms of a reduction in criminal behaviour.

Whilst the evidence to date does not offer definitive answers, it provides useful guide lines for planning work with offenders, demonstrating that there are a number of readily identifiable programme features which are more likely to be effective than others. These factors, sometimes referred to as the 'What Works' principles, can be summarised in the following ways:

1. Target high risk offenders who are most likely to re-offend again. The indiscriminate targeting of treatment programmes is counterproductive in reducing recidivism.

2. Concentrate on offence behaviour or behaviour closely linked to it.

3. Use of structured programmes i.e. with a clear and more directive approach based on specific well researched model that must be linked with the learning style of the group.

4. Multi-modal, skills orientated and cognitive behaviour focus. 'More structured and focused treatments (e.g. behavioural, skill-orientated) seem to be more effective than the less structured and focused approaches e.g. counselling' (Lipsey 1992). The most successful programme, while behavioural in nature, include a cognitive component in order to focus on the 'attitudes, values and beliefs that support anti-social behaviour' (Andrews *et al.* 1990).

5. Use of community-based programmes; interventions have a stronger effect in a community rather than in a prison/residential setting.

6. High programme integrity; what is planned is carried out in practice. The treatment is carried out by fully trained staff and there is effective management of a sound rehabilitative programme.

7. With respect to the type and style of service, Andrews and Gendreau suggest that some therapeutic approaches are not appropriate for general use with offenders. Specifically, they argue that 'traditional psycho-dynamic and non-directive client-centered therapies are to be avoided with general sample of offenders' (Andrews *et al.* 1990, p.376).

When the above conditions are met, the meta-analysis suggests that the high-effect studies can reduce the likelihood of recidivism in the order of 20 to 40 per cent. In the light of such compelling evidence, offence-focused programmes (whether theatre-based work or not), have incorporated the key principles outlined above, sound in the knowledge that their work is more likely to be effective.

Why evaluate?

The debate on effective ways of working provides both the rationale and the reason for incorporating evaluation into any piece of work with offenders: without the limited evaluation that has already taken place, the 'Nothing Works' doctrine would still dominate; without continued evaluation of new projects, the development of the 'What Works?' debate would stagnate. Most arts and probation practitioners have informal ways of knowing whether a piece of work has achieved its objectives, but without the evidence from a more formalised evaluation, a generalisation of their findings or replication of the work elsewhere can become problematic. As McGuire *et al.* point out:

'Dear John' (1995)
Insight Arts Theatre Company, part of Insight Arts Trust
Picture by Chris Johnston

...many excellent projects have disappeared at least in part because of an absence of evidence supporting their usefulness; such evidence simply not having been collected. (McGuire *et al.* 1992, p.103)

Whilst it is misleading to imply that evaluation in itself would make an effective programme, there is evidence that undertaking the process of evaluation leads probation and theatre practitioners to consider more carefully the principles of the 'What Works?' debate. Projects with evaluation as integral have been found to be associated with more successful outcomes (McGuire *et al.* 1992). Further, practitioners who are concerned enough to know whether their work has been successful are also more likely to pay attention to the careful planning and delivery of that work.

Arts practitioners have not been slow to waken up to the demand for more evidence on their effectiveness. There are also reasons internal to an arts organisation that make effective evaluation a good prospect. It stimulates a curiosity about the effectiveness of one's own work, a way of developing and improving programmes and sharing with colleagues your experiences, as well as enabling people who receive the service to have a voice in its development.

There are a number of reasons why practitioners do not evaluate effectively, a perception of a lack of time and/or resources being chief among them. However, if drama in prisons and probation is to maintain itself in a sensitised political and public arena, it needs to develop its own critical authority, supported by objective evidence and rigorous methodology. An over-dependence on personal accounts, subjective reports, anecdotal evidence and insubstantial research will ensure a slow and uneven progress towards developing expertise.

Our final point is that evaluation need not be dull. The research process can be creative, innovative, informative and can add value to a piece of work. It can provide arts practitioners with sensitive antennae that feed back valuable insights on the strengths and weaknesses of our practice. Evaluation is ultimately about good practice, and about making good practice better.

Theories and methodologies

Evaluating drama work presents opportunities for imaginative research staff, but also creates practical difficulties in almost equal and opposite proportions. Whilst most drama work lends itself to process evaluations (for example through observation), problems may arise when trying to demonstrate the outcomes of the work, particularly in terms of attitudinal change. Likewise, whilst the use of drama techniques can demonstrate the clients' depth of understanding of the work in a way that more traditional methods (such as pen and paper exercises) cannot, recording the largely visual results in a systematic way can be problematic.

Evaluation is characterised by its use of social research methods and is therefore informed by much of the theory of this discipline. The application of positivist research methods to social situations raises questions about the selection of appropriate methodologies. However, the qualitative and quantitative methodologies used in social research may be equally valid in determining the effectiveness of a project and it is therefore important to have an overview of the relative merits of each approach.

The quantitative approach to collecting information is typified by numerical measures which can create tables and statistics, and calculate behavioural trends. One example of this in the criminal justice field is the interest in reconviction scales which use static factors such as 'type of offence', 'age at first offence' and 'number of previous convictions' to generate a probability statistic which acts as a baseline measurement for effectiveness.

The qualitative (or interpretative) standpoint offers an alternative approach. The qualitative approach is directed towards not only the actions of individuals but the discerning of the context, subtexts and meanings for those actions. As a result, the information that such a social scientist is interested in is concerned with individual testimonies and is often interpretative. Typically, the work will seek to reconstruct the perspective of its subject using description first and explanation second.

In our experience, arts and probation practitioners find the application of quantitative methods to their practice contrary to their understanding of the nature of their work. For example, the use of the experimental design and in particular the use of control groups can appear to condense complex processes into single variables. It can raise ethical questions and may often in reality prove to be impractical and unmanageable. Both probation officers and drama workers appear to be far easier with the notion of purely qualitative methods of research such as observation despite the immense time that is needed in order to undertake a systematic analysis of such data.

The two approaches, the quantitative and the qualitative, may have different methodologies, but most researchers attempt to connect these two polarised perspectives in order to present a composite picture of a given social subject that suggests meanings rather than conclusions. As Kerlinger argues, 'subjective belief must be checked against objective reality' (for objective read quantitative) (Kerlinger 1970, p.4). Researchers now tend to avoid conclusive arguments for and against quantitative or qualitative data, preferring to concern themselves with a 'combination of both which makes use of the most valuable of each' (Merton and Kendall 1946, p.541). It can be extremely difficult to reconcile the aims and assumptions of these two traditions, but given the respect and current emphasis on numerical statistics (education and health league tables, for example), it would be foolish simply to ignore the merits of bringing together both approaches. The challenge to arts practitioners is to develop methodologies that produce data which is insightful, manageable, reliable and that is underpinned by the value-base of the work.

The debate about the use of scientific methods in social research spills over into discussions of who are the best people to be undertaking such research. There is a compelling argument which considers that the needs of objectivity are met by using external researchers to evaluate programmes of work; such researchers have expertise, skills and knowledge about research methods and, not being directly involved in pieces of work, are less likely to be accused of being subjective in their analysis. Conversely, others debate that a true understanding of outcomes and actions can only be gained through inside knowledge and professional expertise which independent researchers lack; they would argue that the methodology alone can provide the necessities of objectivity. The assumption that paid external consultants do not have an interest in the particular findings of a piece of evaluation ignores the context of work, as does the assumption that the professional expertise of probation or arts practitioners will include a willingness and ability to critically assess their own work. A more realistic picture incorporates practicalities that this dichotomy seems to overlook. Whatever ideals are preferred, at the end of the day most arts projects are run on a shoestring and other ways of demonstrating effectiveness need to be sought apart from relying on external expertise. As McIvor states:

> On a purely pragmatic level, it is likely to be the case that if practitioners do not evaluate the effectiveness of their work with clients then no one else will. (McIvor 1995, p.210)

Within the probation context, evaluation of effectiveness is moving away from a task only undertaken by the 'experts' and towards becoming an expectation of practitioners. Evaluation forms one of the key competencies for probation officers and much of the discussion around professional development includes the role of the 'research-minded practitioner' operating within the context of a 'culture of curiosity'.

Regardless of who is undertaking the work, or which approach is adopted, it is important to have a clear understanding of what a rigorous methodology might look like. Evaluation procedures should be systematic, agreed from the outset to demonstrate the aims and objectives of the piece of work, and applied equally and continuously throughout the programme of work.

Evaluation and practice

At the heart of arts evaluation practice in prisons and probation is a concern to understand in what way a project has affected the participants. Evaluation and research is an attempt at picking up clues from a number of areas, of which none on their own provide conclusive evidence. In this respect evaluation has less to do with a scientific process than with one akin to a court of law which gathers information from a number of sources to ascertain a truth. One must ascertain what the participant thinks she/he has learnt, discover what has been learnt and monitor what she/he applies in practice.

It would be impossible to construct an ultimate evaluation process for all the diverse artistic projects that happen in prison and probation contexts. Evaluation needs to acknowledge the diversity of programmes and practitioners, their different purposes and approaches. Therefore there are no uniform methods of evaluating a project but a collection of techniques which can be matched to a project's needs and resources. Each technique has limited value when used in isolation but, when combined with other techniques, helps to demonstrate outcomes more convincingly. For example, the 'CLEVER' project, a multi-agency collaboration between Greater Manchester Probation Service, the TIPP Centre and Hindley Young Offenders Institution, used a number of different evaluation techniques. The name of the project was an acronym derived from the main themes of the work: Creativity, Leisure, Employment, Values, Education and Rehabilitation. The basic aim of the project was to challenge the thinking and the behaviour that was associated with the young offenders' criminal activity. A further aim of this work was to bring the young people into contact with those providing training and employment back in the 'outside' world. The evaluation methodology examined the outcomes as well as the process of the work. It sought to look at effectiveness from the perspective of those immediately involved and the context in which the work was operating.

Changes in the attitudes of the young people on the programme were seen as a key indicator of success. The quantitative approach was undertaken by using two questionnaires designed to measure attitudes and administered on a pre- and post-test basis. A comparison group was drawn from young men choosing to spend time in the education department to ensure that any change in the drama group was not due to a maturation effect. The qualitative approach entailed a student on placement with the Practice Development Unit acting as an observer, taking notes from the day's work and collecting the participants' feedback. Permission was granted by the prison to take photographs of the drama work as it unfolded, again providing useful qualitative data.

After the performance some of the employers attending the performance were contacted by telephone to ask for their views on the project through a semi-structured interview and the prison governor was consulted for his comments about the impact of the project.

This evaluation was comprehensive and demonstrated that the process of the programme had been very positive. However, it was apparent that the boundaries between the evaluation and the work became blurred. The 'observer' who had originally been briefed to maintain an 'objective' distance from the drama work, found that the participative way the work was structured made it impossible not to become part of the drama. Before the end of the first day our impartial observer was playing the role of the girlfriend in the drama.

The quantitative methods also demonstrated limitations. The prison population has been shown to have a disproportionate number of people with literacy problems and our group was no exception. For some the questionnaires were daunting or an untimely reminder of their less pleasant form-filling experiences at school.

A number of problems were created in the methodology by the security restrictions of an institutional setting. For example, the use of video equipment was limited for security reasons and although permission was given for use of a camera, there were few opportunities to use it. Concern was given to issues of confidentiality of the offenders involved in the project, particularly where the camera was used. However, all offenders gave their permission for their comments to be used in the evaluation report and were also happy that the photos were used to show the work they had undertaken.

Dramatic forms of evaluation

The use of drama as an evaluatory tool is still relatively unexplored. It may be that it takes more organisation than simply handing out a questionnaire, but there are advantages in being able to integrate drama-based evaluation techniques with other drama exercises.

For example, in the first session of the TIPP Centre's challenging violence programme, group members brainstorm what specific situations trigger their anger or violence. From this material the group are asked to: short-list five 'trigger' situations which might lead to violence; make a tableau of each situation; and then stand on a continuum line to identify how much of a personal provocation they thought it was. The tableau images are then photographed and the position on the continuum lines recorded. These trigger situations may then be reintroduced in the last session, and any changes can be discussed in the group. The data revealed through this process should not be viewed as a precise appraisal of a participant's attitude, but it can be a strong lead into the issues which are important for group members. As an evaluation process the material gained from the continuum exercise needs to be put in context and properly interpreted. For example, participants can quite easily deny they have a problem with any of the trigger situations and stand at the lower 'no risk' end of the continuum. However, depending on the participants, and what the team knows about the individual, his denial of anger can be identified through this process because he constantly (and quite probably) stands at the 'low risk' end of the line.

Another similar technique for measuring attitudes and points of view within a group is: 'Where do I stand?' The exercise involves a member of the team standing in the centre of the room and asking 'Where do you stand in relation to the attitude that [for example] all drugs should be legalised?' Group members then stand close to the chair if they agree with this statement or further away if they disagree. This information can also be recorded and used in a later session to measure any changes in viewpoint. The strength of these techniques is that they form a part of the sessions process, and even help to set out what problems exist in the group and can be a starting point for discussion.

It is worth noting that theatre practitioners in other fields have tried out drama-based styles of evaluation. The Theatre in Health Education Trust (THE Trust) document a technique that uses drama to test the impact and acceptability of a programme about HIV and AIDS on schoolchildren. The exercise encouraged young people to apply their knowledge about the issues (learnt on a programme they had recently attended) to a case study, Mike, who was role-played by an actor. The young people were asked to take part by collectively playing volunteers for an AIDS helpline which Mike, who had recently contracted HIV, was phoning. The group were told that they could disagree with advice that was being given, by offering their own alternative so that Mike could make up his own mind. Using two telephones as props the evaluation was carried out by setting up Mike's situation and hearing his first question to the helpline. A researcher then put down one of the phones and asked the group to write down their own responses to the question. Once the responses were written down, the researcher picked up the phone and invited the group to talk to Mike about his options. This is an imaginative way of using drama to see what knowledge has been gained from a programme. The participants in this evaluation provide both written evidence of their knowledge and show through giving their advice what their attitudes towards a particular issue might be.

Practical guidelines for evaluating projects

From our own and other people's experiences of evaluating drama-based work with offenders and from the instruction offered by what is sometimes referred to as the 'What Works' principles, we would like to offer some rough guidelines.

Starting questions

Careful consideration should be given to the type of data that needs to be collected, who is to collect it and at what point in the piece of work this should be done. If you are using other people's monitoring or data systems, ensure that you have permission to use the data in the way you intend and try to consider any ethical implications of sharing such information. If you are looking for client responses try to get these when you have the participants in the room. Probationers can be very difficult to track down, even a short time after you have seen them and will be a less reliable source of feedback after the event. Thinking through the evaluation can be very beneficial and will require you to address a number of questions; but even before setting out these plans, it is worth going back to the most basic of questions: Who is doing the evaluation? Will the evaluation be undertaken by the arts company, or by the organisation in which the work is done, or by an independent researcher? Who is the audience for the results of the evaluation? Is the report for the arts company, the organisation, or a funding body? All these factors will influence the style and content of an evaluation. What aspects of the project will be evaluated? A project is often a sum of many parts. Will the evaluation cover the designing and devising of the project? The running of the project? Is the evaluation to examine processes or outcomes of the work or both? What is the range of work to be evaluated? Are the outcomes of the project to be short or long term? Will the evaluation consider the immediate impact of the work (i.e. change in attitudes) or wider questions (i.e. effect on offending behaviour)?

Research-minded practitioners

In any piece of work, the primary resource available is the staff that are undertaking the tasks. This extends to every level from clerical and support staff to drama practitioners and the management structures that may be overseeing the work. The driving motivation to evaluate a piece of work should ideally lie with the practitioners as it is their craft that is under inspection. However, the support and encouragement given by others is invaluable in ensuring the evaluation proceeds smoothly. The more time devoted to informing and training all staff in the purposes of the evaluation before the work takes place, the more likely staff are to respond positively to requests for assistance in gathering evidence. Staff who feel involved in the process will be more curious about the work and are far more likely to be committed to its outcomes. Conversely, staff who feel that evaluation is dumped on them, who have had little say in the development of the methodology, may actively resist attempts to evaluate. You may go through the motions of evaluating the work only to discover that the quality of data collected is poor.

Clarity on the theoretical basis of the work that is being undertaken

Before thinking about the actual content of a piece of work, consideration needs to be given to the underlying knowledge base of the work, its theoretical grounding and, in particular, what such knowledge would suggest you could hope to achieve. This requires thinking through the processes by which change takes place in drama-based work and how people will be able to apply your work to their own life situations. In doing this, the overall aims of the piece should become explicit.

Knowledge of the identified target group

A clear idea is needed of who you will be working with, what factors may enhance or restrict their learning, what their preferred learning styles may be and how they may feel about the demands of evaluation techniques. This information can help you to think through what the outcomes of the work may be for this group and how they may respond to the practicalities of the evaluation. Ethical issues need to be considered, particularly if using a camera to record work. How you go about ensuring that data collected for research will not be used for other purposes is important. Consider how to get the participants' informed consent to being part of the research and in particular if you need to access specific information (for example, records of previous convictions).

Stated objectives of the work

Often practitioners fail to articulate properly the objectives of the work they are undertaking, frequently because it is felt either to be apparent or not significant enough to mention. However, the objectives will not only define the work you are undertaking but will also direct you towards a particular style of evaluation, helping to define the methodology. The assumption that other people will understand what the work is about often leads practitioners to be dismissive of their greatest achievements. Writing objectives is not always easy but ideally, as Vennard states, objectives should be translatable into research questions (Vennard 1996). In other words, objectives should be able to be measured by their ability to demonstrate specific outcomes. For example, 'to reduce reoffending amongst the client group' is a very worthy objective but would require a researcher to pursue the clients 24 hours a day in order to be reasonably sure of a success. 'To reduce reconviction rates' may be a more researchable objective of the same overall aim. If evaluation is integral to an arts project, questions will be asked at the very inception of the project. Basic aims and objectives with achievable goals (which can be assessed properly) can help to provide focus for the project.

A planned programme of work

The more detailed a plan of work can be, the easier it will be to ensure that you have covered what you intended to do and maintained programme integrity. Likewise the easier it will be to ensure that you will be able to replicate the piece of work in the future and to know what amendments need to be made. The inclusion of timings of each session within the programme are important and adequate time needs to be allocated to evaluation tasks at the relevant point. The evaluation should be part of the programme rather than an added-on extra and adequate time should be allocated as some of the data collection could prove time-consuming.

Conclusion

In the introduction we argued for the benefits as well as the necessity of evaluating the effectiveness of the arts in prison and probation. The evaluation process is more than a way of satisfying the demands of a criminal justice system sensitised by political and economic concerns. Mouly writes:

> Research is best conceived as the process of arriving at dependable solutions to problems through the planned and systematic collection, analysis and interpretation of data. (Mouly 1978, p.40)

The challenge for arts practitioners is to find ways of integrating the evaluation process into their creative practice in order that it may demonstrate effectiveness as well as provide informed feedback from participants. The purpose of this research, whether the methodology is quantitative or qualitative (or a combination of both), is to understand better the creative learning environment as different people experience it. While evaluation does not reveal ultimate truth, it may help to make sense of the learning process involved with the arts, and the way in which creativity and imagination impact on people. Evaluation can offer explanation, clarification and a better understanding of the potential of the arts in prison and probation. Far from being a boring formality, or a cynical attempt to win political acceptance of the penal system from the wider public, evaluation may ensure theatre in prisons a maturity and a sense of progression that is essential to the development of an evolving field.

References

Andrews, D.A., Zinger, I., Hoge, R.D., Bonta, J., Gendreau, P. and Cullin, F.T. (1990) 'Does correctional treatment work? A clinically relevant and psychologically informed meta-analysis.' *Criminology 28*, 369–404.

Everitt, A. and Hardiker, P. (1996) *Evaluating for Good Practice.* Basingstoke: British Association of Social Workers.

Gutierrez-McDermid, G. (1990) 'Something works.' Unpublished article. (For other materials contact Arts in Corrections, Department of Corrections, PO Box 942883, Sacramento, CA 94283–0001, USA.)

Kerlinger, F.N. (1970) *Foundations of Behavioural Research.* New York: Holt, Rinehart and Winston.

Lipsey, M.W. (1992) 'Juvenile delinquency treatment: a meta-analytical inquiry into the variability of effects.' In K.W. Watcher and M.L. Straf (eds) *Meta-analysis for Explanation: A Casebook.* New York: Russell Sage Foundation.

Lipton, D., Martinson, R. and Wilks, D. (1975) *The Effectiveness of Correctional Treatment.* New York: Praeger.

McIvor, G. (1995) 'Practitioner evaluation.' In J. McGuire (ed) *What Works: Reducing Reoffending. Guidelines from Research and Practice.* Chichester: Wiley Publishers.

McGuire, J., Broomfield, D., Robinson, C. and Rowson, B. (1992) *The Probation Evaluation Project Report.* Manchester: Greater Manchester Probation Service.

Merton, R.K. and Kendall, P.L. (1946) 'The focused interview.' *American Journal of Sociology* *51,* 541–557.

Mouly, G.J. (1978) *Educational Research: the Art and the Science of Investigation.* Boston: Allyn and Bacon.

Vennard, J. (1996) 'Evaluating the effectiveness of Community Programmes with Offenders.' *Vista,* 2,1, May, pp.15–27.

Further Reading

Dunne, N. (1993) *An Evaluation of the Staffordshire HIV and AIDS Theatre in Health Education Programme.* Birmingham: T.H.E. Trust.

Gendreau, P. and Andrews, D.A. (1990) 'A tertiary prevention: What the meta-analyses of the offender treatment tells us about "What Works?".' *Canadian Journal of Criminology 32,* 173–84.

Raynor, P., Smith, D. and Vanstone, M. (1994) *Effective Probation Practice.* Basingstoke: British Association of Social Workers.

Van Voorhis, P., Cullen, F.T. and Applegate, B. (1995) 'Evaluating interventions with violent offenders: a guide for practitioners and policy makers.' *Federal Probation 59,* 2, 17–27.

CHAPTER 13

Rebellion and Theatre in Brazilian Prisons

An Historical Footnote

Paul Heritage

When the TIPP Centre began its second Brazilian project in the State of São Paulo, it was assumed that the success of the work in Brasília would make it easier to begin again in Brazil's largest city in the south of the country. However, an historical incident meant that we had to fight that much harder to convince the authorities that theatre should occupy a place in their system. We were told that the last time theatre had been allowed in prison it had ended in a full-scale rebellion with many injured in the process. The name of the director of that project was invoked with a venom and odium that belied the fact that the incident had taken place almost 15 years before this meeting with the prison authorities. Of course we assured them that we were not in the business of riot and revolution, and with the same betrayal and compromise that accompanies so much theatre in prison, we have succeeded in establishing a new project. However, my interest had been aroused by the story of our predecessors who, perhaps, had remained true to some of those revolutionary dreams which I imagine still haunt many of us engaged in this work. I was particularly intrigued as the person held responsible for the previous project was one of the most established figures in Brazilian theatre of the past 30 years and is today the director of a prestigious international theatre festival in São Paulo: Ruth Escobar. As there is little in the way of historical documentation in this field, I thought that it might be of interest to try to see what happened in 1980 that could have been powerful enough to put at risk a theatre project in 1995...

In a theatre that is dominated by male directors, Ruth Escobar is a unique and singular voice in the history of contemporary Brazilian theatre. Producer, director, actress and elected politician, she has both a theatre and a festival that carry her name in São Paulo. Over the 35 years of a dynamic and highly-charged

career at the forefront of Brazilian culture, she has brought an extraordinary array
of artists to Brazil and taken her productions across Europe, Asia, Africa and the
Americas. Her theatre at its best marked the polemical heartbeat of Brazil, and
took her to the forefront of cultural opposition to the 20 years of military rule. Her
own rebellious career has been accompanied by some of the most notable names
of international theatre including Jerzy Grotowski, Núria Espert, Fernando
Arrabel, Victor Gracía, Robert Wilson, Vanessa Redgrave, Stephen Berkoff and a
name that will forever be associated with both prisons and theatre, Jean Genet.

The fragments of historical documentation that still exist to bear witness to the
events that led up to the rebellion in the State Prison of São Paulo tell a story that
is both particular to the Brazilian political situation at the time and strangely
familiar to anyone that has produced theatre in prison. Before the Escobar
company began the project that finished in such violence and bloodshed, they
had already been showing their work in prisons as part of a general policy to take
work to diverse audiences. The play which they had produced prior to the prison
theatre project was a cabaret show that was attempting to respond to the uncertain
space which was being opened in the military dictatorship's grip on the nation. By
1978 the worst years of the repression were over, but it would be almost ten years
before democracy would return in a form that allowed direct participation in
elections. In the meantime there was a period known as the *Abertura* (opening)
which would increasingly see an opportunity for political and cultural opposition.
In a climate of tentative uncertainty, Ruth Escobar produced a political satire
called *Revista do Henfil* using the recognisable forms of the popular Brazilian
cabaret tradition. After opening in theatre spaces the show was subsequently
toured to *favelas*,[1] Trade Union headquarters, streets and prisons, before it finished
in Brasília in June 1979 amidst bombs in the auditorium, personal threats of
violence to Escobar and her cast, and a commotion in Congress (Fernandes
1985).

Many of the performances throughout the tour had been given as benefits for
pro-amnesty committees and the initial impetus to perform in prison came from a
desire to pay homage to the considerable number of political prisoners in the
Brazilian penitentiary system. The performance and reception of any theatrical
text is conditioned by the particularities of those who appear both on stage and in
the audience. The impact of these performances was heightened by the presence
in the cast of a leading actor from the television soap opera *Gabriela* that the
prisoners (and perhaps 90 per cent of Brazil) were watching at this time. But no

---

1   The *favelas* are the haphazard and unofficial dwellings that grow up around Brazilian cities,
     famously climbing the mountainsides of Rio de Janeiro. Commonly translated in English as
     'slums', there is no word that can adequately do justice both to the social deprivation of the
     favelas and the level of autonomous organisation that characterises those who in every sense
     live on the peripheries of Brazilian society.

less significant was the presence in the audience of political prisoners imprisoned under the infamous National Security Law. Normally sectioned off from 'common' prisoners, they were allowed to watch these performances and on rare occasions talk to the press who accompanied the show. For example, a performance at the Penitenciária Barreto Campelo on the island of Itamaracá in the State of Pernambuco was recorded by one of the newspapers at the time and gives some idea of the conditions and response – from the political and non-political prisoners. The total population of the prison at the time was 421, of which 14 were kept under the National Security legislation. In an interview given at the time, Escobar explained that she and her company of 22 actors were there to show their solidarity with the political prisoners and their 'love for those who are here for trying to make our country free' (Fernandes 1985, p.134).

However, it became apparent to the actors on this and other occasions that the division between political and non-political prisoner was largely a false one and the company was also to express its solidarity with the so-called 'common criminal' who was imprisoned as a result of social injustice and a grotesquely unequal economic system. The bias of the newspaper report imagined that the political impact of the play was only appreciated by the 14 political prisoners while the rest of the audience concentrated on the humorous delights and the physical presence of the six actresses. The journalist claimed it was only the political prisoners who paid attention to the text. However, Escobar made it clear in a testimony given at the time that what was most impressive during the performances was the way in which the prison population as a whole responded to the issues that were raised in the play: the amnesty, inflation, international debt, and democracy (although she acknowledged that the sexual jokes were clearly effective and vociferously appreciated).

This level of audience comprehension was tested further when the group took the play to Carandiru (the Casa de Detenção in São Paulo) in May 1979. The largest prison in Latin America, Carandiru is a part of the most terrible recent and past history of the Brazilian prison system and the site of the bloodiest rebellions and repressions.[2] In an interview given to the Folha de São Paulo[3] at the time, Escobar said that the visits to the prisons were a balloon being raised for work that must follow in the future. She highlighted one area of particular interest for the company, which was to test the type of theatrical language that could be used in performing in prisons. The play was constructed using techniques of popular theatre that Escobar claimed had largely disappeared from the Brazilian stage. The company distributed questionnaires amongst the audience and conducted interviews with the inmates after the performances to see how much was

2   See Chapter 1, p.33.
3   1 June 1979.

understood of the text. With the results of their research it was hoped to modify the way in which theatre could be most effectively performed in prison.

In the Salão Nobre, where 15 years later the TIPP Centre would come to begin the workshops for their own theatre project, the play was presented to 1500 men sitting on the floor. Those that were not able to get inside watched through the bars from beyond. The play lasted one hour and ten minutes and the actors were greeted as so many other performers have been in prison, by shouts and whistles which gradually diminished as the play began. In one of the interviews with an inmate recorded after the show, Pedro (who was serving a 16-year sentence) commented, 'We are not very used to theatre, but we understand what the play is saying, the message. It's clear that not everyone wants to know this, there are those that come just to see the woman on stage. But these people don't count'(Folha de São Paulo 1979). The journalist who covered the event for Brazil's most prestigious newspaper commented:

> It is difficult to analyse the reactions of an audience of prisoners, faced by a play about liberty…but judging from the feedback given by the spectators as a result of the performance, the level of understanding was very high. (Osmar Freitas Jnr in Fernandes 1985, p.136)

The director of the prison commented to the same journalist after the show that he thought theatre was an excellent activity for the prison because it would give the inmates something to talk about for months to come. It is, he claimed, 'a little tranquillity in the prison'. Such words are resonant in the light of what occurred the following year and begin to push the extremities of the boundaries that mark our performances. In entering the prisons, do we seek to create that tranquillity or inspire the rebellion?

In May 1980, the Teatro Ruth Escobar was able to announce a follow-up to their prison tour which would allow seven actors, a psychologist and a social worker to begin a five-month project based in Carandiru. Whereas the initial impetus for the prison work had been the presence of the political prisoners, the actors' contact with the general prison population had shown them that such facile divisions were not easy to make:

> Too often the verb 'to torture' is conjugated as if in the past tense. It is important to remember that it is conjugated in the present tense everyday, victimising more common prisoners than political prisoners. With the same violence and the same significance.[4]

---

4   Programme note for *The Chocolate Factory* by Ruy Guerra (this play was performed the months immediately prior to the prison project started in May 1980).

The project reached its first performance in October 1980 with a series of short plays written and performed by the inmates and subversively titled *Aqui Há Ordem e Progresso* (*Here there is Order and Progress*[5]). Not only did this invoke the words of the national flag, but also challenged public perception with the very notion that from the disorder of prison could be produced work that was in any way progressive. From the beginning there were problems, when the Director General of the prison, Sr. Bruno Vizotto, banned the performance, announcing to the *Folha de São Paulo* that the play was 'pernicious and negative and would interrupt the work of the rehabilitation and social readaption of the inmates' (*Folha de São Paulo* 9 October 1980 in Fernandes 1985, p. 158). The fight that must be so familiar to those that work in prison theatre began to be played out, although on this occasion in a more public arena as the presence of Ruth Escobar in the debate inevitably assured that attention was paid by the media.

The case was taken to the Secretary of Justice for the State of São Paulo and in the face of threats by Escobar to do public readings of the play using professional actors and tapes of the inmates in rehearsal, he allowed the play to be performed with two substantial cuts. It was presented in the prison throughout the month of November to an audience of inmates and invited guests, thus fulfilling the various aims that the group had set for themselves at the outset. The performances took what had been learnt by a small group of inmates out to the rest of the prison population, described by one of the inmate actors at the time as the 'most demanding audience in the world, because we are going to show them their own reality'[6] (Fernandes 1985, p.160). But as with so many prison theatre projects there was an important function in these performances to provide a bridge between the closed world of the prison and the world outside its walls. In the press reports about the performances given to an invited audience, it is this function of the project that attracted the journalists' attention. According to one report in a Catholic publication, it was now the moment for anyone concerned with human rights to follow the path opened up by Ruth Escobar's team:

> Now is the time to demystify a system which is supposed to rehabilitate men, but in reality only demonstrates its vindictive character. It is the time to make a firm commitment to the prisoners and the first step is to support their basic demands: an end to censorship, access to newspapers and publications, and conjugal rights.[7]

5   'Ordem e Progresso' are the words that appear on the Brazilian national flag.

6   Inmate known as *Grandão* (the Big One) cited in an anonymous review for the *Globo* newspaper on 17 November 1980.

7   *O São Paulo* 7–13 November 1980 in section entitled 'Justice and Peace for all' (Fernandes 1985, p.159). The lack of sexual rights is seen by other critics, most notably Betty Milan in the *Folha de São Paulo* (11 November 1980), as a part of the dehumanising of the prisoner. Perhaps it is worth noting here that Brazilian prisons do now allow inmates one conjugal visit per week, conditional on the availability of space and both parties submitting to a test for HIV.

Sábato Magaldi, today one of Brazil's most important and honoured theatre critics, commented at the time that the project had a dual function: for the prisoners to make themselves aware of their own lives and in the process making aware the society that had incarcerated them. He anticipated that the performances should ease the tensions in the system and create a dialogue with the authorities. In his review for the *Jornal da Tarde* he quoted one of the inmates as saying that as a result of the experience his behaviour had changed from irrational revolt to a new understanding which was affecting not only his relationship with the guards but also with his own family (Fernandes 1985, p.160).

In her own report on the project, Escobar also drew attention to the positive effect on the families of the prisoners, some of whom for the first time in their lives were able to take pride in the men who performed for them. Her conclusions for the project as a whole are the same as so many other theatre workers have made: that the next stage has to be with the guards because they are the ones who live in daily contact with the inmates. This has particular relevance in Brazil where, as Escobar notes, the guard and the prisoner come from the same social group. Although society has put them on opposite sides they are not in essence torturers and victims, and 'it falls to theatre to bring them together' (Ruth Escobar in Fernandes 1985, p.163). The review in the newspaper *O Estado de São Paulo* on 5 December finished optimistically with the proclamation that the seed that Escobar had planted could now grow and develop throughout the prisons of Brazil and beyond. While the critic may have been prescient in his world view, the possibilities in Brazil were virtually destroyed within only three weeks.

On 21 December the theatre group performed again. Once more uniting the professional team led by Ruth Escobar with roughly the same group of inmates (allowing for the normal disruptions of transfers and punishments), the group organised a Christmas party for 1200 inmates and their families. The festivities took place from 8.00 a.m. to 4.00 p.m. in the exercise yards of each pavilion where the majority of the inmates normally spend their day. The group organised music shows, children's entertainment and at night a special presentation of *O Auto do Burrinho de Bélem* by Chico de Assis. On the following day a second performance of the play was staged for invited groups of psychiatrists, theatre critics, actors, writers many of whom were also asked to talk about the work they had seen for a film made by David Lindenbaum entitled *Os Artistas Condenados (The Condemned Artists)*. At the end of the session all talk was of the future with the extension of the project to other prisons across the country, even perhaps to the capital city of Brasília.

On Christmas Day 1980 it began to rain in São Paulo and a game of football that was taking place in the prison had to be stopped. Five of the inmates carried on playing until one of the guards took the ball away and they were escorted back to their cells. As punishment for insubordination the guards began beating these five inmates on their return. This in turn led to wider scenes of violence as other inmates and guards arrived. This minor incident ended quickly and the inmates were escorted back to their cells. But retribution was to follow as a shock troop of 600 military police with dogs were twice sent into the prison over the next 48 hours, despite the prisoners being held individually in their cells throughout this period. Journalists watching the event from outside the prison gates saw the police emerging with broken batons and the dogs with bloodied jaws. Someone from the military police shouted out: 'You missed the best party!'.

Quick to apportion blame and never to assume it, the prison authorities lashed out at the easiest target: the actors. In a statement to the press on the following day, the Director of the prison declared that the rebellion was ignited by the theatre group of Ruth Escobar. This in turn launched a emotional debate about theatre in prisons which was conducted on a public and polemical level which has rarely been witnessed since. Away from the heat of the events, Escobar's words at the time still carry resonance for those working on theatre projects in prison today:

> For six months we were observers of the rights of these men and we tried to raise various questions. We tried to establish a dialogue, establishing a new dynamic in the relationship between prisoner and prison, prisoner and guard, prisoner and administrator, the prisoner and his family. It was a great advance; they performed various plays for the other prisoners, which were followed by debates, and hundreds of people – lawyers, politicians, students – were witnesses to the work we have done. We are all RESPONSIBLE FOR THIS MASSACRE. Because the system and the security forces did not support these changes that were happening... The prison system does not support the idea that these men can think. They were always treated like animals. In order to reform the prisoner it is first necessary to reform the system and the authorities who run it. These offenders are also human beings who were created by the system; the State owes them re-education. For many of them the theatre was a revelation of a secret ingredient that maintains the essence of human integrity. (Ruth Escobar, *Folha de São Paulo*, 30 December 1980 in Fernandes 1985, p.166)

The events in São Paulo in 1980 posed questions for us in 1995 as we embarked on a new theatre project in the same prison where so much had already been achieved and so much had been violently destroyed. They reminded us of the responsibilities and failures, the transformations and stasis of so much of this work. Each will find their own lesson or reflection from reading about these events. For me they are a reminder not to forget that the concentration on rehabilitation that informs so much contemporary work in theatre in prisons is contingent on ideologies that hide collective responsibilities and limit the possibility of change to the individual agent. This is a limitation and distortion of the role of theatre. People make theatre; theatre does not make people. In that Brazilian prison during seven months in 1980 prisoners made theatre in such a way that change was effected and resisted in its most violent form. Fifteen years later, re-entering the *Salão Nobre* in Carandiru to begin our first workshop we are carrying on a path that was begun elsewhere: a timely reminder that to participate in any theatre is a collective and incomplete act. It must never be otherwise.

References

Fernandes, R. (1985) *Teatro Ruth Escobar: 20 Anos de Resistencia.* São Paulo: Global Editora.

Folha de São Paulo (1979) Interview with Ruth Escobar, 1 June.

List of Useful Addresses

Clean Break Theatre Company
37/39 Kings Terrace
London NW1 0JR
Tel: 0171 383 3786

Geese Theatre Company
Cannon Hill Park
Birmingham B12 9QH
Tel: 0121 446 4370
Fax: 0121 446 5806

Insight Arts Trust
9 Islington Green
London N1 2XH
Tel: 0171 359 0772
Fax: 0171 359 4217
e-mail: insightartstrust.demon.co.uk

The Scene Through Project 4 ARTS
PO Box 12512
London W9 3GS
Web site: www.giraf.demon.co.uk/scene/

The Theatre in Prisons and Probation (TIPP) Centre
Drama Department
Manchester University
Oxford Road
Manchester M13 9PL
Tel: 0161 275 3047
Fax: 0161 275 3349
e-mail: tipp@man.ac.uk

The Unit for the Arts and Offenders
34 Victoria Road
Dartmouth
Devon TQ6 9SA
Tel: 01803 835278
Fax: 01803 832982

The Contributors

Michael Balfour has worked for the TIPP Centre since 1994, contributing to the development of its programmes, and teaching on the MA in Applied Drama and undergraduate courses at the University of Manchester. He has recently completed a PhD in Prison Theatre at Lancaster University.

Robert Clare has worked with the RSC, the Royal National Theatre, the Royal Exchange Theatre (Manchester) and Compass. He has worked in various prisons, most notably in Manchester (Strangeways) and Maghaberry (Northern Ireland). His work in Maghaberry was honoured by the Butler Trust, and was the subject of a BBC television documentary.

Murray Cox was Consultant Psychotherapist at Broadmoor Hospital from 1970 until his death in 1997. He was an Honorary Research Fellow of the Shakespeare Institute, the University of Birmingham and series editor for Forensic Focus, Jessica Kingsley Publishers.

Mark Farrall was a founder member of LEAP TIE and trained with LEAP Confronting Conflict in the use of drama for mediation and conflict resolution. Now in his sixth year with Geese Theatre Company, he is currently researching a PhD in Drama in Education focused on Geese's Theatre Violent Illusion Trilogy prison residency for violent offenders. He is founder and Director of *ignition* Theatre Projects.

Pauline Gladstone is the Education Development Coordinator for Clean Break Theatre Company. She designs and manages the company's theatre education and training programme, as well as taking responsibility for national outreach and training. She is on the Standing Committee for Arts in Prisons and the Steering Committee for Theatre in Prison and Probation.

Martin Glynn has spent time working with individuals and educational organisations internationally developing literature initiatives, directing perform-ances and arts policies, alongside pursuing a career as a professional writer/performer. He has gained recognition for commissioned work in areas such as theatre, radio drama and live performance. As a workshop facilitator, he has conducted workshops in a diverse range of educational institutions, including schools, colleges, prisons, special needs and youth arts establishments.

Victor Hassine has a degree in Law from the New York School of Law. In 1981 he was found guilty of first degree murder and sentenced to serve life imprisonment without the chance of parole. He has written extensively about his life behind bars and has had some of his fiction and non-fiction published in prison journals in the US, Canada and the UK. His writings have won recognition in the prestigious national Pen American Prison Writing Contest. In 1993 a play he wrote, 'The Circles of Nod' was successfully performed in prison. 1996 saw the publication of his first book, *Life without Parole: Living in Prison Today* by Roxbury Publishing Company.

Paul Heritage is Head of Drama at Queen Mary and Westfield College, University of London, having previously worked at Manchester University where he co-founded the TIPP Centre in 1992. Extensive work in Brazilian prisons since 1993, has resulted in theatre projects in Brasília, São Paulo and Rio de Janeiro. Previously he worked as a director with Gay Sweatshop. His publications include work on AIDS, British contemporary theatre, Shakespeare and most recently (with Maria Delgado) *In Contact with the Gods? Directors Talk Theatre* (1996, Manchester University Press).

Jenny Hughes trained as a drama leader specialising in work with offenders with the TIPP Centre, University of Manchester. She worked within the criminal justice system in the North West of England for three years. She is currently working with children with emotional and behavioural difficulties and is training as a person-centred therapist.

Chris Johnston is currently Projects Director for Insight Arts Trust. He was trained at the Drama Centre, North London and has worked variously as Theatre Director, Writer and Tutor in subjects varying from improvisation to witchcraft. He is author of *Theatre, House of Games* due to be published in 1998 by Nick Hem Books.

Angus McLewin is the Director of 4 ARTS and the Scene Through project. He develops and delivers arts projects with vulnerable groups, focusing particularly on work within prison and probation, including training staff on drama-based approaches to groupwork. He is also a dramatherapist.

Alun Mountford is the Senior Trainer for Geese Theatre Company. He has worked extensively with Probation Services throughout the UK designing and co-facilitating violent offender, sex offender and offending behaviour programmes. He is an actor and Eriksonian therapist who has worked with many forms of theatre as communication.

Anne Peaker, Director of the Unit for the Arts and Offenders (an independent charitable trust set up to support the development of creative and participatory arts activities in criminal justice settings), worked as an artist in prison, ran an organisation which placed other artists to work in a variety of social contexts including prison, probation and special hospital and undertook a study of the arts in prisons for the Home Office and the Arts Council of Great Britain whilst employed by the Centre for Research in Social Policy, at the University of Loughborough. She sits on the Prison Service Standing Commitee for the Arts in Prisons.

Lindsey Poole is the Senior Officer (Research and Education) for Oxfordshire and Buckinghamshire Probation Service. Prior to this she worked as a research officer for Greater Manchester Probation Service, specialising in the use of evaluation as a practice and service development tool.

Sally Stamp is a dramatherapist at a Regional Secure Unit. She has worked extensively with offenders in a range of settings. She sat on the Arts Therapies in Prisons Working Party and has a Certificate in Forensic Psychotherapy from the Portman Clinic.

James Thompson is the Co-Founder and Director of the TIPP Centre and a visiting lecturer at Manchester University Drama Department. He is a former Harkness Fellow having spent a year in the US researching theatre/arts based juvenile justice programmes. He has worked in prisons in the UK, the US, Brazil, and Sri Lanka.

Joe White is an actor, director and writer. As a serving prisoner (1985–1997) his theatre in prisons included: Berkoff's 'East'; Barker's 'Love of a Good Man'; Wertenbaker's 'Our Country's Good'; Wilson's 'For King and Country'; Dostoyevsky's 'Crime and Punishment'; Dorfman's 'Death and The Maiden' (Tricycle Theatre) and Barker's 'The Possibilities' (Tricycle Theatre/Royal Court Theatre Upstairs).

Subject Index

References in italic are to photographs or figures.

Author Index